Soft Threats to National Security

This book explores the Boycott, Divestment, and Sanctions (BDS) phenomenon – its impact and implications for Israel and the Palestinian-Israeli conflict, as well as the inextricable linkage between its anti-Israeli/anti-Zionist propaganda and antisemitism, unraveled from yet unknown perspectives.

The edited volume offers groundbreaking research: while Israeli public diplomacy focused on security, Palestinian diplomacy focused on a fabricated history. The book analyzes the old Russian anti-Zionist propaganda and its application by the BDS. The public space of BDS activity projects a humane façade, yet the covert part harbors antisemitic and violent supporters including terror groups and Iran. Western universities turned into incubators of pro-Palestinian groups that portray Israel as the source of evil. The academic boycott of Israel worked to isolate and stigmatize Jewish scholars in America because of a presumed Jewish occupation of the American academe. Western "liberals" wish to build bridges with the Muslim world, unable to overcome differences on democracy, secularism, women's rights, etc., they focus on what they agree: animosity towards Israel. So has the UN; the ICC; Bedouin advocacy; and Human Rights Watch.

The chapters in this book were originally published as a special issue of the journal, *Israel Affairs*.

Dana Barnett is an expert on post-Zionism in the academe. She has demonstrated a direct connection between the critical, neo-Marxist scholarship mainstreamed by the social sciences, and the anti-Israel sentiments espoused in scholarships. Barnett is the co-founder and CEO of Israel Academia Monitor, a group which follows BDS and anti-Israel writings of academics. She is the author of *Post Zionism and Israeli Universities: The Academic Political Nexus* (2016).

Efraim Karsh is Professor Emeritus of Middle East and Mediterranean Studies at King's College London and Editor of the scholarly journals *Middle East Quarterly* and *Israel Affairs*. He is the author of over 120 scholarly articles and 16 books, including *The Tail Wags the Dog: International Politics and the Middle East; Palestine Betrayed; Islamic Imperialism: A History; Empires of the Sand: the Struggle for Mastery in the Middle East 1798–1923;* and *Fabricating Israeli History: the "New Historians"* (Routledge).

Soft Threats to National Security
Antisemitism, BDS and the
De-legitimization of Israel

Edited by
Dana Barnett and Efraim Karsh

LONDON AND NEW YORK

First published 2022
by Routledge
2 Park Square, Milton Park, Abingdon, Oxon, OX14 4RN

and by Routledge
605 Third Avenue, New York, NY 10158

Routledge is an imprint of the Taylor & Francis Group, an informa business

© 2022 Taylor & Francis

All rights reserved. No part of this book may be reprinted or reproduced or utilised in any form or by any electronic, mechanical, or other means, now known or hereafter invented, including photocopying and recording, or in any information storage or retrieval system, without permission in writing from the publishers.

Trademark notice: Product or corporate names may be trademarks or registered trademarks, and are used only for identification and explanation without intent to infringe.

British Library Cataloguing-in-Publication Data
A catalogue record for this book is available from the British Library

ISBN13: 978-1-032-14091-9 (hbk)
ISBN13: 978-1-032-14092-6 (pbk)
ISBN13: 978-1-003-24315-1 (ebk)

DOI: 10.4324/9781003243151

Typeset in Minion Pro
by codeMantra

Publisher's Note
The publisher accepts responsibility for any inconsistencies that may have arisen during the conversion of this book from journal articles to book chapters, namely the inclusion of journal terminology.

Disclaimer
Every effort has been made to contact copyright holders for their permission to reprint material in this book. The publishers would be grateful to hear from any copyright holder who is not here acknowledged and will undertake to rectify any errors or omissions in future editions of this book.

Contents

Citation Information	vii
Notes on Contributors	ix
Introduction *Dana Barnett*	1
1 From underdog to occupier: Israel's tarnished image *Yoav Gelber*	7
2 The unspoken purpose of the academic boycott *Martin Kramer*	27
3 Human Rights Watch's anti-Israel Agenda *Gerald M. Steinberg*	34
4 Israel in modern Jewish identity: an internal debate *Evyatar Friesel*	57
5 The Palestinian campaign against Israel at the United Nations Human Rights Council *Eytan Gilboa*	68
6 Birds of a feather vote together? EU and Arab League UNGA Israel voting *Leah Mandler and Carmela Lutmar*	89
7 The ICC's Prosecutor in the service of Palestinian Lawfare *Assaf Derri*	105
8 The Negev Bedouin as a de-legitimization tool *Havatzelet Yahel*	121

9	The coalescence of anti-Zionist ideologies *Henri Stellman*	144
10	The Covert War: From BDS to De-legitimization to Antisemitism *Lev Topor*	166
11	The BDS as an example of Soviet political warfare *Nelly Atlan*	181
	Index	203

Citation Information

The chapters in this book were originally published in the journal *Israel Affairs*, volume 27, issue 1 (2021). When citing this material, please use the original page numbering for each article, as follows:

Introduction
Dana Barnett
Israel Affairs, volume 27, issue 1 (2021) pp. 1–6

Chapter 1
From underdog to occupier: Israel's tarnished image
Yoav Gelber
Israel Affairs, volume 27, issue 1 (2021) pp. 7–26

Chapter 2
The unspoken purpose of the academic boycott
Martin Kramer
Israel Affairs, volume 27, issue 1 (2021) pp. 27–33

Chapter 3
Human Rights Watch's anti-Israel Agenda
Gerald M. Steinberg
Israel Affairs, volume 27, issue 1 (2021) pp. 34–56

Chapter 4
Israel in modern Jewish identity: an internal debate
Evyatar Friesel
Israel Affairs, volume 27, issue 1 (2021) pp. 57–67

Chapter 5
The Palestinian campaign against Israel at the United Nations Human Rights Council
Eytan Gilboa
Israel Affairs, volume 27, issue 1 (2021) pp. 68–88

Chapter 6

Birds of a feather vote together? EU and Arab League UNGA Israel voting
Leah Mandler and Carmela Lutmar
Israel Affairs, volume 27, issue 1 (2021) pp. 89–104

Chapter 7

The ICC's Prosecutor in the service of Palestinian Lawfare
Assaf Derri
Israel Affairs, volume 27, issue 1 (2021) pp. 105–120

Chapter 8

The Negev Bedouin as a de-legitimization tool
Havatzelet Yahel
Israel Affairs, volume 27, issue 1 (2021) pp. 121–143

Chapter 9

The coalescence of anti-Zionist ideologies
Henri Stellman
Israel Affairs, volume 27, issue 1 (2021) pp. 144–165

Chapter 10

The Covert War: From BDS to De-legitimization to Antisemitism
Lev Topor
Israel Affairs, volume 27, issue 1 (2021) pp. 166–180

Chapter 11

The BDS as an example of Soviet political warfare
Nelly Atlan
Israel Affairs, volume 27, issue 1 (2021) pp. 202–223

For any permission-related enquiries please visit:
http://www.tandfonline.com/page/help/permissions

Notes on Contributors

Nelly Atlan, International Relations, University of Saint Andrews, UK.

Dana Barnett, Israel Academia Monitor, Israel.

Assaf Derri, Haim Striks Law School, The College of Management, Rishon LeZion, Israel.

Evyatar Friesel, Modern Jewish History, Department of Jewish History, Hebrew University of Jerusalem, Israel.

Yoav Gelber, Department of Land of Israel Studies, University of Haifa, Israel.

Eytan Gilboa, Begin-Sadat Center for Strategic Studies, Bar-Ilan University, Ramat Gan, Israel.

Martin Kramer, Department of Middle Eastern and Islamic Studies, Shalem College, Jerusalem, Israel.

Carmela Lutmar, Division of International Relations, School of Political Sciences, University of Haifa, Israel.

Leah Mandler, Division of International Relations, School of Political Sciences, University of Haifa, Israel.

Gerald M. Steinberg, Bar-Ilan University, Ramat Gan, Israel.

Henri Stellman, Independent Researcher, London, UK.

Lev Topor, Center for Cyber Law and Policy, University of Haifa, Israel.

Havatzelet Yahel, Study of Israel & Zionism, Ben-Gurion University of the Negev, Beersheba, Israel.

Introduction

Dana Barnett

ABSTRACT

From its modest beginning in the 2000s, the Boycott, Divestment, and Sanctions (BDS) movement has grown into a worldwide phenomenon that changed the discourse on Israel. Commentators pointed out that, at a minimum, the BDS has transformed the Israeli-Palestinian debate. More ominously, the BDS spawned an entire discursive tradition of delegitimizing Israel and played an essential role in increasing antisemitism. Empirical evidence seems to indicate that the dramatic increase in antisemitic rhetoric and attacks is at least partially related to the BDS campaign. Most recently, the BDS activists took credit for the International Criminal Court decision in Hague to try Israel for war crimes. This special issue explores the BDS phenomenon – its impact and implications for Israel and the Palestinian-Israeli conflict, as well as the inextricable linkage between its anti-Israeli/anti-Zionist propaganda and antisemitism.

Palestinian and pro-Palestinian groups run numerous student organisations on Western campuses, helped by faculty who provide the 'ideological pedagogy,' a reference to a narrative deriding Israel as the source of all evil in the Middle East. The vast body of research on this topic demonstrates that universities serve as incubators for new antisemitism and de-legitimisation of Israel. These activists also reject the International Holocaust Remembrance Alliance (IHRA) Working Definition of antisemitism.[1]

Omar Barghouti, who co-founded the Palestinian Campaign for the Academic and Cultural Boycott of Israel (PACBI) in 2004, is portrayed as the architect of the BDS movement. In 2007, when the BDS National Committee (BNC) was created, Barghouti was appointed to head it.

However, the idea was conceived in the late 1990s by the Islamic regime in Iran in conjunction with its Palestinian proxies and 'human rights' NGOs and was brought to fruition during the UN-sponsored World Conference Against Racism (WCAR) in Durban, South Africa, in 2001. For the Iranian regime, which had previously relied on its terror proxies' hard power, the BDS domain represented a diversification into soft power, a term denoting the use of discursive assets to influence policy outcomes. By all accounts, Barghouti, the Qatari-born Palestinian, was brought in to provide a Palestinian face and Qatari connections to what was mostly an Iranian-international 'humanitarian' collaboration.

The BDS concept was used as a catch-all phrase for all negative depictions of the Jewish state. Such an approach is in line with de-legitimisation's intuitive definition: Destroying the legitimacy, prestige, or authority of a person or an entity. Social psychologists noted several de-legitimisation strategies, including trait characterisation, political labels, ostracising, and using a delegitimized group to stigmatise another group. However, a wholesale de-legitimisation of a state entity is a complex process that requires a more accurate view of how it was possible to subvert the legitimate Israeli claims of being a democracy in good international standing.[2]

At its core, the BDS movement's effort at de-legitimisation is subsumed in Israel's definition as a 'fascist, settler-colonial state.' Since de-legitimisation is a discursive process, BDS proponents are not compelled to rely on facts. However, even a cursory analysis of Max Weber's seminal theory of legitimacy demonstrates the case's fallacy. As is well known, Weber posited that in modern states, rational-legal authority is the norm, as opposed to traditional societies where the authority system is based either on numinous or traditional claims. Democracy, a popular way to satisfy Weber's requirements of the rational-legal authority, has been at the centre of Israel's political system since independence. The Economist Intelligence Unit (EIU), a popular index of democratic qualities in countries, shows Israel, in 2019, with a score of 7.86 compared to the United States with a rank of 7.96. Authoritarian regimes, such as Iran or Syria, on the other hand, score below three.[3]

The 'settler-colonial state' stigma is based on an equally deceptive misrepresentation of events. Weber conceptualised the membership/territory legitimacy in terms of *Gemeinschaft–Gesellschaft* society. In the former, the societal bond is underlaid by 'subjective feeling' that may be 'effectual or traditional.' In the latter, 'rational agreement by mutual consent' is legitimising the society. Weber postulated that as societies progress, the *Gesellschaft* mode takes over, an observation principally based on membership/territory legitimacy's organic nature. Arguably, Israel lacked the Weberian time spectrum, but the UN 1947 Partition Proposal recognised the ancient roots of its *Gemeinschaft* bond by granting the Jews the right to a part of historical Palestine. In other words, far from considering Israel a settler-colonial state, the international community added its considerable legitimacy to creating the Jewish state.

What enabled the BDS movement to ignore basic historical facts was the growth of the critical, neo-Marxist scholarship, a somewhat incongruous mixture of critical theory and post-modern themes pioneered by Michel Foucault and elements of radical structuralism derived from classic Marxism. Unlike the traditional realistic approach of positivism anchored in the belief that social phenomena ought to be studied empirically, the new approach considered social facts a fabrication by the 'hegemonic' classes marshalled to retain their domination. In deconstructing the 'hegemonic' narrative, the critical, neo-Marxist scholarship has challenged the dominant realistic school of International Relations (IR) by espousing the postcolonial theory. Pioneered by Edward Said, postcolonialism posits that white colonial and imperialist powers have shaped the international reality and structured its institutions to marginalise indigenous populations. According to the postcolonial theory, the United Nations, a representative of the white international hegemons, lacked the legitimacy to grant the Jews land rights. Not surprisingly, postcolonial theorists and their followers would increasingly describe Israel as an 'illegitimate,' 'racist,' or 'apartheid state.'

A better understanding of the discursive practices of the BDS movement is required. Few realise that the BDS practitioners followed the blueprint for communication developed by Antonio Gramsci, an Italian Communist with a later contribution by Jurgen Habermas, a neo-Marxist German philosopher. Gramsci noted that the middle classes developed a hegemonic culture by dominating the public discourse and infusing it with their values and norms. The working classes could not challenge these values because of a lack of what Habermas later described as 'linguistic competence.' Gramsci believed that it was incumbent on public intellectuals and academics to produce a counternarrative representing the working classes and subaltern groups' voices, which postcolonial theory adopted to describe the marginalised native populations. There was little doubt that the Palestinian BDS activists and their Western academic supporters had the 'linguistic competence' to voice the Palestinian subalterns' grievances. However, they were keenly aware of the antismitic nature of their delegitimisation campaign. To deflect charges of antisemitism, the BDS campaign preferred to use Jewish and especially Israeli scholars who played a crucial role in pushing the themes that showed Israel to be a 'fascist, settler-colonial' country with 'apartheid' thrown in for dramatic effect.[4] Pushing for an academic boycott, Israeli scholars such as Tanya Reinhart, Ilan Pappe, Anat Matar, Rachel Giora, Kobi Snitz, and Neve Gordon have led the trend. They were helped by a large circle of followers who promoted and pushed the BDS ideas to academic audiences. In response, Israeli universities did next to nothing.

There is a greater need to analyse the extensive web of alliances that the BDS movement has relied on to bolster its effectiveness. In terms of soft power, alliance building is considered a potent force multiplier. However, it is hard to discern because the linkages are not always clear or, occasionally, are counterintuitive.

Intersectionality is the foremost mechanism in the BDS alliance. The intersectionality concept was first introduced in 1989 in a black feminist treatise to describe an intersection of concerns of oppressed minorities. From its original formulation, intersectionality expanded to a prominent concept in critical sociology, primarily because of two additional theoretical innovations. One was the so-called matrix of domination, also referred to as 'vectors of oppression and privilege,' which gave birth to the dichotomy of white privilege vs. minority disadvantage. In this view, Israeli Jews and the state they created were the epitome of white privilege, whereas the Palestinians were the poster-children of racist-driven disadvantage.

The other innovation, known as the standpoint theory, identifies knowledge as a product of a specific social position. As one scholar put it: 'One's standpoint (whether reflexively considered or not) shapes which concepts are intelligible, which claims are heard and understood by whom, which features of the world are perceptually salient, which reasons are understood to be relevant and forceful, and which conclusions credible.' Also, another analyst put it, 'intersectionality privileges experiential authority,' which gives any distinctive identity group the 'experiential authority' to speak 'conclusively and decisively only about their own experience.'

For instance, if a race issue comes to the fore, the community of people of colour takes the lead. The rest of the intersectional community is required to act as their allies and speak out in their favour. The Palestinians, the alleged victim of 'white privilege,' are automatically supported by the entire intersectional community of people of colour, women, and LGBTQ, to name a few,[5] without questioning Palestinian cases of abuse of people of colour, women, or LGBTQ.

There has been a spirited debate about the BDS movement's real impact on various facets of Israeli politics, economy, and culture. In the absence of agreed-upon empirical criteria for evaluation, this debate is difficult to solve. The instances of antisemitism are also not investigated enough.

In the last two decades, the rise of antisemitism has reached a peak. Some observers point to Israeli Professor Shlomo Sand, who published two bestsellers, in 2008 and 2012, delegitimizing Israel's right to exist and negating the right of Jews for self-determination, themes considered antismitic according to the IHRA Definition of antisemitism. While it was not entirely a dormant feeling, Sand provided the reasons for it to sprout. According to Sand, Jews are not people and, therefore, not connected to the Land of Israel. Arguably, Sand provided the antismites an academic stamp of approval for their claims since he is a Tel-Aviv University professor. After deconstructing the Zionist 'nation-and-identity building' project, Sand offered his own version of history that tried to undermine the 'false mythistory' of the Old Testament to denote contentions.[6] In his haste to nullify Jewish affinity to the Land of Israel, Sand described Ashkenazi Jews as converts to Judaism, thus breaking their connection to the land. Simultaneously, Sand ignored Sephardic lineage to ancient Jewish history, which destroys his theory. However, the damage is done. For example, on 2 September 2018, the Musawa satellite channel, owned by Palestinian Public Broadcasting, broadcasted an Arabic interview with Sand, titled 'Shlomo Sand: I do not think that Israel will remain in place in the Middle East!' The host presented Sand as following:

The guest of "Dialogue of the Hour" today is the Israeli historian, who wrote a series of publications that exposed the falsity of the Zionist narrative, and refuted the term the Jewish people and denied their existence ... and who holds the highest academic degree in History from Tel-Aviv University, and a specialist in the history and theories of peoples and nationhood and political history of the twentieth century.

In another example, a British Labour Party member and a Tower Hamlets official, Puru Miah, has been 'administratively suspended' by the Party for antisemitism. In one case, Miah wrote on Facebook on 6 August 2014:

The invention of the Jewish People by Israeli historian Shlomo Sand. This is an absolutely "must read" for everyone who wants truth and justice for Palestine/ Israel. The essential historical evidence will amaze you - there is no factual basis whatsoever for a Jewish race, nation or homeland, it is all a recently invented propaganda called "Zionism." Download and read now.[7]

Sand is, of course, but one contributor to the resurgent trend of antisemitism. However, tackling the de-legitimisation of Israel, BDS and antisemitism requires constant monitoring, exploration, and re-examination. By way of facilitating this process, this special issue seeks to provide cutting-edge analyses on the various aspects of this soft threat to Israel's national security: from the growing assault on Israel's image and legitimacy in world public opinion in the post-1967 era; to the constant de-legitimisation campaign at the United Nations and its specialised agencies; to the hugely disproportionate (and vastly unjustified) censure of the Jewish state by 'human rights' non-governmental organisations (NGOS) while turning a blind eye to massive atrocities by serial human rights violators; to the misuse of the Palestinian problem and Israel's relations with its Arab citizens for de-legitimisation purposes; to the BDS's operational and propaganda techniques; to the coalescence of anti-Zionist and antisemitic ideologies in general, and their convergence in BDS precepts and ideology in particular.

Notes

1. The International Holocaust Remembrance Alliance, an intergovernmental organisation founded in 1998 in Stockholm by the-then Swedish Prime Minister Göran Persson, developed a definition of antisemitism several years later. Referring to Israel, the Definition notes that, 'Denying the Jewish people their right to self-determination, e.g. by claiming that the existence of a state of Israel is a racist endeavor'; 'Applying double standards by requiring of it a behavior not expected or demanded of any other democratic nation'; and, 'Drawing comparisons of contemporary Israeli policy to that of the Nazis,' can be construed as antisemitic.
2. Volpato, "Picturing the Other."
3. The Economist Intelligence Unit (EIU) is the research and analysis division of The Economist Group which produces reports for almost 200 countries and provides analysis to understand how the world is changing.
4. Barnett, *Post-Zionism*.

5. Sprague-Jones, "The Standpoint"; and French, "Intersectionality."
6. See note 4 above.
7. "Dialogue of the Hour," *Musawah Channel*; and "Councilor Suspended."

Disclosure statement

No potential conflict of interest was reported by the author(s).

Bibliography

Barnett, D. *Post-Zionism and Israeli Universities: The Academic-Political Nexus*. Saarbrücken: Lambert Academic Publishing, 2016.

Dialogue of the Hour, Palestine 48. "Shlomo Sand: I Do Not Think that Israel Will Remain in Place in the Middle East!." with dubbing voice, *Musawah Channel*, September 3, 2018. (#بأن أعتقد زاند:لا شلومو ٤٨ #فلسطين_٨_# حوار_الساعة (إسرائيل ستبقى قائمة في الشرق الاوسط!،ح5،حوار الساعة،2-9-18،مدبلج،مساواة). https://www.youtube.com/watch?v=7mEI0gBSwRo

French, D. "Intersectionality, the Dangerous Faith." *National Review*, March 6, 2018. https://www.nationalreview.com/2018/03/intersectionality-the-dangerous-faith/

"The International Holocaust Remembrance Alliance Definition of Antisemitism." https://www.holocaustremembrance.com/working-definition-antisemitism

Mandel, J. "Councilor Suspended for Saying 'No Basis for a Jewish Race, Nation or Homeland'." *Jewish News*, November 27, 2020. https://jewishnews.timesofisrael.com/councillor-suspended-for-saying-no-basis-for-a-jewish-race-nation-or-homeland/

Sprague-Jones, J., and J. Sprague. "The Standpoint of Art/Criticism." *Sociological Inquiry* 81, no. 4, September 29 (2011): 404–430. doi:10.1111/j.1475-682X.2011.00385.x.

The Economist Intelligence Unit (EIU). https://www.eiu.com/topic/democracy-index

Volpato, C., et al. "Picturing the Other: Targets of Delegitimization across Time." *International Journal of Conflict and Violence* 4, no. 2 (2010).

From underdog to occupier: Israel's tarnished image

Yoav Gelber

ABSTRACT

The purpose of this article is to show that most problems that Israel has faced in the public opinion domain in recent decades were evident already in the wake of the Six Day War. Israel either ignored or miscomprehended their significance. While it has become a struggle over the consciousness of the world in general, and the younger generations in Israel and abroad in particular, Israel treated it as a problem of internal and external *'Hasbara'* (explaining) and has been unprepared and ill equipped to cope with it.

The transformation of Israel's image

After statehood, Jewish intellectuals in the diaspora and some of their Israeli counterparts found it difficult to comply with the new reality of the Jewish State that seemed opposed to their idyllic academic worldview in Britain, France the US or Jerusalem.[1] After 1967, they could hardly identify with the "'Greater Israel'" that ruled the territories and their Arab inhabitants. The persistence of fighting after the war widened the gap. Men of spirit such as Isaiah Berlin, Raymond Aron, George Steiner, Jacque Derrida abroad, or Yaakov Talmon and Yehoshua Arieli in Israel, wished the Jewish State to be Athens while she increasingly turned into a Sparta. Israeli patriotism deterred them, and the tribalism and provincialism of the Israelis appeared to contrast the cosmopolitism and liberalism of Western Jewry. They still admired Israel and continued to hope that one day she would become 'a light unto the nations' but the continued domination of the territories frustrated their hopes.

In the waiting period before the war, many Israelis felt threatened with annihilation, and abandoned by the enlightened world that did nothing to remove the tightening Arab siege. After the triumph, these feelings beefed up and reinforced distrust of the international system and the morality of statesmen and intellectuals whose origin dated back to the Holocaust. Criticism of Israel's position after the war exasperated the public, and many Israelis argued that the government should act according to Israel's interests, and ignore the condemnations of its opponents and the criticism of its friends. The response to criticism, wrote the British ambassador Michael Hadow in his first half-annual report after the war, was xenophobic and distanced foreign governments and friends alike though not yet all of western public opinion.[2]

Harvard sociologist Seymour Lipset, a strong supporter of Israel, wrote in the midst of the war that in the Arab-Israeli conflict it was possible to argue morally for both sides. If one believes that recognising Israel's legitimate right to exist, and not just the recognition of the fact of its existence, is a precondition for peace he should endeavour to achieve such a recognition. Israel did not accomplish it in the past because after signing the armistice accords in 1949 and withdrawing from Sinai in 1957, nothing was left to give the Arabs in return for their recognition. Hence, the US should do everything to prevent the UN from enforcing withdrawal on Israel, and Israel should not withdraw before the signing of peace agreements based on recognition of its legitimate right to exist.[3]

After the war, the issue became not just legitimacy but also demography. Between 1949 and 1967, the Arab minority in Israel did not threaten the Jewish nature of the state, but the war revived the demographic issue. Demography presented the question of the state being 'Jewish", beyond its legitimacy as a state. Subsequently, the question surfaced: what is 'a Jewish state' and how it can be reconciled with democracy.

The change

The shift from the underdog icon to that of the triumphant 'occupier' was rapid.[4] One week, the weekly *Economist* devoted the front page to Israel under the title 'They Did It!' describing how its audacity made Israel victorious. In the next week's edition, Israel was put on the docket and won a considerable amount of moral lecturing. Other newspapers shifted from describing the festivities in Israel in the first week after the war to portraying the misery of the Arabs in the next one.

Newspapers in the West published reportages about the wretched Egyptian soldiers that roamed the dunes of Sinai, the use of NAPALM bombes by the IAF, and the expulsion of hundreds of thousands from their homes in the Western Bank and the creation of a new problem of Palestinian refugees. Israeli legations across the globe warned of the quick spread of Israel's image as 'cruel towards the civilian population.'[5]

An editorial in the *New York Times* preached to Israel to demonstrate generosity towards the defeated, adding that occupation is not peace.[6] The London *Times* wrote that Israel's conditions for a settlement (that had not been decided yet and certainly had not been published) were 'those of a conqueror.' The media in the West, its editors and correspondents did not reflect public opinion but endeavoured to shape it. Polls revealed a different picture from the press, and although support for Israel diminished in the two years after the war it was still far higher than support for the Arabs that remained static. Those who withdrew their support moved mainly to the camp of the neutrals and a little less to the camp of 'I don't know.' Yet, it was only a matter of time until the criticism of Israel among journalists would affect the public and the polls.

Defensive or offensive war?

The uncompromising image of Israel derived primarily from its determination to hold all the occupied territories until the signing of peace treaties, and part of them forever. Israel justified its stance claiming that the Six Day War was a defensive war launched by the blockade of the Tiran Straits, and being the attacked party she was entitled to retain the territories.

Most members of the UN did not accept the Israeli contention. Many member states backed the Arab and Russian demand for Israel's prompt withdrawal to the line of 4 June 1967, and the opinion that Israel opened the war was widespread. It relied on paragraph 51 of the UN charter that distinguished between aggression (such as blocking the straits) and an act of war (what Israel did on June 5). Nonetheless, the Arabs failed to mobilise a majority of two thirds of the votes because of a controversy between member states that thought that withdrawal should take place first, and then the other problems could be handled, and other members who stood for the handling of all problems simultaneously.[7]

Foreign minister Abba Eban analysed the reasons for the consecration of existing territorial borders by the international community. Since World War II, he said, no border was changed as a result of a war. The approach to terminating wars relied on three principles: cease fire; return to the status quo ante; negotiating a solution. The main cause for this procedure was the shared assumption that any existing situation is preferable to its forceful change.[8] Despite all their profound disagreements, on this matter Dayan agreed with Eban:

> We want something unacceptable by the world: to expand the borders of the country. All states go to war, but they don't go to make a new state and take from another state. We want it ... a lot of time and many struggles will be necessary in order to succeed in achieving it.[9]

The shift of world public opinion

Public opinion in the West was shaped by sentiments rather than juristic arguments or political considerations. The world was flooded by rumours of

Israeli atrocities in the occupied territories. War stories were replaced with accounts of the Arabs' expulsion from the Jewish Quarter of Jerusalem's old city and from the West Bank, and Israel was urged to allow refugees to return to their homes. Some rumours had factual basis, but the source of many others was inventions of local employees of UNRWA and foreign consulates. Other fictitious narratives emanated from the USSR and its satellites.[10]

The communist media's hostility had been known for a long time. The novelty was a new position among liberal newspapers in the West that had sympathised with Israel before the war. The change began in France, continued to Britain and ultimately spread over all Western States. The official French media represented the government, namely De Gaulle's position. The French president once described the Jews as a chosen people, sure of itself and domineering, and warned them of replacing the aspiration for independence with frantic urge for occupation. His statement provoked a wave of responses across the globe that blamed him for antisemitism. Israel still hoped at the time for an alteration of the French embargo policy and its official reaction was moderate. All PM Eshkol had to say about the statement was that De Gaulle failed to comprehend what Zionism is.[11]

In addition to De Gaulle, Eban blamed 'the communist press as well as a circle of Jews that belongs to the intellectual Left and makes a lot of noise, but has no real influence on public opinion.' *Le Monde* appeared to him the central organ of this anti-Israeli propaganda campaign.[12] He comforted himself with the fair treatment of Israel in the French commercial TV, but his persuasion of the Left intellectuals' lack of influence on French public opinion was no more than a wishful thinking.

Early in 1969, the Israeli embassy in London organised a visit to Israel of four editors of central newspapers. They interviewed Eshkol and had discussions with ministers, army generals and senior officials of the Foreign Ministry. The interview with Eshkol covered political topics such as his opinion of potential successors, resolution 242, Israel stance on opening the Suez Canal and Russian influence in the region. However, the guests also asked the PM what was his reaction to the assertion that the Jews robbed Arab lands already before statehood? A question that implied doubts about the very legitimacy of the Jewish State.[13]

The BBC held a prominent place among the hostile media. For Example, it published regularly the announcements of the Palestinian terrorist organisations about imaginary accomplishments on the battlefield together with the IDF spokesman's statements and under a mask of journalistic neutrality, granted them legitimacy. The Israeli protests were to no avail, either ignored or dismissed.[14]

In the spring of 1968, Eban went on a tour of the Scandinavian States, where the change of attitude to Israel could be easily noticed. During the war, more than thousand Swedes, mostly non-Jews, volunteered to go to Israel and help it. Less than a year later, Eban heard from the Swedish premier, Tage Erlander, that if Israel aspired to change its borders he would not support it. Eban was impressed that the higher the position of his interlocutors, the greater was their friendship to Israel. In the street parades, however, protestors shouted slogans against Israel and in support of *Fatah*. Sweden was the pioneer, and other Scandinavian countries followed suit. Eban, however, convinced himself that the problem was not Israel's policy but its image.[15]

He was widely off the track. He might have been annoyed by the image, but the Scandinavians were irritated by the essence. Long before the Palestinians appeared on the international scene as an independent factor, the Swedish social-democratic press published sympathetic reports describing the Palestinians as the third player in the Middle East conflict, alongside Israel and the Arab States.[16]

Eban denied the assertion that a total collapse of public opinion on Israel was taking place. Back from another tour in Western Europe he told the members of the Knesset: 'There is stability and continuity of the basic attitude of both governments and public opinion, and nothing fundamental has changed since the war.' Eban was closed in a diplomatic bubble and detached from reality.[17] His self-confidence contradicted what every newspaper reader could have noticed. He did not distinguish between diplomacy and *Hasbara* and between *Hasbara* and a struggle for the younger generation's minds and hearts. He was impressed by statesmen and diplomats with whom he talked and turned a blind eye to the deep undercurrents among parts of the general public.[18]

American public opinion and Israel

The transformation of Israel's image in the US was slower than in Europe. In certain circles, support for Israel grew and in others it diminished. Critics of Israel, professors of government, political science and international relations, and diplomats who had served in the Middle East and feared for the US status in the region, rushed to outline the details of their preferred settlement. Israel's insistence on direct negotiations and peace treaties, they accused, was an excuse for doing nothing.[19]

By contrast to some American and Israeli professors' sophisticated suggestions that appealed to the State Department's officials, the polls revealed ordinary Americans' view of the conflict, as McGeorge Bundy reported to President Lyndon Johnson: 'This view is far more sensible and rational than that of certain officials in the State Department.' According to the polls, the Americans thought that: (1) The Arab started the war; (2) The Russians were behind the Arabs' initiative; (3) The Israelis cleared the ground; (4) The UN is a joke; (5) The Arabs (and the Russians) have to pay for their re-education. Bundy further told the president that the American public was not opposed to Israel's annexation of Jerusalem, but was perplexed to see apparently wise persons think that the Israelis should give up the fruits of their triumph. He finished his report reminding the president that according to a basic American principle, losers should pay for their loss.[20]

Public sympathy notwithstanding, in the eyes of the haughty American media the underdog of May-June turned into triumphant conqueror. Sympathy for the weak shifted to the side of the Arabs both in the conservative press that had not felt compassion for Israel before the war, but also in friendly magazines such as *Time*. The shift was not swift, and began with the idea of separating between Israel's existence in its prewar borders and its right to keep the newly gained territories. Magazines such as *Life* or *Look*, and a daily like the *New York Times* were ambivalent on the second issue already at the end of June 1967.

Israeli visitors to the US reported on the effects of the press attitude on American Jewish young people. Back from a long tour of America, Golda Meir, then secretary general of the ruling *Mapai* party, revealed that the critics of Israel are not just Arabs and communists but also people who had previously backed Israel. The worst, she said, were the people of the intellectual Left, many of them Jews and even former Zionists.[21]

The conspicuous presence of Jewish youth in the ranks of the New Left worried the American Jewish establishment. Many articles and essays in the American Jewish press dealt with the phenomenon, analysed it and offered various ways of responding to it. Israelis, too, were curious about the linkage between the New Left and young Jews. Israeli emissaries' attempts to converse with few leaders of the Jewish radical students failed and the efforts to strengthen the connections with Jewish students in general also gained little success.[22]

The Old Left blamed Israel for being a proxy of the administration and serving the big oil companies (in fact, the oil companies criticised the administration for its support of Israel). The New Left accused Israel of imperialism and regarded it as a threat to the revolutionary Third World. Comparing Israel with Apartheid South Africa began already in 1967, and the leaders of the Black Power called the Israeli victory 'a Genocide.'

Disapproval of Israel grew as the efforts to reach a negotiated settlement proved stillborn and the US seemed to lose its grip of the Arab World. The *New York Times* wrote in July 1968 about American isolation in the Arab World and quoted Nasser's mouthpiece Hassanin Heikal arguing that the American Jews shaped the US image in the moderate Arab countries. He further quoted an American diplomat (probably Donald Bergus) asking whether support for Israel was worth the economic and political loss of the Arab World?[23]

Three months after his arrival in Washington, Israel's new ambassador, Yitzhak Rabin, estimated that not only the administration but also 80% of American public opinion disagreed with Israel's control of a million Arabs in the territories. This attitude did not clash with their support for Israel's right to live in peace and security, its sovereignty and independence. American opposition to annexation, Rabin said, derived from the issue of the territories' population.[24]

Two years later, on a visit to Israel, Rabin explained that below the ripple of the Arab-Jewish conflict, American public opinion on Israel was shaped by undercurrents emanating from different mentalities. One of American society's basic principles was the separation of State and Church. The unique linkage in Judaism between religion and nationality was hard to explain and difficult to digest, and the Jewish nation-state linked not only state and nationality, but also state and religion. The Palestinian propaganda underscored the supposedly racist nature of the Law of Return, claiming that 'you, the American Jew from Boston are allowed [to enter Israel and automatically naturalise] and I, who have lived there 800 years, am forbidden [to enter].' These matters, he told Knesset members, bring the debate back to the basic problems of Zionism, but the Americans are superficial and have no time and patience for profound discussions: 'There are no Jewish refugees nowadays, there are Palestinian refugees', and from their viewpoint this is the determinant fact.[25]

The old and the new left

During the 1960s, a new version of radical Left emerged in Western Europe that did not accept the authority of the USSR and was detached from the established communist parties. This new version did not focus on a struggle against class discrimination but against other forms of injustice: racial, gendered and colonialist. Its basis of power was in the universities, not the factories, and the sources of its inspiration were professors who introduced Western versions of Marxism based on Antonio Gramsci and the Frankfurt School of Marxism-. A parallel movement emerged in the US from the struggles for women and Afro-Americans rights, and primarily from the opposition to the Vietnam War. Jews held a prominent place in the New Left on both sides of the Atlantic Ocean.

The New Left was not a coherent movement but an assortment of groups that vied for a variety of goals, from non-proliferation of nuclear arms to animal rights. Some of them stressed anti-colonialism, others emphasised feminism and all opposed the US and the political establishments of their own countries. Rabin once reported after meeting a group of radical Jewish intellectuals: 'I was overwhelmed. They are for Israel, but say: keep distance from the American scum. You are OK, America is not. Don't be linked to America.'[26]

The old and new European Left ignored older forms of colonialism, such as Arab, Turk or Russian. By contrast, they had aversion to the former Western colonialism and regarded Israel as a bastion of Western colonialism/imperialism in the Middle East. They were obsessed with the Palestinian problem. This obsession was common to Israel's partisans and opponents alike.[27]

As long as the hub of the conflict was Israel's relations with the Arab states, the intellectuals of the New Left were a secondary factor in shaping public opinion vis-à-vis Israel. Only after the 1973 war, when the Palestinians returned to the heart of the conflict, the New Left's role was upgraded. In Western Europe there was almost an overlap between Intellectual and Leftist, and between the Left and support for the Palestinians.

Already before the outbreak of the protests in France in May 1968, Golda Meir asked Israel ambassador to France, Walter Eitan, if his estimate that French public opinion sympathised with Israel related 'also to the left-wing intellectuals.' Eitan replied that 'almost all our opponents are Jewish intellectuals. However, these circles are not France, they are small groups of people who voice their opinions loudly.'[28] In the course of the riots a few months later it was clear that Eitan underestimated the left-wing intellectuals, who became the protestors' main source of inspiration.

Minister of Information Israel Galili was aware of the influence of the New Left on the Israeli Left, and warned of 'accommodation to the values of the hostile propaganda also among Israelis.' He proposed to summon a group of intellectuals for a brainstorming on how to respond, with an emphasis on the polemics with the New Left. Galili mentioned the names of poet Haim Guri, writer Hanoh Bartov, historian Zvi Ya'abetz and philosopher Natan Rotenstreich. It is highly doubtful if these were the befitting persons to cope with the buds of the New Left in Israel.[29]

The impact of Palestinian propaganda

A principal cause for the change in Israel's image in the eyes of public opinion was the return of the Palestinians to the conflict. A main goal of the Fedayeen organisations was elevating the Palestinian question from a humanitarian problem of refugees to a national issue, and the attainment of international recognition of their national liberation movement. The war was a significant milestone on their road. In certain circles of the European public and American campuses the Palestinian status ascended in direct relation to the increasing question marks about Israel's legitimacy.

Fatah propaganda presented the organisation in the West as a movement deeply interested in freedom, also of Jews, that strove to establish a democratic secular state in Palestine, free from the chains of Jewish theocracy. At the end of 1968, the two central dailies in the US, *The*

New York Times and *The Washington Post*, published articles that called for an American dialogue with the Palestinian organisations. On 13 December 1968, *Time Magazine* published a long reportage on Yasser Arafat and *Fatah*, describing them as the principal source of instability in the Middle East. Arafat's portrait appeared on the Magazine's front page.[30]

In early February 1969, the British *Guardian* wrote that the *Fedayeen* were rapidly gaining international recognition like other national-liberation movements in the Third World.[31] Two weeks later, after *Fatah* took over the PLO, the *Washington Post* editorial called the great powers and the UN secretary-general to acknowledge reality and negotiate with PLO representative in New York.[32] These were only preliminaries, but after Black September 1970 massacres, the US administration looked for ways to involve the Palestinians in a political settlement of the conflict.

At the beginning of 1969, the head of Israeli military intelligence, Maj. Gen. Aharon Yariv, warned that it was difficult to prevent international recognition of the PLO.[33] Prof. Yehoshafat Harkavi, a former head of intelligence, warned of the implications of the Palestinians' return to the political stage: unlike its predecessors that were satisfied with abominations and anti-Semitic slogans, he said, *Fatah* waged an ideological struggle and contesting it was a complex matter.

Harkavi was the first Israeli academic to notice the Palestinians' central role in the struggle for the world's consciousness. Since the beginning of Zionism, he said, there had not been times in which its basics were challenged like the present days. Israeli students abroad, he complained, failed in debates with Palestinians because of their ignorance of both the Arab and the Zionist positions. The conflict preoccupied the Arab students more than it interested their Jewish counterparts and they were better informed. The Arabs portrayed Israel as a colonialist state and claimed that the Balfour Declaration had been made without asking for Arab opinion. Israel did not put forward counter-arguments, did not emphasise the Arab pomposity as a national stance and related to it as rhetoric: 'we are afraid to present the Arab position as a national one and describe it as a diplomatic posture', Harkavi said, and summed up that '*Fatah* has turned to be a dangerous and serious matter in the public opinion.'[34]

Rabin expressed similar observations. Palestinian propaganda, he said, stopped talking about destroying Israel. Instead, it described the supposedly idyllic coexistence of Muslims and Jews until the appearance of Zionism and asked why the Muslim world should pay for the maltreatment of Jews by the Christian world. The Palestinians spoke about separating religion from the state (something natural for Americans but virtually non-existent in the Arab world), portrayed the Law of Return as religious discrimination and contended that the solution should be a bi-national state (euphemised in today's politically correct terminology as 'a state of all its citizens'). This propaganda,

Rabin maintained, appealed to Jewish students, who constituted a third of the demonstrators in support of the *Fatah* in American universities. Luckily enough, he added, after their graduation the students – Jews and non-Jews alike – return to be typical Americans and forget the rebellious years of their youth.[35]

'The Fifth International'

The Palestinian propaganda appealed to both the radical left and the radical right. The pro-Palestinian propaganda in Italy, as well as in other West European countries, linked what was labelled the 'Deir Yassin massacre,' namely 1948, with the situation after the Six Day War and questioned the very legitimacy of Israel's existence. Attempts by Jewish youth and students' organisations to cope with it were usually futile.[36]

Similar conditions prevailed in West Germany. Socialist students who had supported Israel before the war turned against it, encouraged by Arab students who fed them with anti-Israeli propagandist materials. Their anti-Israeli stance interlaced well with the German socialist students' anti-establishment postures on other issues. A top rating TV programme screened in May 1968 a film that had been photographed in Jordan and portrayed *Fatah* terrorists as volunteers fighting for freedom and heroes combatting for the return of their plundered homeland.[37] Emigrants from Israel, members of the *Matzpen* radical group, served as their alibi and verified their allegations. Israeli students who studied in Germany attempted to cope with both the Arab students and their Israeli partners. However, they were inferior quantitatively, and especially were not well versed in issues of the Arab-Jewish conflict and needed guidance that was not forthcoming.[38]

Yaakov Zur, a veteran spokesman for Zionism and Eitan's predecessor in Paris, argued that the problem was not one of explaining Israeli policy but one of ideology. Marxist hostility accompanied Zionism from its infancy and the arguments of conservatives and the big oil companies were also known before Jewish statehood. In 1968, the innovation was the joining of the anti-Zionist chorus by the anti-establishment New Left, mainly because of the central role played by the Jewish youth in it. Zur attributed the New Left's anti-Israeli stance to its inclination to view realities in black and white and to its rebellion against consensus when sympathy for Israel was almost consensual in established America. In Europe, Israel suffered from the general hostility of the left to the US because of the Vietnam War. The New Left sympathised with the losers and the oppressed and regarded the Arabs as such. All these, Zur summed up, could not be remedied by *Hasbara*. To cope with them, Zionism should resume its nature of a national liberation movement.[39]

The foundations of the Fifth International – the ostensibly impossible alliance of the radical left with the radical right, financed by Arab petrodollars – were laid in that period in West Germany and spread over Europe. Thus, for example, Uri Avneri's book *The War of the Seventh Day*, was published in Germany under the title *Israel ohne Zionisten* (Israel without Zionists) by the publishing house of the Neo-Nazi newspaper *Deutsche National Zeitung* and was popular among its readers alongside Hitler's speeches, the memoirs of the commando hero Otto Skorzeny and the letters of Nazi prisoners from the Spandau prison.[40]

Occasionally, the propaganda struggle turned violent. Upon his return to Israel at the end of his term in Bonn, ambassador Asher Ben-Natan contended that out of his 23 presentations in German universities during his mission only four were interrupted. He forgot to mention that these were the last four and all the others had taken place before the war. Nonetheless, he was convinced that the interruptions and protests reflected a minority and the vast majority of the German students supported Israel even when criticising its policy.[41]

Similar incidents took place in France. Israel's embassy in Paris traced the activities of Palestinian students and their fans, using volunteers from among the Israeli students for that purpose.[42] In the summer of 1969, violence escalated. In France, the Jewish community was larger and less restrained than in West Germany. In December members of Betar youth movement assailed a rally of Palestinians and their fans at a university in Paris. At the end of January 1970, another clash took place in Paris between Jewish students and hundreds of leftwing students who assaulted a rally of the Jewish Students Front shouting 'Death to the Jews!' Fourteen persons were wounded and property was damaged. A few months later the riots spread from the campuses to the immigrants' slums around Paris, where squabbles broke out between Jews and immigrants from North Africa.[43]

In the spring of 1970 the repercussions of the 'Goldman Affair' in Israel spread from newspapers' headlines in Europe to the streets. In various places, parades of Arab and leftwing students, reinforced by leftwing MP's, demonstrated against 'Israeli and American imperialism.' The protesters burnt flags and puppets in the image of Moshe Dayan, and a few passers-by were stabbed.[44]

Things came to a head at the World Youth Conference that convened in New York to celebrate the 25th anniversary of the United Nations. The delegations from East Europe and the Third World dominated the debates and passed a resolution that expressed solidarity with the Palestinian People and demanded to establish 'a united and democratic Palestinian State.' For the first time, an international forum under UN auspices called for the foundation of a Palestinian State 'united and democratic', namely instead of Israel and not alongside it.[45]

Was it a Hasbara problem?

Two weeks after the 1967 war, Eshkol convened a team of advisors to discuss the deterioration of Israel in world public opinion. The director general of the PM Office, Yaacov Herzog, emphasised the need to reinforce *Hasbara* abroad, but added that it could not be a substitute for action. After the meeting he noted in his diary: 'This was a totally depressing get-together.' Galili, who wrote down the protocol, ordered to destroy it and described the meeting as 'shocking.'[46] Following the consultation Eshkol decided to appoint a ministerial committee for *Hasbara*. Eban was offended and threatened to resign from the Foreign Ministry, the government and the Alignment (party). Having been asked why he wouldn't resign also from the Knesset, he calmed down and did not raise the issue again.[47]

The deterioration in Israel's image provoked a discourse on its reasons. Netanel Lorch, for example, maintained that Israeli *Hasbara* addressed the intellect and tried to persuade people by using rational arguments. By contrast, Arab propaganda was emotional and aimed at provoking compassion. The Arabs stressed the misery of the refugees and the allegedly persecuted population of the West Bank and portrayed them as hapless victims. Israel, he wrote, should consider counter-measures and decide whether they are desirable or not. He suggested emphasising topics like the conditions of Jews in the Arab countries, the Egyptians' war crimes in Yemen, the Syrians' attitude to prisoners of war and the murder of shot down pilots.[48]

A year after the war, Eban pointed to four issues that affected Israel's international standing: (1) A feeling that Israel was more interested in territories than in peace; (2) the military government and the assertion that a liberal occupation is still an occupation; (3) the situation along the ceasefire lines and what the world perceived as disproportionate retaliation by the IDF; (4) The old (1948) and new (1967) refugees that raised the question of 'how many hundreds of thousands people should wander, migrate, to fortify the positive phenomenon of Jewish sovereignty?'[49] The first three issues referred mainly to Israel's policies. The fourth issue was more profound and concerned its legitimacy.

In his interviews with the local press on the eve of the 1969 Jewish New Year, Eban found himself under attack over the impotence of Israeli *Hasbara*. He explained that since the war Israel had been encountering unprecedented issues: controlling another people, military administration, laws of occupation, Hague and Genève conventions and international law. In the post-colonial age, no other Western state was facing such a situation. Israel had good answers to most questions, but they were not easy and it was impossible to separate the policy from explaining it. Statesmen, he said, should occasionally take steps that have price in terms of *Hasbara*, and demolition of houses cannot leave positive impression even if there are reasons for it.

Defending his ministry, Eban mentioned articles in the Arab press that criticised the Arab *Hasbara* and complained that the Zionists took over the world, the voice of the Arabs is mute, Israel had been holding Arab lands for more than a year and the world was not shaken, Israel had the most efficient propaganda in the world, etc. Israeli *Hasbara* was far from being the best in the world as some Arabs claimed, but it also was not the most inferior as the rightwing opposition and a few Israeli newspapers asserted.[50]

The foreign ministry viewed *Hasbara* in short range terms and concentrated its efforts on politicians and 'opinion shapers,' mainly media personalities. He invited them to visit Israel and instructed its ambassadors and senior officials to grant them interviews and background talks abroad. The significance that Eban assigned to the British press did not derive from its influence on the British public but from the fact that it was read regularly in many foreign ministries around the world. He briefed his people to meet as many editors as possible, to prepare a seminar for opinion shapers and to submit diplomatic complaints on every partiality on the part of the BBC.[51]

The foreign media asked questions that did not conform with the Israeli ethos and usually did not accept it. Foreign correspondents regarded East Jerusalem as an occupied Arab city. For them, the Palestinian refugees were dispossessed people striving to return to their homes and the Arab *Fedayeen* were freedom fighters like the Jewish underground organisations that fought against the British in pre-statehood years. The answers did not convince the interviewers, and gradually also a growing part of the readers, listeners and watchers abroad.[52]

One of Eshkol's last interviews was granted to Arno De Borshgrave of the magazine *Newsweek*. The interviewer pressed Eshkol with difficult questions like 'how do you justify the ongoing Israeli occupation of Arab lands?' 'How Israel intends to solve the refugee problem and will it be prepared to allow part of them to return to their homes?' 'Why the terrorists are not freedom fighters and their organization are illegitimate?' 'Why the Jews deserve a national home and the Palestinians do not?' 'Where does he stand on the issue of a Palestinian State?' 'Hasn't the time come for an Israeli peace initiative?'

Eshkol coped well with the questions. Sometimes he bypassed them, in other cases he calmed down the journalist and occasionally refuted them. However, his historical knowledge was not something to be proud of:

What are the 'Palestinians'? When I arrived in this country [1913] there were a quarter of a million non-Jews, mainly Arabs and Bedouin. It was a desert more than a primitive region. Nothing. Only after we blossomed the desert and straightened it they wanted to take it from us.[53]

This was not a slip of the tongue. Eshkol gave a similar figure in an interview to Hanna Zemer of *Davar* at the end of March 1968. He spoke of 200,000 Arabs in 1913 and apparently believed it. The real number was more than three times bigger.[54]

Confronting Palestinian propaganda

De-colonisation shaped a world that was empathic to the old Palestinian allegation that Zionism was a colonialist movement. This assertion dated back to the first Palestinian Congress in January 1919, but carried little weight in a world that had not regarded colonialism as a derogatory word. As Israel's domination of the territories continued, it was increasingly perceived as colonialist.

Israel's official *Hasbara* failed to cope with the New Left, with the young generation in Europe that was free from the guilt feelings for the Holocaust of its parents and with the Protestant churches that led the missionary activities in the Middle East. Partly, the difficulties emanated from obsolete techniques, an anachronistic approach and unqualified personnel. Many Israeli diplomats who stood at the forefront of the *Hasbara* campaign had not lived in Israel for years. They were slow to adapt to the transformation caused by the war, and all the more so to explain it to others. The traditional written or visual *Hasbara* materials were bound to raise funds, not to clarify ideological and political disputes and were irrelevant to the struggle over consciousness and legitimacy. They preached to the converted and had no chance of persuading the unenlightened.[55] A potential group that might help in this campaign were Israeli academics who went abroad on sabbaticals, conferences and lecture tours. The politicians, however, felt that they often served the Arab propaganda more than the Israeli *Hasbara*, and rather than persuading the professors and students of the New Left they were influenced by them. Golda Meir mentioned Talmon 'who compares us with South Africa and Rhodesia. What else should be said about us? Unfortunately, he is not the only one.' Many MKs agreed, and some recalled that 'we have never gotten satisfaction from Mount Scopus.'[56]

Confrontations between Israeli and Arab students abroad exposed not only the Israelis' weakness in terms of knowledge, compared to their Arab rivals, but also their doubts about representing the just side: 'They are confused about the very right for existence. They are perplexed when the issue of dispossession comes forward. They are embarrassed when a guy from Jaffa tells them: I was born in Jaffa ... where have you been born? You are a vuz-vuz who came from Poland or Romania.'[57]

In May 1969, a joint symposium of the foreign ministry and Hebrew University professors discussed Israel's reflection in the eyes of the world and its relation to *Hasbara*. The professors did most of the talking, but spoke mainly about the policy and little about explaining it. Yirmiahu Yovel elaborated on academe as a possible channel to the New Left abroad, but insisted that the contacts could not be established by people who identified with Israel's policy. Michael Rabin warned that recognition of the Palestinians might open an outlet to the New Left, but would certainly distance King Hussein.[58] Dan Patenkin complained about how unpleasant it had become to be an Israeli abroad, especially in academic and intellectual circles. Natan Rotenstreich remarked that the debate on Israel's legitimacy had not begun after the war: 'We are portrayed not as imperialists of 1967, and not of 1948, but as if the Zionist enterprise in its entirety is a project of Boors from South Africa. We have to cope with it as a matter of our destiny, to explain its various faces and our relation to the heritage of the Jewish People.'[59]

An exceptional voice was the last speaker, Israel Kolat, who objected to his colleagues' total negation of the 'Greater Israel' idea: 'I think it is a positive idea in all aspects. As long as we keep the territories and don't have an alternative, why shouldn't we say that we have a right for them? If we are going to concede, we can say explicitly that we have a right but are ready to concede it for the sake of compromise.'[60]

Two years after the Six Day War, Israel's foreign ministry was surprised to discover that Palestinian spokesmen were received abroad as representatives of a liberation movement and the Palestinians were viewed as the forgotten people of the Middle East who were exploited by Israel – and to a lesser extent by the Arabs – and were entitled to play a central role in the resolution of the conflict.[61] The Palestinians were welcomed not only by traditional opponents of Israel but also by non-hostile progressive circles and even by American and European Jews who were unfamiliar with the details of the conflict and its history. American and British official policies lagged behind but not out of sympathy with Israel but because of Jordanian insistence on its exclusive right to speak for the Palestinians.

Eban ascribed the erosion of Israel's position in American public opinion to its tough political position. In Europe, by contrast, he ascribed the decline to Israel's actions in the territories, or 'the occupation': 'They [the Europeans] demand that our measures in the territories comply with the Fourth Geneva Convention ... We cannot abide by the Geneva Convention and at the same time fight against *Fatah*. The convention requires the population to obey. It does not submit to this duty.' Most of the criticism of Israel concerned the arrest and interrogation of suspect terrorists.[62] Israel denied allegations of torture, but Eban admitted that the life of those interrogated was hard and acknowledged the difficulties it created for Israeli *Hasbara* in Europe. Beyond the Palestinian front, Eban understood well that targeting civilian objectives harmed Israel's image in Europe. The horrors of WWII were still vivid in European memory and people above

22   SOFT THREATS TO NATIONAL SECURITY

a certain age remembered how factories were bombed and their workers were killed:

> What irritates Europe is not our insistence on peace, but their associations of relations between government and populace. This is far more significant in Europe than in America. The word 'curfew' has [in Europe] a meaning and so are the words 'demolishing a house'. Words such as "collateral" or "collective" punishment trigger memories [of WW II].[63]

The foreign ministry responded to the new challenges but did not really comprehend them. It mobilised the services of leading commercial advertisers who proposed to promote Israel as they used to advertise products or political parties in election campaigns. They failed because the problems and requirements of Israel's image were different from those of the political or commercial world of marketing. Organisational changes within the ministry also yielded marginal results. Another short-lived initiative was the establishment of a 'public council for *Hasbara*' to advise the ministry on the principal issues of *Hasbara*.[64]

Eban wanted the Israeli *Hasbara* to broaden the one-dimensional image of Israel as a fighting nation and portray it as 'a democratic, civilised state that worked on scientific development and social progress, a state that has created original values ... Our challenge is to bring back into the world's cognisance the true Israel ... that continues its creative life as a multi-dimensional society in spite of the security situation.'[65]

Eban's line might be appropriate for the Israeli media of the time, but their foreign colleagues were interested in topics, such as occupation, peace or political settlement, settling in the territories, demolishing houses and arrests.[66] Eban agreed that the deterioration of Israel's status in the field of public opinion was not an outcome of Arab propaganda, but stemmed from the growing suspicion towards its policy in the territories and its alleged aim to retain all of them.[67]

Before the war, Israel handled the *Hasbara* front mainly with official adversaries – foreign and propaganda ministries in the Arab world and some times in the Eastern Block. Its tools were created for this encounter. In the duels between diplomats, Israel usually had the upper hand, at least if we accept Arab self-criticism of their own propaganda.

The transformation of Israel's image in the wake of the war took the Israeli leadership and public by surprise. Long forgotten or apparently self-explaining subjects such as nationalism, colonialism, refugeedom, land and settlement, returned to the fore. Their application to the territories has been controversial within Israeli society, and with the passage of time more cracks appeared in the national consensus. The main pillar of this consensus remained security, a vague and subjective term, given to various interpretations.

While Israeli *Hasbara* focused on security because it was the broadest uniting element of Israeli society, its Arab, mainly Palestinian opponents focused on justice, based mainly on history. Their historical arguments have been mostly fake, but official Israeli *Hasbara* abandoned this field a long time ago to the Palestinians and their Israeli post-Zionists partisans. How long can safeguarding the life of every Jew in the country from every hot-headed or insane Palestinian terrorist justify Israel's rule in the territories?

The Six Day War changed the rules of the game. A struggle for the Israeli, Arab and world consciousness replaced the former diplomatic contest and fund-raising campaigns. The quintessential victim of this change was Eban, described by a fellow Israeli politician after one of the UN General Assembly's sessions as 'the most brilliant, fluent and witty speaker in the entire assembly. He speaks in the name of the most justified subject that the assembly debates. Yet, when he steps down after his speech, no one modifies his view or vote.'

Notes

1. Eisenstadt, *Israeli Society*, 331; and Keren, *The Pen and the sword*.
2. UK National Archives (hence: TNA), Prem 13/1624, Michael Hadow's report to Foreign Minister George Brown on the situation in Israel half a year after the war, 16.11.1967.
3. Lyndon Baynes Johnson Library (hence: LBJL), NS-Defence files, Box 193, Seymur Lipset to Vice President Hubert Humphrey, 8 June 1967.
4. Avineri, "Western Anti-Zionism: The Middle Ground," 173–4; and Muravchik, *Making David into Goliath*.
5. LBJL, History files, Box 23, folder 3, Charles Bohlen (American ambassador to Paris) to Secretary of States, 12 June 1967; ISA, 7460/10/A, Gershon Avner (Israeli ambassador to Ottawa) to Arthur Lurie (Ministry of Foreign Affairs, hereafter: MoFA) Same date; ibidem, Meir Ezri (head of the Israeli legation in Tehran) to MoFA, same date; ibidem Yaacov Shimoni (Israeli ambassador to Sweden) to MoFA, 14 June 1967.
6. Editorial, *New York Times*, 19 June 1967.
7. ISA, 8161/7-A, protocol of the Knesset Foreign Affairs and Defence Committee's meeting, 11 July 1967, 4–5; Ibid, Gideon Rephael (Israel's ambassador to the UN) survey at the Protocol of the Knesset Foreign Affairs and Defence Committee's meeting, 8 August 1967, 13–17.
8. Labour Party archives (hereafter: LPA), 2/14/67-33, Aubrie Eban (Abba Even) in the meeting of Mapai's ideological forum, 23 December 1967, 7–9.
9. IDF archives, 1/12/75, Dayan in the meeting of the IDF General Staff, 6 January 1969, p. 15.
10. LBJL, SCNC files, Box 8, folder 5, USA embassy in Moscow to Secretary of State, 12 and 13 June; LBJL, History files, Box 21; Israel-Arab situation report of the CIA, 18 June; LBJL, SCNC files, Box 109, folder 4, USA embassy in Moscow to Secretary of State, 22 June 1967.
11. Heiman, "The Relations between Israel and France under De Gaulle," 338–9.
12. ISA, 6434/45-C, Eban to Minister of Tourism Moshe Koll, 21 January 1968.

13. ISA, 6420/7-C, Shimshon Arad to Adi Yaffe, 6 February 1969.
14. For a discussion of British public opinion's attitude to Israel in the wake of the Six Day War, cf. Blass, From a threatened state to a dangerous state, chapter I.
15. ISA, 8161/12-A, Eban's review in the meeting of the Knesset's defence and foreign affairs committee, 21 May 1968, 6–8.
16. *Aktuellt*, 27 November 1968 and 18 December 1968.
17. Cf. Yoav Gelber, *Ha Kheth Ve'Onsho: Darka Shel Israel LeMilchemet Yom HaKipurim* (Crime and Punishment: Israel's Road to the Yom Kippur war), Dvir, forthcoming 2021.
18. ISA, 16707/5-A, Eban review in the protocol of the meeting of the Knesset committee for defence and foreign affairs. 13 March 1970, 7–8.
19. ISA, 6490/15-C, Talmon's speech in the protocol of a symposium of the Foreign Ministry and a group of professors of the Hebrew University, early May 1969, 28–31.
20. LBJL, Country Files, Box 110, folder 1, Bundy's memo to Johnson, 10/7/1967.
21. LPA, 2/24/1967-90, Golda Meir's report on her tour of the USA in a meeting of *Mapai* secretariat, 3/12/1967, 3.
22. Geoffrey Vigoder, "Dmuta HaMesulefet Shel Israel BeEiney HaNo'ar HaYehudi BeAmerica" (The Distorted Image of Israel in the Eyes of Jewish Youth in America), *Davar*, 10 March 1969, 7.
23. *The New York Times*, 17 July 1968.
24. ISA, 8161/12-A, protocol of the Knesset committee for defence and foreign affairs' meeting, 20 May 1968, 8.
25. ISA, 16707/8-A, protocol of the Knesset committee for defence and foreign affairs' meeting, 29 June 1970, 32.
26. ISA 8162/12-A, protocol of the Knesset committee for defence and foreign affairs' meeting, 29 May 1969, 10.
27. Israel Neuman, 'an interview with Albert Memmi', *Davar*, 23 February 1968, 9.
28. ISA, 8161/8-A, protocol of the Knesset committee for defence and foreign affairs' meeting, 13 December 1967, 9–10.
29. ISA, 7466/7-A, protocol of the Director Generals' committee for *Hasbarah*, 23 December 1968.
30. *Time Magazine*, 13 December 1968, 29–32 and 35–36.
31. *Guardian*, 6 February 1969.
32. The *Washington Post*, 21 February 1969.
33. ISA, 8162/4-A, protocol of the Knesset committee for defence and foreign affairs' meeting, 25 February 1969, 22.
34. ISA, 8162/4-A, protocol of the Knesset committee for defence and foreign affairs' meeting, 18 February 1969, 5–14. Cf. also Harkavi's essay "The camouflage Slogan: A Palestinian Democratic State," *Ma'ariv*, 3 April 1970, 19.
35. ISA, 8162/5-A, protocol of the Knesset committee for defence and foreign affairs' meeting, 20 May 1969, 10.
36. *Ma'ariv*, 2 May 1969, 17; LPA, 4–031-1969-5, Newsletter to Israeli Legations Abroad, 16 September 1969.
37. ISA, 7456/4-A, Israel's embassy in Bonn to the foreign ministry, 27 May 1968.
38. David Lipkin, "Israelim mesay'im LaFatah BeGermania" (Israelis help the Fatah in Germany), 6.
39. Ya'acov Zur, 'Lo Vikuach Srak – Ela Mitkafa Ra'ayonit' (not a futile discussion but an ideological offensive), *Davar*, 22 August 1969, 3.
40. Inge Deutschkron in *Ma'ariv*, 19 September 1969, 3.

41. ISA, 16707/6-C, protocol of the Knesset committee for defence and foreign affairs' meeting, 10 April 1970.
42. ISA, 4232/11-FA, Ilya Akerman to Arie Levin of the Israeli embassy in Paris, 20 May 1969.
43. *Ma'ariv*, 10 December 1969, 2; 1 February and 16 June 1970, 3.
44. Cf. for example items on anti-Israeli demonstrations in London and in Ankara, *Ma'ariv*, 17 and 18 May 1970. On the Goldman affair see Chazan, "Nachum Goldman's initiative"; and Gelber, *Attrition: the forgotten war*, 603–11.
45. *Davar* and *Ma'ariv*, 14 and 19 July 1970.
46. ISA, 4511/3-A, entry in Herzog's diary for 22 June 1967.
47. ISA, 7231/1-A, Eban to Eshkol, 7 August 1967.
48. ISA, 7466/7-A, Lorch to the Director Generals' committee for *Hasbarah*, 29 December 1967.
49. ISA, 18161/12-A, protocol of the Knesset committee for defence and foreign affairs' meeting, 18 June 1968.
50. A symposium of Eban and the foreign ministry's top officials and the editorial committee of the daily *Yedi'ot Acharonot*, 22 September 1968, and Eban's interview to the daily *LaMerchav* of the same date.
51. ISA, 5254/16-FA, minutes of a consultation at Eban's office on relations with Europe, n.d. but apparently end of April 1969.
52. Cf. for example the text of Dayan's interview to the BBC's *Panorama* program in *Jerusalem Post*, 17 January 1969.
53. De Borshgrave's interview with Eshkol, *Newsweek*, 17 February 1969.
54. ISA, 7231/1-A, text of Eshkol's interview to Hanna Zemer, 29 March 1968, 3.
55. ISA, 8162/1-A, protocol of the Knesset committee for defence and foreign affairs' meeting, 5 July 1968, 2–4.
56. ISA, 8162/5-A, protocol of the Knesset committee for defence and foreign affairs' meeting, 3 June 1969, 17.
57. ISA, 16707/9-C, protocol of the Knesset committee for defence and foreign affairs' meeting, 24 July 1970, 16–17.
58. ISA, 6490/15-C, protocol of the joint symposium, early May 1969, 37–38 and 45.
59. Ibid., 47–9.
60. Ibid., 56.
61. ISA, 6889/4-C, "Israel and the Palestinian Entity," attached to Eliashiv Ben Horin's circular letter to Israel's heads of legation across the world, 20 June 1969.
62. ISA, 7437/13-A, Aron Remez to Herzog, 5 November 1969.
63. ISA, 16707/3-C, protocol of the Knesset committee for defence and foreign affairs' meeting, 26 December 1969, 13.
64. ISA, 5254/4-FA, minutes of consultations on *Hasbarah* at Eban's office, 12 February and 10 March 1970.
65. ISA, 5254/16-FA, protocol of the meeting of the public council for *Hasbarah*, early May 1970.
66. ISA, 7428/10-A, Aluf Har-Even to the members of the public council for *Hasbarah*, 20 September 1970.
67. ISA, 16707/9-C, protocol of the Knesset committee for defence and foreign affairs' meeting, 24 July 1970, 13–15.

Disclosure statement

No potential conflict of interest was reported by the author(s).

Bibliography

Avineri, S. "Western Anti-Zionism: The Middle Ground." In *Anti- Zionism and Antisemitism in the Contemporary World*, edited by R. Wistrich. Basingstoke: New York University Press, 1990.

Blass, Y. "From a Threatened State to a Dangerous State: The Causes for the Change of Israel's Status in the UK, 1967-1982." PhD dissertation submitted to the Hebrew University, 2017

Chazan, M. "Yozmat Nachum Goldman LeHipagesh 'Im Nasser BiShnat 1970." [Nachum Goldman's Initiative to Meet Nasser in 1970.] *'Iyunim BiTkumat Israel* 14 (2004): 255–284.

Eisenstadt, S. N. *Israeli Society*. London: Weidenfeld and Nicolson, 1967.

Gelber, Y. *Hatasha: HaMilchama ShNishkecha* (Attrition: The Forgotten War). Dvir, Hevel Modi'in, 2017.

Heiman, G. "The Relations between Israel and France under De Gaulle, 1958-1967." PhD dissertation submitted to the Hebrew University of Jerusalem, 2009

Keren, M. *The Pen and the Sword: Israeli Intellectuals and the Making of the Nation-state*. Boulder: Westview Press, 1989.

Muravchik, J. *Making David into Goliath: How the World Turned against Israel*. New York: Encounter, 2014.

The unspoken purpose of the academic boycott

Martin Kramer

ABSTRACT
The academic boycott of Israel, ostensibly targeting Israeli academe, is actually meant to isolate and stigmatise Jewish academics in America. It serves the aim of pushing Jewish academics out of shrinking disciplines, where Jews are believed to be 'over-represented.' That is how diehard supporters of the Palestinians find academic allies who have no professional interest in Palestine, in fields like American studies or English literature.

What is behind the spread of the academic boycott movement? The usual explanation is that Israel's policies, particularly Israel's blockade of Gaza, the way it wages its war on Hamas, and its settlement policy in the West Bank, have pushed American academics over the edge. American academe, with its overwhelming liberal-left bias, has grown alienated from the Jewish state. This has created an opening for boycott advocates, who trade on the analogy between Israel and South Africa. If a boycott worked to end apartheid, it can work to end the occupation – so goes the argument.

Let us begin by asking a simple question: who does the boycott seek to stigmatise and isolate? The simple answer would be: Israeli institutions of higher education, since they are the ostensible targets of the boycott. But that answer is way too simple. I am going to anticipate my more complex answer, and then explain it.

The academic boycott of Israel is actually meant to isolate and stigmatise Jewish academics in America. It serves the aim of pushing Jewish academics out of shrinking disciplines, where Jews are believed to be 'over-represented.' That is how diehard supporters of the Palestinians find academic allies who have little interest in Palestine, in fields like American studies or English literature.

For these allies, it is not about the Israeli occupation of Palestinian territories. It is about the presumed Jewish occupation of American academe by Jewish faculty and administrators. Decades ago, a litmus test on Israel and

Palestine was used to push Jews to the margins of Middle Eastern studies. Now the strategy is being imitated in other fields, where academic positions are scarce and Jews have some of the best of them. In the words of the American congressman Tip O'Neill, all politics is local – and so are the politics of the academic boycott.

But first, let me dispense with the conventional argument: that the academic boycott is meant to stigmatise and isolate Israel's research universities. This cannot be done, and the boycotters know it. Israel's universities are highly productive, and their research output cannot be ignored. They aren't South African universities. They also have highly developed institutional partnerships all over the world, in both North America and Europe, in fields as diverse as computer science, business, and medicine.

The targets aren't individual Israelis either. The boycott applies to institutions, not individuals. For example, when the American Studies Association (ASA) passed its boycott resolution in 2013, it announced that Israelis could still attend the ASA and deliver papers. The ASA even announced that Israeli university presidents could present at their annual conference, in their personal capacities. So the academic boycott doesn't do much to stigmatise or isolate individual Israelis. Despite an academic boycott, an Israeli can go off to an ASA conference, present a paper, and safely put it down on his or her resume as a credential for appointment or promotion.

But let us say that the person in question is a young doctoral student or assistant professor in an American university in some field of the humanities. Quite possibly she is Jewish, and someone in Israel has heard of her work. She opens an email, and there it is: an invitation to an academic conference in Jerusalem or Tel Aviv. The theme is right up her alley. The organisers will fly her over, put her up, show her around, and will edit the proceedings of the conference.

Normally, she wouldn't think twice – she would shoot back an email saying 'I accept your kind invitation,' and call her dad to tell him she is finally going to Israel. But her professional society has just passed a boycott resolution at its annual conference. What does she do?

If she does go to Israel, someone might point a finger at her: she's a boycott buster, she's acted outside the bounds of her discipline, she's been unprofessional. If she is up for appointment or tenure, does she want that conference in Israel on her c.v.? What if someone on the academic committee sees himself as a boycott enforcer, and spots it? Will this torpedo her candidacy or promotion? Sure, she doesn't agree with all of Israel's policies; she might even be openly critical of them. But is she going to shun her Israeli peers by refusing their invitation? What does she do?

And let me give you an example of the language of these enforcers – this, from a professor of history at the University of California at Irvine, published on Facebook in 2014. (I apologise for the language.)

SOFT THREATS TO NATIONAL SECURITY

> '*Machers*' in the American Jewish community get up in arms about BDS. Well ... fuck you. Call me uncivil, but still, fuck you. Fuck all of you who want to make arguments about civility and about how Israel wants peace ... and how you are in fact a 'critic' of Israel. There is only one criticism of Israel that is relevant: It is a state grown, funded and feeding off the destruction of another people. It is not legitimate. It must be dismantled, the same way that other racist, psychopathic states across the region must be dismantled. And everyone who enables it is morally complicit in its crime, including you.[1]

This is the intimidating language of the boycott enforcers, they have tenure, and they show no quarter.

She, the young academic, can accept the invitation and take the risk – and it is a risk. If she's up for a rare job in her field, it could kill her chances. She can turn down the invitation, say nothing, and become a Jew of silence. Cary Nelson is the former president of the American Association of University Professors. He has written the following: 'I know many secret Zionists who avoid expressing public support for Israel. They worry that to do so might torpedo their jobs. They worry it might limit their chance at presenting a conference paper or being appointed to a committee.'[2] One option is to become one of these crypto-Zionists.

But perhaps even silence isn't enough if you are in the humanities. Nelson goes on to add this: 'Only virulent hostility toward Israel wins broad approval among American humanities faculty.'[3] You need broad approval to advance. So a third option is to show some virulent hostility yourself – especially if you are a Jew, and therefor naturally suspected of secretly being a Zionist. And virulent obviously doesn't mean supporting a two-state solution; that doesn't count. The boycotters on your faculty expect you to denounce Israel as an apartheid state, support the Palestinian right of return, perhaps even accuse Israel of genocide.

It is this young Jewish American graduate student or junior professor who is stigmatised and isolated by the academic boycott of Israel. She has to pass a litmus test, and it is one that's hardest to pass for Jews.

Now litmus tests for Jews in the academy are nothing new. In the 19th century, in universities in Germany and Russia, a Jew couldn't be appointed to a professorship unless he renounced Judaism and converted to Christianity. In the early 20th century, in the Ivy League, a Jew couldn't be appointed to a professorship unless he shed his 'clannishness' and detached himself from Jewish life.

All these litmus tests were meant to restrict the Jewish presence in the academy. Since World War Two, it seemed as though the litmus tests had disappeared: this was a 'golden era' for Jews in academe. But we are now seeing the re-emergence of the litmus test: if a Jew wishes to take his or her place in certain parts of the academy, he or she must first renounce Zionism and denounce Israel. And the motive for imposing this litmus test is the same as all past litmus tests: it is to restrict the Jewish presence in the academy.

Why would a litmus test reemerge? We are used to thinking of American academe in the past few generations as a welcoming place for Jews. As early as 1969, according to the largest survey ever, Jews constituted 9% of the faculty nationwide, and 17% of the faculty in the highest-ranked universities. And at the highest-ranked universities, Jewish faculty made up 36% of law, 34% of sociology, 28% of economics, 28% of medicine, and 26% of physics (all figures for the upcoming faculty under 35).[4] This, at a time when Jews had fallen to 3% of the population. Today, the figures may be even higher, while Jews have fallen to under 2% of the population.

Jews also had more exalted status within the academy. Reviewing the same data, sociologist Seymour Martin Lipset noted that

> academic achievements of the Jewish faculty are reflected in their rank and financial status. Although slightly younger on the average than non-Jews ... a larger percentage of Jews were full professors. And the salaries of the Jewish professors were considerably higher than those of other faculty.[5]

In recent decades, Jews also have risen to high positions in university administration, including the presidencies of major universities. It began in 1968, when Edward Levi became president of the University of Chicago. The list is now long, and includes past and present presidents of Harvard, Princeton, Yale, Cal Tech, and MIT. We like to believe that the university, as a place of liberal enlightenment, is perfectly at ease with this Jewish 'over-representation.' Academe is a meritocracy, and Jews enjoy their outsized place by virtue of their merit, which, we assume, is universally acknowledged.

But this situation evolved under particular conditions. After the Holocaust, antisemitism in America declined, and quotas restricting Jews became an embarrassment. But just as important, after World War Two, rising enrolments created a faculty shortage, which gave Jewish academics an initial rung on the ladder.

Today the situation is reversed. The Holocaust has receded in memory, and Jews are regarded not as targets of prejudice but as bearers of privilege. And in much of academe, especially the humanities and social sciences, student demand is weak and falling, full-time academic jobs are rare, and budgets are being cut. For every tenured position, the competition has become cutthroat.

And where competition is cutthroat, anything goes. Academe now seethes with struggles over diversity, ethnicity, gender and race, and it would be naïve to think that Jewish 'over-representation' isn't an issue anymore.

Of course, no one will stand up and say that there are too many Jews in a discipline – that would be deemed blatantly antisemitic. Instead, sociological theses are advanced. For example, one can now encounter the thesis, dressed up as an empirical study, that Jews are being admitted to elite colleges at rates that aren't justified by their merit.[6] The suggestion is then made that Jews on university faculty and in higher administration are unconsciously doing what WASPs did in the early 20th century: skewing admissions criteria so that their own kind are preferred over others.

This thesis can then be extended from student admissions to faculty appointments. These, so it is suggested, are subject to the subtle influence of 'ethnic networking.' Such networking is common and legitimate in economic activity. It's not supposed to happen in well-regulated universities. The insinuation is that it does happen, and while Jews aren't the only ones who do it, Jews do it better than anyone else, perhaps because their network includes not just faculty and administrators but also donors.

The academic boycott is the answer: it is agitation to establish a moral litmus test that Jews will have the hardest time passing. It is thus no accident that the associations that have passed academic boycott resolutions represent fields in the humanities and social sciences which are in the deepest crisis.

Consider the analysis of almost a thousand academics who had signed or endorsed one of the statements calling for an academic boycott of Israel. Fully half came from the humanities, another third from the social sciences; the largest single disciplinary affiliation, by a large margin, was English and literature. The compiler of this study was perplexed. After all, she wrote, 'there is no obvious connection between the discipline of English and the Israeli-Palestinian conflict.'[7]

Of course there isn't, but that isn't the point. The relevant points are these: First, English literature is a field in which the job market has been in a free fall since 2008. In the decade between 2007 and 2017, the number of jobs on offer fell by more than half.[8] Most PhDs don't get jobs and feelings of betrayal and distrust are rampant.

Second, English lit was one of the very last bastions of academe which was breached by Jews. When, in 1969, Jews formed more than a quarter of the faculty in law, physics, sociology, and economics, they were only 7% of the faculty in English. Historically, this was the discipline most resistant to appointing Jews. But eventually, in they came. Now the discipline leads the way in imposing the litmus test of the academic boycott that Jews will have the hardest time passing.

At the time Israel was created, such a test wasn't needed. When Lionel Trilling became the first Jew tenured in Columbia's English department back in 1944, he was told straight out not to think of himself 'as a wedge to open the English department to more Jews.'[9] Today, those who fear 'ethnic networking' by Jews need a more subtle tactic. They have found an ideal one in the academic boycott of Israel.

The other fields that make up the boycotters' specialities are almost as troubled, every one of them is contracting, and in every one of them, Jews are 'over-represented.' In this setting, the Israel-Palestine issue gets blown out of proportion, not because it gives rise to special outrage, but because one side of it is, by association, 'over-represented' and thus resented in disciplines undergoing a wrenching downsizing.

The debate over Israel and the Palestinians is mostly a proxy fight for the real fight. Some have argued that Israel's conduct is prompting antisemitism. In the case of American academe, the opposite is true: rolling back the 'disproportionate' Jewish presence is served by the disproportionate inflation of Israel's supposed crimes. Israel in Gaza becomes a useful stick with which to beat the local Jews. The boycotter who isn't an Arab wants a boycott, not to keep Jews out of the faraway West Bank, but to keep Jews out of the downstairs faculty lounge – to make room for someone else.

I have not used the word antisemitism here. But the remedy, if there is one, is to begin speaking frankly about what is really at work, and to avoid euphemisms. The academic boycott isn't mostly Israel's problem. It is America's problem – and specifically the problem of American Jews. They must decide if the place earned by Jews in American academe is worth preserving. If it isn't, then at least Israel has vibrant universities and colleges that can make up the difference.

Notes

1. History professor Mark Levine, quoted by Nelson, "Conspiracy Pedagogy"
2. Nelson, "Am I a Zionist?"
3. Ibid.
4. This was the 1969 survey by the Carnegie Commission Survey on Higher Education, as analysed by Steinberg, *The Academic Melting Post.*
5. Lipset, "Jewish Academics".
6. Unz, "The Myth".
7. Rossman-Benjamin, "Interrogating".
8. Kramnick, "What We Hire".
9. Diana Trilling, "Lionel Trilling".

Disclosure statement

No potential conflict of interest was reported by the author(s).

ORCID

Martin Kramer (iD) http://orcid.org/0000-0002-2560-2679

Bibliography

Kramnick, J. "What We Hire in Now: English by the Grim Numbers." *Chronicle of Higher Education*, December 9, 2018.

Lipset, S. M., and E. C. Ladd Jr. "Jewish Academics in the United States: Their Achievements, Culture and Politics." *American Jewish Year Book* 72 (1971): 102.

Nelson, C. "Am I a Zionist?" *Jerusalem Post*, October 25, 2014.

Nelson, C. "Conspiracy Pedagogy on Campus: BDS Advocacy, Antisemitism, and Academic Freedom." In *Anti-Zionism on Campus*, edited by A. Pessin and D. S. Ben-Attar, 196. Bloomington: Indiana University Press, 2018.

Rossman-Benjamin, T. "Interrogating the Academic Boycotters of Israel on American Campuses." In *The Case against Academic Boycotts of Israel*, edited by C. Nelson and G. N. Braham, 222. Detroit: Wayne State University Press, 2014.

Steinberg, S. *The Academic Melting Post: Catholics and Jews in American Higher Education*. New York: McGraw-Hill, 1974.

Trilling, D. "Lionel Trilling, a Jew at Columbia." *Commentary* 67, no. March (1979): 46.

Unz, R. "The Myth of American Meritocracy." *The American Conservative*, November 28, 2012.

Human Rights Watch's anti-Israel Agenda

Gerald M. Steinberg

ABSTRACT

The influence of Human Rights Watch (HRW) is reflected in the organisation's intense involvement in institutions that emphasise human rights, including the United Nations and the International Criminal Court. However, HRW and its leaders have been strongly criticised for intense political and ideological bias against Israel and for proliferating unsubstantiated accusations to fit this bias. This article documents the role of Kenneth Roth, Executive Director since 1993, in this politicisation. Roth's direct involvement with Israel-focused activities is fundamentally different from his role on other topics and countries on HRW's agenda, and contrasts strongly with norms of universality and political neutrality.

On 19 November 2020, U.S. Secretary of State Pompeo issued a declaration categorising anti-Zionism as a form of anti-Semitism, and particularly the 'Global BDS Campaign as a manifestation of anti-Semitism.' He also directed the Office of the Special Envoy to Monitor and Combat Anti-Semitism to identify organisations that support such campaigns.[1] According to media reports, US-based Human Rights Watch (HRW) is one of the groups most likely to be included in this policy.[2] In this context, the description and analysis of the activities and campaigns undertaken by this organisation that focus on Israel, Zionism, and BDS (boycotts, divestment and sanctions) are of major significance.

Human Rights Watch was founded as Helsinki Watch by the late Robert Bernstein in 1978, and has grown to become one of the most influential international non-governmental organisations active in this arena. As of 2019, HRW had an annual budget of 92 USD million, and its influence is reflected in the organisation's media visibility, as well as intense involvement in many institutions and platforms that emphasise human rights, including the United Nations and the International Criminal Court.

However, the organisation and its leaders have been strongly criticised, including by its own founder, Bernstein, for acting against its original mission, and for deep-seated political and ideological bias, accompanied by the proliferation of unsubstantiated accusations to fit this bias. In an opinion piece published in the *New York Times*, Bernstein accused HRW officials, including Roth, of abandoning their 'original mission to pry open closed societies' and instead focusing on Israel, an open society, in order to 'turn Israel into a pariah state.'[3]

As demonstrated in this article, Roth's direct involvement with Israel-focused activities are fundamentally different from other topics and countries on HRW's agenda. Former board members have referred to 'a palpable hostility toward Israel among the HRW brass.'[4] In 2011, in the wake of Judge Richard Goldstone's renunciation of his UN report on the Gaza conflict, a report heavily influenced by HRW's 'research,' Bernstein urged Roth to follow this example and 'issue his own mea culpa.'[5]

The systematic analysis of Roth's personal attitudes on Israel and his control of HRW's agenda for almost three decades are significant because of the influence he and HRW have had on key international institutions, as well as in universities (specifically law schools and human rights programmes), liberal think tanks, media coverage of these issues, and other realms. Furthermore, Roth's exercise of soft power is amplified by the absence of external review mechanisms or checks and balances within the structure of HRW.

Background: the principle of universality in human rights

International conventions and compacts highlight the centrality of universality and neutrality in human rights. The 1948 Universal Declaration of Human Rights (UDHR) emphasises equality in the title as well as repeatedly in the text. This document was composed in the shadow of the Holocaust, with the objective of marking a clear departure from Nazi racial hatreds and antisemitism. The introduction declares: 'all human beings are born free and equal in dignity and rights,' and Article 7 proclaims 'All are entitled to equal protection against any discrimination in violation of this Declaration and against any incitement to such discrimination.'

Numerous individuals and institutions, including NGOs such as Human Rights Watch, claim to derive their moral authority from the UDHR, and proclaim a commitment to political neutrality. In practice, their activities often reflect biased agendas. A number of systematic analyses provide evidence of such bias, including detailed studies by Robert Charles Blitt[6] and by Vennesson and Rajkovic, who describe a history of double standards, discriminatory behaviour, and disproportionate criticism, citing bias and contradictory HRW 'fact finding' in making accusations.[7] As Michael Ignatieff noted, many NGOs and their officials 'espouse the universalist language of human rights but actually use it to defend highly particularist causes.' Ignatieff cites the example of 'persons who care about human rights violations committed against Palestinians [who] may not care so much about human rights violations committed by Palestinians against Israelis.'[8]

The role of Kenneth Roth, HRW executive director

Kenneth Roth has served as HRW's Executive Director since 1993 and has met with success in expanding its public profile, influence, and fundraising. He is a public figure, frequently representing HRW in the media, the United Nations, international conferences (such as the Davos World Economic Forum) and other venues.

He is also primarily responsible for the biases, disproportionality, and violations of universality in HRW's activities pertaining to Israel, and for the major impact of these activities on the worldwide perceptions of Israel regarding human rights and international law.

Prior to Roth's appointment, the Middle East, and Israel specifically, had not been significant aspects of HRW's agenda. This changed in the mid-1990s, with the addition of staff members with advocacy backgrounds in radical politics criticising Israel.[9] In parallel, HRW began to issue frequent reports of 'grave violations of international humanitarian law' and 'collective punishment' by Israel.[10] It is notable, as reflected in Bernstein's criticism, that as HRW increased the emphasis on Israel, the surrounding countries, undemocratic and with poor human rights records (to understate the case), received far less coverage from HRW.

To some degree, this can be attributed to the political environment which singled out the Jewish state, as reflected in UN General Assembly Resolution 3379 labelling Zionism as a form of racism (1975), and in the UN human rights frameworks, which are major sources of disproportional condemnation.[11] In parallel, extensive media coverage created a feedback loop in which HRW and other NGOs provided media content in the form of allegations of egregious human rights violations, and gained visibility and funding in return.[12]

But beyond these factors, the evidence indicates that Roth has been personally and ideologically invested in HRW's disproportionate focus on Israel. During the period from 2001 to 2004, which was characterised by Palestinian mass bombings and Israeli responses, Roth wrote letters to world leaders backing the Palestinian cause, including the 'right of return' (the Arab/Palestinian euphemism for Israel's destruction via demographic subversion), published opeds, gave numerous media interviews and spoke in international frameworks, repeatedly condemning Israel.[13]

His views and animus were directly reflected in HRW activities. In early 2002, after deadly Palestinian suicide bombings inside Israel killed and wounded hundreds, the IDF entered the Jenin refugee camp, the hub of these attacks. HRW issued 10 reports, press releases, and UN statements accusing Israel for 'indiscriminate' and 'disproportionate' attacks, 'willful killings,' 'summary executions' and 'war crimes.'[14] In examining HRW's record during this period with respect to other conflicts (for example, Kashmir, Columbia, Sri Lanka), or regimes with the worst human rights records (Syria, Saudi Arabia, Iraq, Iran) the level of activity was significantly reduced relative to issues related to Israel.

Furthermore, the condemnations of Israel for the Jenin incursion, an operation in a very crowded urban area in which 52 Palestinians, a majority of them combatants, and 23 Israeli soldiers were killed,[15] contrasted sharply with the nearly complete absence of HRW comments on the dozens of deadly Palestinian mass terror attacks during that period. In response to criticism of this discrepancy, Roth and HRW provided technical excuses, claiming that human rights and international law applied only to states, and not to non-state actors, including the PLO and Hamas.[16]

In 2004, Roth travelled to Israel to launch HRW's report, 'Razing Rafah,' which excoriated Israel over measures to prevent Palestinian weapons smuggling into Gaza, and repeated accusations of deliberate Israeli attacks against civilians.[17] Roth again denied 'giving Israel disproportionate attention' while emphasising Israel's power and contrasting it with the perceived weakness of the Palestinians.[18]

A detailed study of the number of reports focusing on each of the countries in HRW's Middle East and North Africa (MENA) division between 2005 and 2010 demonstrates the disproportionality.[19] Led by HRW, Israel was 'at the top of human rights hit lists.'[20] Five years later, as the torrent of allegations continued to grow, journalist Jonathan Foreman observed that, 'the overall amount of material put out on Israel, measured by words and pages, is strikingly out of balance and because HRW's reports on Israel are uniquely accompanied in almost every case by high-profile press releases and press conferences. As its executive director, Roth has devoted much of his letter writing and public work to alleged Israeli crimes, to the exclusion of other matters.'[21]

In this and many other cases, the issues, facts and gross human rights violations (in the form of attacks and war crimes committed against Israelis) on which Roth and HRW choose to be largely silent – add to the evidence of built-in bias. Commenting on these blatant omissions compared to Roth's activism during the 2006 Lebanon War, Abraham Foxman observed: 'If the intentions of Syria and Iran are not to be examined, if the takeover of part of a country by a terrorist group committed to the destruction of Israel is not something important ... then ultimately why should anyone take seriously what Human Rights Watch has to say?'[22]

As the criticism of this bias increased, Roth changed his response: 'It's not that we're exclusively focusing on Israel. But if the question is, "Why are we more concerned about the [Gaza] war rather than on other rights abuses [in Israel]?" Well, we've got to pick and choose – we've got finite resources.'[23]

Roth's biases

In the absence of concrete and consistent criteria, particularly in the realm of human rights, the process of 'picking and choosing' reflects personal opinions, biases and ideology. Roth's statements on Israel as the nation-state of the Jewish people are clearly reflective of these opinions and biases.

In 2004, responding to criticism, he told an Israeli interviewer, 'I recognize Israel as a Jewish state.' Yet, at the same time, Roth supports the Palestinian claim to a blanket 'right of return,' which would be tantamount to reversing the establishment of Israel.[24] In 2000, he sent letters to President Clinton, PLO Chairman Arafat, and Prime Minister Barak asserting (in contrast to all other historical examples) that this 'right ... persists even when sovereignty over the territory is contested or has changed hands.'[25] In a 2019 interview with journalist Eran Cicurel, Roth repeatedly declined to express support for the core concept of Zionism. Israel, he said 'can define itself any way it wants. I mean, lots of governments define themselves in nationalist terms.' But for him, a Jewish state is unacceptable 'because there are many Palestinians who live in Israel too who are citizens who deserve full rights.'[26]

In reference to Israel, Roth frequently uses language not found in his statements on other issues. In Foreman's view, 'it often feels as if Roth has a religious sense of mission regarding Israel; it's his crusade.'[27] In an exchange with critics who accused him of systematic bias, Roth responded: 'An eye for an eye – or, more accurately in this case, twenty eyes for an eye – may have been the morality of some more primitive moment. But it is not the morality of international humanitarian law.'[28] His use of the phrase 'an eye for an eye' is a highly pejorative reference to the Hebrew Bible, and clearly not the policies of the Israeli government or the IDF, neither of which utilise such language or concepts. As ADL head Abraham Foxman wrote, Roth repeated 'a classic anti-Semitic stereotype.'[29]

Roth often goes further, accusing Israel of being inherently racist. In justifying HRW's prominent role in the infamous NGO Forum of the 2001 UN Durban anti-racism conference that launched the anti-Israel boycott movement, Roth declared, 'Clearly Israeli racist practices are an appropriate topic.'[30] No other country was targeted similarly. In a Foreign Policy article (2013), ostensibly about eight countries other than Israel, Roth began by criticising President Obama for refusing to stop the alleged 'Jim Crow-like separate-and-unequal treatment of Palestinians in Israeli-controlled parts of the West Bank.'[31]

He often falsely accuses Israel of deliberately killing civilians in responding to and defending against terror attacks. During the 2006 Lebanon war, in addition to his 'eye for an eye' smear, Roth claimed that the IDF was 'turning southern Lebanon into a free-fire zone' by 'targeting civilian homes and vehicles where there was no Hezbollah military presence.'[32] In another instance, responding to criticism that he was driven by ideology,[33] Roth referred to alleged civilian deaths as a 'roadway casualty of Israeli bombing.'[34] Subsequently, when even HRW acknowledged that the 'homes' and vehicles were used by Hezbollah for storage and transport of missiles and personnel, Roth did not retract his accusations, nor did he withdraw his blatantly false claim that 'Even the Israeli government hasn't produced a single fact to refute Human Rights Watch's findings.'[35]

Again during the 2014 Gaza conflict, before the battles were over and investigations could be conducted, Roth's tweets and media statements frequently labelled Israel's actions as 'war crimes,' 'indiscriminate,' 'unlawful,' and 'collective punishment.'

Roth posted more than 400 tweets from 5 July to 2 September 2014, of which one-quarter condemned Israel; in some weeks, more than half were in this category.[36] In one instance, Roth even appeared to use international law to justify the kidnapping of Israeli soldiers or snatching their bodies to hold for ransom: 'Tunnels used to attack or capture civilians is a rights violation. Tunnels used to attack or capture soldiers isn't.'[37] In the same period, there were over 1,700 deaths due to Syria's civil war, and in Iraq, where ISIS took control, forces drove out the Christian population. 'Roth did tweet about the crises in both places ... but with nothing remotely like the obsessive energy he brought to the Israel issue.'[38]

Roth's Israel agenda is typically reflected in significant levels of sarcasm, vitriol, and deep-seated hostility. He frequently refers to Israel using, at best, contested terms such as 'racist' and 'apartheid' that expose his personal hostility. He denigrates those speaking out against antisemitic attacks linked to the conflict as 'Israel partisans' and part of the 'Hasbarah crowd.'[39]

Roth's bias has also approached or crossed the line into antisemitism and hate speech. His 2006 reference to 'an eye for an eye' in condemning the Israeli response to the Hezbollah attack was a 'classic anti-Semitic stereotype', according to the head of the Anti-Defamation League at the time, Abraham Foxman.[40] And in 2017, in the context of the white supremacist march in Charlottesville, Roth tweeted a link to a propaganda piece headlined 'Birds of a feather: White supremacy and Zionism.'[41] Roth included a picture depicting a Confederate and Israeli flag, commenting 'Many rights activists condemn Israeli abuse & anti-Semitism. Some white supremacists embrace Israel & anti-Semitism.'[42] Yehuda Mirsky of Brandeis University noted that Roth's link to a 'piece casually calling all us Zionists racists is foolish & offensive.'[43]

Invoking the Holocaust and dismissing antisemitism

In 2004, an Israeli journalist asked Roth 'What's a good Jewish boy from Chicago doing at the helm of Human Rights Watch, the famous NGO that many accuse of singling out the Jewish state?' His response referred to his father's 'stories of life in Nazi Germany until he fled in summer 1938.'[44] Similarly, for many years, Roth's official HRW biography cited his father's experience in Germany.[45] Rosa Brooks, a former HRW employee, defended Roth in the *Los Angeles Times* by again highlighting his father's experience in Nazi Germany, and dismissed the evidence and allegations of bias as attempts to silence 'anyone rash enough to criticize Israel'.[46] (Her piece was cited in Mearsheimer and Walt's tendentious book, *The Israel Lobby*.[47])

On a number of occasions, Roth has referred to the Holocaust in order to condemn Israel. In a 2006 article in the *Weekly Standard*, Joshua Muravchik criticised Roth's silence regarding Hezbollah's terror attacks and repeated threats to destroy Israel. Roth's response ignored the specifics and instead, evoked the Holocaust to minimise the implications of the threats:

> For Muravchik, the killing of 39 Israeli civilians by Hezbollah rockets is in the same league with such real genocides as the slaughter of six million Jews in the Holocaust ... but to call them genocide cheapens a concept whose continued vitality could be a matter of life and death for those who really face it. It also does a disservice to a people whose ancestors have experienced the real horror of genocide. [48]

In 2009, Roth published an op-ed piece in *Haaretz* ('Human Rights Watch Applies Same Standards to Israel, Hamas') again attempting to allay criticism of bias against Israel. As in the past, Roth did not deal with the specifics raised by his critics, but substituted an imagined claim involving the Holocaust, declaring: 'At the heart of our critics' arguments lies the view that we should hold Israel to lower standards. There is no dispute that the country was founded on the ashes of genocide and is surrounded by hostile states and armed groups. But some believe that these circumstances give Israel's democratic government the right to take whatever steps it deems necessary to keep the country safe.'[49]

Roth is also criticised for ignoring or whitewashing genocidal threats against Israel from the Iranian regime, Hamas and others. David Feith observed, 'Tehran will continue to call for Israel's obliteration – and Human Rights Watch will continue to sit back and watch.'[50] HRW founder Bernstein, joined by another former board member and Professor Irwin Cotler, wrote, 'Silence is not a moral option when states threaten genocide – especially when they are on the verge of acquiring nuclear weapons and boast that they can bring about a holocaust in a matter of minutes.'[51] Repeating his justification regarding Hezbollah, Roth responded but did not address the substance of their criticism, 'Many of [Iran's] statements are certainly reprehensible, but they are not incitement to genocide. No one has acted on them.'

Roth's avoidance of engagement on the subject of antisemitism has also drawn criticism. In 2004, he turned down an invitation from former Israeli Minister Natan Sharansky to participate in the Global Forum on Antisemitism, explaining: 'we tend to focus on violence. We have sort of decided not to get involved around attitudes per se ... For [antisemitism] to be a human rights violation one would need to see governments in Europe either embracing antisemitism, condoning antisemitic violence, not genuinely trying to stop the violence.'

On other occasions, Roth 'dismissed Jewish concerns about anti-Semitism by holding up the banner of 'free speech' or by suggesting ... that Israel's occupation of Palestinian territories is the reason' for the rise in murderous attacks on Jews and on Jewish institutions.[52]

Roth has also embraced memes that compare Israeli actions to those of the Nazis – an example of antisemitism cited in the International Holocaust Remembrance Association's working definition of antisemitism. During the 2014 Gaza confrontation, he endorsed an advertisement from a shadowy group calling itself the Jewish Anti-Zionist Network in the *New York Times* and *Guardian* that equated 'Nazi genocide' with 'the massacre of Palestinians in Gaza.' The text condemns Israel for 'colonialism, racism, and genocide,' and unnamed 'right-wing Israelis' are compared to Nazis.[53] Following a series of attacks on Jews in Germany, Roth blamed Israel's conduct during the Gaza War, and journalist Jeffrey Goldberg issued a sharp rebuke: 'Just as Jews (or Jewish organizations, or the Jewish state) do not cause antisemitism to flare, or intensify, or even to exist, neither do black people cause racism.'[54]

Roth's references and attitude towards the Holocaust and to antisemitism broadly and particularly in comparisons of Israel to Nazi-like behaviour reinforce the perception that his relationship with and criticism of Israel is influenced by personal views. In this regard, as with other dimensions, Roth undermines his and HRW's position as 'neutral and impartial' analysts of universal human rights.

Focusing on the UN and ICC

In many of their activities related to Israel, Roth and HRW effectively mirror the political environment which singles out the Jewish state, as reflected in UN General Assembly Resolution 3379 labelling Zionism as a form of racism (1975), and in the UN Commission on Human Rights (changed to Council in 2006), which added a specific permanent agenda item focused on Israel and has none for other countries.

Roth and HRW have played leadership roles aimed at involving the United Nations and the International Criminal Court in the Israeli-Palestinian agenda. Already in 1998, during the final negotiations for the Rome Treaty that created the ICC , Roth lobbied intensively to promote the strategy in conference presentations and media platforms.[55]

As noted, Roth guided HRW's role in the 2001 Durban conference, organised by the UN Human Rights Commission. Since then, he has been among the most vocal and visible figures in calling for UN investigations of allegations of violations, which, given the structural biases, were guaranteed to condemn Israel. This pattern was clearly evident in Roth's statements in 2002 (Jenin), 2006 (the

Lebanon war), 2009, 2014, 2019 (regarding Gaza), and in a number of additional cases. He and other HRW employees lobbied intensively in support of the UNHRC's contribution to the BDS movement, in the form of a database, or blacklist, of businesses ostensibly involved in West Bank settlements.

Roth has also advocated for and defended the series of 'experts' appointed to the position of the UN Human Rights Council's Special Rapporteur on the Situation of Human Rights in Palestine. Richard Falk, perhaps the most notorious in this group, who held the post from 2008 to 2014, was on HRW's Santa Barbara (California) fund-raising board until widespread criticism of Falk's obsessive demonisation of Israel forced his removal.

During and after the three week Gaza conflict at the end of 2008 and early 2009, HRW again accused Israel of deliberately killing civilians, demanding an 'independent investigation' under the UN Human Rights Council. Roth wrote a number of articles repeating his standard accusations against Israel, such as acting with 'a determination to make Gazans suffer for the presence of Hamas – a prohibited purpose for using military force.'[56]

Following the standard practice, the Council voted to establish a commission to investigate Israel alone, and Judge Richard Goldstone – who was close to Roth and a member of HRW's International Advisory Board – was selected to head it. In September 2009, Goldstone's UN Commission issued a report that was largely based on NGO accusations, including substantial input from HRW, and ominously concluded that 'some of the actions of the Government of Israel might justify a competent court finding that crimes against humanity have been committed.'[57] (The phrase 'competent court' is a reference to ICC prosecutions.) When the allegations and details were demonstrated to be false or unfounded, Goldstone recanted,[58] effectively ending this phase. Undaunted, Roth insisted 'the report will live on.'[59]

Roth repeated a similar strategy again during the 2014 Gaza war and the violent confrontations along the border between Gaza and Israel in 2018 and 2019. However, when asked about UNHRC's disproportionate focus on Israel and his role, he asserted that this image is a 'caricature that comes up in the Israeli press that the Human Rights Council, somehow, only looks at Israel.'[60]

In parallel, Roth and HRW are active in the lawfare campaigns aimed at Israelis, including the effort (2002–3) to conduct a 'war crimes trial' of Prime Minister Ariel Sharon in Belgium.[61] Roth has lobbied the prosecutor of the ICC directly to open investigations in partnership with Al Haq ('the Law'), the leading Palestinian lawfare organisation. In 2011, Roth appointed Al Haq's executive director, Shawan Jabarin, to HRW's MENA advisory board. Jabarin was convicted and served time in prison for membership in the Popular Front for the Liberation of Palestine terror group, and in 2007, the Israeli High Court of Justice referred to Jabarin as a 'human rights defender by day, and a terrorist by night.'[62] Responding to the appointment of Jabarin, Robert Bernstein declared 'I am of course shocked but even more saddened that an organization dedicated to the rule of law seems to be deliberately undermining it.'[63]

Roth's many media statements and Twitter posts reflect his emphasis on the ICC lobbying effort, including dozens of posts promoting this strategy, with repeated calls for addressing Israel's alleged 'impunity,'[64] in addition to the claim that the court has jurisdiction, despite the fact that Israel is not a signatory and Palestine is not a state. HRW submitted material to the ICC Prosecutor regarding the 2009 Gaza conflict, calling for an investigation.[65] Roth later advocated for Palestinian ratification of the ICC statute, to 'diminish the accountability gap for serious international crimes, including war crimes, and contribute to justice for victims of abuses.'[66]

In April 2012, Roth denounced ICC prosecutor Ocampo's deferral on the jurisdiction decision: 'Today's decision appears to close the door for now on access to the ICC for victims of international crimes committed in the Palestinian Territories.'[67] Roth tweeted 'ICC prosecutor says Palestine statehood status rests with UN General Assembly (which is why #Israel is so worried)'[68] and in November, following more Hamas rocket attacks and IDF responses, he asked: 'Since #Israel insists it doesn't commit war crimes, why not call PA bluff & welcome #ICC to deter Hamas rocket attacks?'[69] He also criticised President Obama for 'protecting Israel' from the ICC.[70]

After Fatou Bensouda replaced Ocampo, Roth met with her,[71] and called for moving beyond the 'endless ICC preliminary examination of Israel-Palestine' by initiating a 'formal investigation.'[72] Between 2012 and May 2020, Roth's Twitter feed contained dozens of posts promoting this effort.[73] In December 2019, when Bensouda seemed to accept the jurisdiction claim, but then requested that a panel of ICC judges endorse her finding, Roth told journalists 'Bensouda's decision to seek guidance from the court's judges nearly five years into her preliminary inquiry means that perpetrators of serious crimes will not face justice at the ICC anytime soon. Palestinian and Israeli victims have faced a wall of impunity for serious violations committed against them for long enough.'[74]

For Roth, ICC investigations and prosecutions of Israelis continue to be a primary objective, reflecting his personal ideological and political priorities, in sharp contrast to the concepts of universality and neutrality that constitute the normative foundations of human rights. This narrow investment of 'finite' resources is another example of what HRW founder Bernstein characterised as Roth's pursuit of an anti-Israel agenda, and a major departure from the original purpose of the organisation.

Bias in HRW senior appointments on Israel

As Executive Director of HRW, Roth is centrally involved in the hiring of senior staff members – particularly those dealing with Middle Eastern and

Israeli-Palestinian issues. An examination of HRW's employees working on areas of armed conflict demonstrates a departure from neutrality though the presence of many individuals with backgrounds in anti-Israel advocacy stands out. By contrast, a comparison of the backgrounds of staffers who work on Columbia, Sri Lanka, central African conflicts or the India/Pakistan dispute, for example, reveals minimal records of advocacy, bias, and lack of neutrality that characterise HRW's Israel-focused personnel.

In the mid-1990s, HRW's first Israel-related reports and advocacy campaigns were led by Joe Stork, Fatemeh Ziai and Shira Robinson, whose prior political activities displayed clear hostility towards the Jewish state.[75] In 2004, Roth hired Sarah Leah Whitson to be the director of the Middle East and North Africa division, a position she retained until January 2020.[76]

Whitson was born in the Armenian Quarter of Jerusalem's Old City (then under Jordanian occupation), and her family reportedly moved to the US in 1960.[77] Prior to joining HRW, she had been active with the Arab-American Anti-Discrimination Committee, MADRE and the Centre for Social and Economic Rights (CESR) – organisations that ran campaigns referring to Israel using charged terms such as 'apartheid,' 'matrix of control,' and 'brutality.'

At HRW, Whitson's intense anti-Israel agenda was reflected in the publications she co-authored and supervised, as well as her media interviews and opinion pieces.[78] In May 2009, Whitson went to Saudi Arabia seeking donors, emphasising HRW's 'work on Israel and Gaza, which depleted HRW's budget for the region,' and the need to stand up to 'pro-Israel pressure groups,' which 'strongly resisted the [Goldstone] report and tried to discredit it.' Critics noted the irony of eliciting support from the repressive Saudi regime to campaign against democratic Israel.[79] Whitson also travelled to Libya in 2009, where she promoted the Qaddafi family as 'human rights reformers.'[80]

Whitson has echoed classic antisemitic tropes and Jewish conspiracy theories. She accused American Jewish supporters of Israel of racism, and compared Israeli responses to Palestinian violence to segregation in the United States (similar to Roth's 'Jim Crow' accusations).[81] In January 2015, Whitson commented on the US Holocaust Museum's display of 'death and torture in Syria,' stating that the Museum should 'also show pics of death and destruction in #Gaza' – equating the 2014 war with Hamas to the Holocaust and the extermination of six million Jews.[82] In February 2019, in reference to intense criticism of antisemitism in the British Labour Party, she asked 'Why is this #Israel interference in domestic UK politics acceptable? Is it only a problem when Russia does this?'[83] In 2020, during the Corona virus pandemic, Whitson (no longer at HRW) posted a tweet referring to Israeli internal quarantine measures, which she compared to the Gaza counterterror blockade, echoing the classic blood libel theme: 'Such a tiny taste. Missing a tablespoon of blood.'[84]

For the position of HRW's 'Israel/Palestine director,' Roth and Whitson brought in a series of political activists including Lucy Mair (2006–7),[85] Sari Bashi (2014–16),[86] and Omar Shakir (2016-present). Like the others, Shakir was an experienced activist, involved in Israel-focused campaigns at Georgetown University and Stanford, including the promotion of BDS. Shakir's 2010 Israel Apartheid Week event at UC Irvine was named 'Apartheid IsReal.'[87]

Shakir's initial application for an Israeli work visa was rejected, citing evidence that 'this organization's public activities and reports have engaged in politics in the service of Palestinian propaganda, while falsely raising the banner of "human rights."'[88] The Interior Ministry labelled HRW as a 'blatantly hostile anti-Israeli organization whose reports have the sole purpose of harming Israel with no consideration whatsoever for the truth or reality.'[89] Roth responded by attacking Israel as joining 'an unsavory group in denying access to an @HRW researcher: Cuba, N Korea, Sudan, Uzbekistan, Venezuela.'[90] (He would repeat similar lines of attack many times over the next three years.)

The Israeli government suddenly reversed the decision in March 2017, for reasons that remain unclear, and Shakir received a one-year visa.[91] From this position, Shakir led an expanded campaign through pressure on high-visibility businesses like California-based Airbnb to participate in boycott activities, on FIFA, the international football (soccer) association, to ban Israel, and in lobbying the UN Human Rights Council for publication of its first and only 'blacklist' of businesses, in this case targeting those allegedly 'in support of the occupation.'[92] In addition, Shakir and HRW hired a number of Palestinian political activists to further amplify the organisation's messaging targeting Israel.[93] This policy is also unique – HRW does not employ local political activists in other conflict zones or priority areas.

Shakir's central role was also highlighted during the Hamas-organised 'March of Return' violence along Gaza's border that began in March 2018. In a flood of opinion articles, media interviews, and social media posts, he repeatedly accused Israel of 'entrenched discrimination,'[94] and 'cag[ing]' Palestinians,[95] while erasing the orchestrated attacks from Gaza. These allegations were repeated in HRW's statement before the UN Human Rights Council. Roth was extensively and visibly involved in these campaigns, as reflected in numerous statements and social media posts.

Citing these and other activities, Israeli courts affirmed that Shakir had violated the terms of his work visa as a 'human rights expert' and was not entitled to a renewal. During this period, Roth made a point of travelling to Israel twice, accompanied by a number of HRW officials and a media team to ensure wide coverage. With Shakir, Roth held highly publicised meetings with diplomats and journalists, gaining endorsements for the campaign. During the lengthy court process, Roth repeatedly compared Israel to North Korea and Venezuela, condemning the final decision of the High Court in November 2019 as part of a campaign to silence 'the human rights violations at the heart of the oppressive, discriminatory occupation.'[96]

Roth's public lobbying and statements during the Shakir campaign again highlighted his commitment to a political agenda that focuses on attacking Israel, under the guise of human rights activism.

Conclusions

HRW is one of the world's most influential NGOs focusing on human rights, a movement that at its core emphasises universality. Given HRW's central role in shaping the soft-power political impact of human rights and international law, the blatant departures from universality and impartiality under the leadership of Ken Roth offer an important lens through which to examine these dimensions of international politics.

Roth has led HRW since 1993, and, as documented, his personal hostility towards Israel has shaped the organisation's publications, policies, staffing and activities. Beyond the evidence of disproportionality, his emotional expressions throughout this period, such as the multiple references to Jewish themes and to the Holocaust in his harsh criticisms of are not found in other aspects of his involvement in human rights issues. The fact that, uniquely, the key HRW officials hired by Roth to report on Israel and the Middle East had backgrounds in political advocacy that were consistently condemnatory adds to the evidence that Israel is subject to unique treatment.

The consistent and preponderant evidence of bias has led to growing criticism of HRW and Roth. His responses that minimise the threats posed to Israel, and on the need to 'pick and choose' [Israel] because 'we've got finite resources' do not address the pointed allegations of bias and persistent immorality. As Daniel Kohn observed in the liberal *Forward*, Roth's 'animus towards Israel and its supporters is expressed regularly and assertively ... For the past two decades, Roth has used his organization to support Israel's opponents.'[97] Similarly, Foxman observed that 'despite painting itself as a great moral arbiter, in fact Human Rights Watch's approach to these problems is immorality at the highest level.'[98]

In 2009, when HRW founder Robert Bernstein denounced HRW's leadership role in campaigns seeking to 'turn Israel into a pariah state,' and a number of the organisation's funders withdrew their support, Roth successfully survived the challenge. He found new funding sources, and greatly increased the available resources. There is no evidence that the members of HRW's board, many of whom joined after the departure of Bernstein and his founding group, were concerned about Roth's personal bias.

The absence of checks and balances on a powerful organisation and its top officials, combined with the lack of transparency, including regarding donors (in 2020, an internal leak exposed a 470,000 USD 'donation' to HRW in 2011 from a Saudi billionaire),[99] further amplify the impact of Roth's biases on HRW and the execution of its mission.

This blatant violation of the norms of neutrality and impartiality in advancing a highly personal agenda is broadly symptomatic of a wider problem among political advocacy NGOs and their officials, particularly in the realm of human rights. The details of Roth's hostility towards Israel highlight the dangers of particularism, in contrast to the universality that is essential to all human rights activities. To the degree that 'the role of moral universalism is not to take activists out of politics but to get activists to discipline their partiality,' the case of Roth and HRW demonstrate the inherent difficulties.[100]

Notes

1. Pompeo, "Identifying Organizations Engaged in Anti-Semitic BDS Activities."
2. Toosi, "U.S. weighs labelling leading human rights groups 'anti-Semitic."
3. Bernstein, "Rights Watchdog Lost in the Middle East."
4. Birnbaum, "Minority Report."
5. Horn, "At 88, a man of morals starts over."
6. Blitt, "Who will watch the Watchdogs?" 261–398.
7. Vennesson and Rajkovic, "The transnational politics of warfare accountability," 409–429.
8. Ignatieff, *Human Rights as Politics and Ideology*, 9.
9. Foreman, "Nazi scandal engulfs Human Rights Watch"; and Stork, "The American New Left and Palestine," 64–69.
10. Human Rights Watch, "Civilian Pawns: Laws of War Violations and the Use of Weapons on the Israel-Lebanon Border"; Human Rights Watch, "Operation Grapes of Wrath"; and Human Rights Watch, "Israel's Closure of the West Bank and Gaza Strip."
11. See, for example, Cohen and Freilich, "War by other means," 1–25.
12. Ron, Ramos and Rodgers, "Transnational Information Politics: NGO Human Rights Reporting," 557–587.
13. See above 4.
14. Human Rights Watch, *Jenin War Crimes Investigation Needed*; and Human Rights Watch, *Jenin: IDF Military Operations*.
15. Israel Ministry of Foreign Affairs, "Israel's Reaction to the UN Secretary General's Report on Jenin."
16. Himel, *Jenin: Massacring the Truth.*
17. Human Rights Watch, *Razing Rafah.*
18. Kreiger, "We Don't Do Comparisons."
19. Steinberg, "International NGOs, the Arab Upheaval, and Human Rights," 123–149.
20. Ron and Ramos "Why Are the United States and Israel at the Top of Human Rights Hit Lists?"
21. Jonathan Foreman, "The Twitter Hypocrisy of Kenneth Roth."
22. Foxman, "No Accident."
23. Hoffman, "Broken Watch: Does Human Rights Watch Have an Israel Problem?"
24. See, for example, Schwartz and Wilf, *The War of Return.*
25. Birnbaum, "Minority Report."

26. Cicurel, International Hour, "Interview with Kenneth Roth and Omar Shakir."
27. Foreman, "The Twitter Hypocrisy of Kenneth Roth."
28. Roth, "Getting It Straight."
29. See above 22.
30. National Public Radio, 14 August 2001, Cited by Bayefsky.
31. Ken Roth, "Barack Obama: Dump These 8 Unsavory Allies."
32. Ken Roth, "On Human Rights Watch, etc."
33. Muravchik, "Human Rights Watch vs. Human Rights."
34. Roth, "On Human Rights Watch."
35. Steinberg, Herzberg and Berman, *Best Practices for Human Rights and Humanitarian NGO Fact-Finding*, 1–201.
36.. NGO Monitor, "Kenneth Roth Twitter Activity."
37. Roth, Tweet, July 30 2014.
38. See above 27.
39. NGO Monitor, "Kenneth Roth Twitter Activity."
40. See above 22.
41. Elia, "Birds of a feather: White supremacy and Zionism."
42. Roth, Tweet, 27 August 2017.
43. Mirsky, Tweet, 1 September 2017.
44. See above 18.
45. Human Rights Watch. "Kenneth Roth", This version was replaced in 2009 with a text which does not refer to his father.
46. Brooks, "On Israel, kid gloves – or else"; and Murray, "Human Rights Watch director (and former lawyer) Ken Roth."
47. Mearsheimer and Walt, *The Israel Lobby and U.S. Foreign Policy*, 329.
48. Roth, "On Human Rights Watch, etc."
49. Roth, "Human Rights Watch Applies Same Standards to Israel, Hamas."
50. Feith, "Dancing Around Genocide."
51. Bernstein, Cotler and Robinowitz, "Inciting Genocide Is a Crime."
52. Cohen, "Suddenly, Human Rights Watch discovers anti-Semitism."
53. Roth, retweet of Andrew Stroehlein, August 23 2014.
54. Goldberg, "Does Human Rights Watch Understand the Nature of Prejudice?"
55. Roth, "We Need an International Court"; Roth, "An International Criminal Court". See also Anderson, "The Ottawa Convention Banning Landmines."
56. Roth, "The Incendiary IDF."
57. United Nations Human Rights Council, *Report of the Fact Finding Mission on the Gaza Conflict*, 1–29.
58. Goldstone, "Reconsidering the Goldstone Report on Israel and war crimes."
59. Roth, "Gaza: the stain remains on Israel's war record."
60. Cicurel, Weekly Journal. "Interview with Kenneth Roth and Omar Shakir."
61. Human Rights Watch, "Belgium Anti-Atrocity Law Limited."
62. Israel High Court of Justice, "Shawan Rateb Abdullah Jabarin vs The Commander of IDF Forces in the West Bank."
63. *Jerusalem Post*, "HRW appoints alleged terrorist to Mideast Board"; and Bernstein, "HRW Defends Shawan Jabarin."
64. Human Rights Watch, *Promoting Impunity: The Israeli Military's Failure to Investigate Wrongdoing*; and Roth, Tweet, 24 March 2015.
65. Human Rights Watch, "Implement Goldstone Recommendations on Gaza."
66. Human Rights Watch, "Newest 'Observer State' Should Act on Rights Treaties."

67. ICC's Israel war crimes probe halted pending UN decision, Agence France-Presse, 3 April 2012https://www.rawstory.com/2012/04/iccs-israel-war-crimes-probe-halted-pending-un-decision/
68. Roth, Tweet 3 April 2012.
69. Roth, Tweet 29 November 2012.
70. Roth, "Barack Obama: Dump These 8 Unsavory Allies."
71. International Criminal Court, Tweet, 17 February 2019.
72. Roth, Tweet, https://twitter.com/KenRoth/status/739459685380706304?s=20; and Human Rights Watch, "ICC Should Open Formal Probe."
73. Roth, Tweet, 5 June 2016.
74. Associated Press, "International prosecutor preparing to open Palestinian probe."
75. Foreman, "Nazi scandal engulfs Human Rights Watch"; and Stork, "The American New Left and Palestine."
76. In January 2020, Whitson suddenly departed HRW and joined the Quincy Institute – neither Whitson nor HRW provided an explanation. However, by April 2020, she had left this position, again without explanation.
77. https://en.wikipedia.org/wiki/Sarah_Leah_Whitson#Early_life_and_education
78. For example: Whitson, "The Middle East through the Looking Glass"; Human Rights Watch "Hezbollah Needs Answers"; Human Rights Watch, "The Protection of Civilians Has No Limits"; and Whitson, "Israel's Settlements are on Shaky Ground."
79. Bernstein, "Human Rights Watch Goes to Saudi Arabia"; Goldberg, "Fundraising Corruption at Human Rights Watch."
80. Whitson, "Tripoli Spring."
81. Whitson, "A Matter of Civil Rights."
82. Whitson, Tweet, 29 January 2015.
83. Keinon, "Human Rights Watch Head Claims Israel Interfering in UK Politics."
84.. Kredo, "Missing a Tablespoon of Blood."
85. Mair's position was defined as 'researcher for Israel and the Occupied Palestinian Territories.'
86. After the appointment of Shakir in 2016, Bashi was listed as Israel/Palestine Advocacy Director before taking a leave of absence in 2017.
87. Cfalcon7688. "Apartheid IsReal with Omar Shakir @ UCI", https://www.you tube.com/watch?v=0v5pqFFDD8A
88. Israel, Ministry of the Interior. "Letter from Moshe Nakashto Adv. Emily Schaeffer Omer-Man."
89. Federman, "Israel denies work visa to Human Rights Watch official."
90. Roth, Tweet, 24 February 2017.
91. It is possible that HRW had led Israel to believe that Shakir and the organisation would press Hamas to release the bodies of two IDF soldiers held since 2014, and the return of two civilians. Initially, Shakir and other HRW officials did show an interest in this issue, but their actions can be described as minimal or token, far below the volume and visibility of the BDS activities.
92. Shakir, Tweet, 2 July 2018.
93. Steinberg and Rockland, *Palestinian Activists at Human Rights Watch.*
94. Shakir, "Israel Wants to Deport me."
95. Shakir, 14 May 2018, Tweet.
96. Agence France-Presse, "Israel first democracy to expel HRW staffer."
97. Kohn, "Human Rights Watch Tweet Exposes Decades-Old Anti Israel Bias."

98. See above 22.
99. Emmons, "Human Rights Watch Took Money from Saudi Businessman."
100. Anderson, "After Seattle: NGO's and Democratic Sovereignty in an Era of Globalisation."

Disclosure statement

No potential conflict of interest was reported by the author(s).

Bibliography

Agence France-Presse. 2012. "ICC's Israel War Crimes Probe Halted Pending UN Decision." April 3. https://www.rawstory.com/2012/04/iccs-israel-war-crimes-probe-halted-pending-un-decision/
Agence France-Presse. 2019. "Israel First Democracy to Expel HRW Staffer: Director." November 24. https://www.france24.com/en/20191124-israel-first-democracy-to-expel-hrw-staffer-director
Anderson, K. "After Seattle: NGO's and Democratic Sovereignty in an Era of Globalization." unpublished essay, Harvard Law School, Autumn 2000a.
Anderson, K. "The Ottawa Convention Banning Landmines, the Role of International Non-governmental Organizations and the Idea of International Civil Society." *European Journal of International Law* 11, no. 1 (2000b): 91–120.
Associated Press. "International Prosecutor Preparing to Open Palestinian Probe." December 20, 2019. https://apnews.com/ffd36215662e80c8dd1323bdb05fb9d0
Bayefsky, A., "Human Rights Watch Coverup." *Jerusalem Post*, April 13, 2004 https://web.archive.org/web/20040620103544/http://ngo-monitor.org/archives/op-eds/041304-1.htm
Bernstein, D. 2009a. "Human Rights Watch Goes to Saudi Arabia." *Wall Street Journal*, June 16. https://www.wsj.com/articles/SB124528343805525561
Bernstein, D. 2011. "HRW Defends Shawan Jabarin." *The Volokh Conspiracy* (blog), February 21. http://www.volokh.com/2011/02/21/hrw-defends-shawan-jabarin/
Bernstein, R., I. Cotler, and S. Robinowitz. 2012. "Inciting Genocide Is a Crime." *Wall Street Journal*, May 1. https://www.wsj.com/articles/SB10001424052702303592404577364283553552766
Bernstein, R. L. 2009b. "Rights Watchdog Lost in the Middle East." *New York Times*, October 20. https://www.nytimes.com/2009/10/20/opinion/20bernstein.html
Bernstein, R. L. "Human Rights in the Middle East: The Shirley and Leonard Goldstein Lecture on Human Rights." University of Nebraska at Omaha. November 10, 2010. https://www.ngo-monitor.org/nm/wp-content/uploads/2019/06/bernstein_nebraska_speech_2010.pdf
Bernstein, R. L. 2013. "Remarks upon Receiving Dr. Bernard Heller Prize." New York: Hebrew Union College. May 2. https://www.ngo-monitor.org/remarks_upon_receiving_dr_bernard_heller_prize/

SOFT THREATS TO NATIONAL SECURITY 51

Birnbaum, B. 2010. "Minority Report: Human Rights Watch Fights a Civil War over Israel." *The New Republic*, April 27. https://newrepublic.com/article/74543/minority-report-2

Blitt, R. C. "Who Will Watch the Watchdogs? Human Rights Nongovernmental Organizations and the Case for Regulation." *Buffalo Human Rights Law Review* 10 (2005): 261–398.

Brooks, R. 2006. "On Israel, Kid Gloves – Or Else." *Los Angeles Times*, September 1. https://www.latimes.com/archives/la-xpm-2006-sep-01-oe-brooks1-story.html

Cfalcon7688. 2010. "Apartheid IsReal with Omar Shakir @ UCI (Part 6)." *YouTube*, 10:00, May 15. https://www.youtube.com/watch?v=0v5pqFFDD8A

Cicurel, E. International Hour, Kan Radio (Israel). "Interview with Kenneth Roth and Omar Shakir." July 24, 2019a. https://www.kan.org.il/radio/player.aspx?ItemId=104315

Cicurel, E. Weekly Journal. Kan Radio (Israel). "Interview with Kenneth Roth and Omar Shakir." July 27, 2019b. https://www.kan.org.il/radio/player.aspx?ItemId=104566

Cohen, B. 2020. "Suddenly, Human Rights Watch Discovers anti-Semitism." *Jewish News Service*, May 26. https://www.clevelandjewishnews.com/columnists/ben_cohen/suddenly-human-rights-watch-discovers-anti-semitism/article_f35fb296-9f78-11ea-889d-e7a731c6851c.html

Cohen, M. S., and C. D. Freilich. "War by Other Means: The Delegitimisation Campaign against Israel." *Israel Affairs* 24, no. 1 (2018): 1–25.

Elia, N. 2017. "Birds of a Feather: White Supremacy and Zionism." *Middle East Eye*, August 24. https://www.middleeasteye.net/opinion/birds-feather-white-supremacy-and-zionism

Emmons, A. 2020. "Human Rights Watch Took Money from Saudi Businessman after Documenting His Coercive Labor Practices." *The Intercept*, March 2. https://theintercept.com/2020/03/02/human-rights-watch-took-money-from-saudi-businessman-after-documenting-his-coercive-labor-practices/

Federman, J. "Israel Denies Work Visa to Human Rights Watch Official." Associated Press. February 24, 2017. https://www.providencejournal.com/news/20170224/israel-denies-work-visa-to-human-rights-watch-official

Feith, D. 2012. "Dancing Around Genocide." *Wall Street Journal*, December 4. http://online.wsj.com/article/SB10001424127887324439804578105691046734674.html

Foreman, J. 2010. "Nazi Scandal Engulfs Human Rights Watch." *The Times* (London), March 28.

Foreman, J. 2014. "The Twitter Hypocrisy of Kenneth Roth." *Commentary*, September 1.

Foxman, A. 2006. "No Accident." *New York Sun*, August 2. https://www.nysun.com/opinion/no-accident/37146/

Friedman, R., and B. Weinthal. 2011. "HRW Appoints Alleged Terrorist to Mideast Board." *Jerusalem Post*, Februrary 18. https://www.jpost.com/international/hrw-appoints-alleged-terrorist-to-mideast-board

Goldberg, J. 2009. "Fundraising Corruption at Human Rights Watch." *Atlantic*, July 15. http://jeffreygoldberg.theatlantic.com/archives/2009/07/fundraising_corruption_at_huma.php

Goldberg, J. 2014. "Does Human Rights Watch Understand the Nature of Prejudice." *Atlantic*, September 21. https://www.theatlantic.com/international/archive/2014/09/does-human-rights-watchs-kenneth-rothunderstand-the-nature-of-prejudice/380556/

Goldstone, R. 2011. "Reconsidering the Goldstone Report on Israel and War Crimes." *Washington Post*, April 1. https://www.washingtonpost.com/opinions/reconsidering-the-goldstone-report-on-israel-and-war-crimes/2011/04/01/AFg111JC_story.html

Himel, M. 2004. "Jenin: Massacring the Truth." Elsasah Productions, for Global Television Network. July.

Hoffman, A. 2009. "Broken Watch: Does Human Rights Watch Have an Israel Problem?" *Tablet*, August 26. http://www.tabletmag.com/news-and-politics/14421/broken-watch/

Horn, J. 2011. "At 88, a Man of Morals Starts Over." *Jerusalem Post*, April 8. https://www.jpost.com/Features/Front-Lines/At-88-a-man-of-morals-starts-over

Human Rights Watch. 1996a. "Civilian Pawns: Laws of War Violations and the Use of Weapons on the Israel-Lebanon Border." May. https://www.refworld.org/docid/3ae6a7e34.html

Human Rights Watch. 1996b. "Israel's Closure of the West Bank and Gaza Strip." July. Vol. 8, No. 3 (E). https://www.hrw.org/reports/1996/Israel1.htm

Human Rights Watch. "Operation Grapes of Wrath - the Civilian Victims." September 1997. https://www.refworld.org/docid/3ae6a7e60.html

Human Rights Watch. "Kenneth Roth." December 20, 2002a. https://web.archive.org/web/20060208065109/http://hrw.org/about/bios/kroth.htm

Human Rights Watch. "Jenin War Crimes Investigation Needed." May 2, 2002b. https://www.hrw.org/news/2002/05/02/israel/occupied-territories-jenin-war-crimes-investigation-needed

Human Rights Watch. "Jenin: IDF Military Operations." May 2002c. https://www.hrw.org/reports/2002/israel3/

Human Rights Watch. "Belgium Anti-Atrocity Law Limited." April 5, 2003. http://www.hrw.org/en/news/2003/04/05/belgium-anti-atrocity-law-limited

Human Rights Watch. "Razing Rafah — Mass Home Demolitions in the Gaza Strip." October 18, 2004. https://www.hrw.org/reports/2004/rafah1004/rafah1004images.pdf

Human Rights Watch. 2006. "Hezbollah Needs Answers." *News Release*, October 4. http://www.hrw.org/en/news/2006/10/04/hezbollah-needs-answer

Human Rights Watch. 2007. "The Protection of Civilians Has No Limits." *News Release*. August 31. http://www.hrw.org/en/news/2007/08/31/protection-civilians-has-no-limits

Human Rights Watch. "Implement Goldstone Recommendations on Gaza." September 16, 2009. http://www.hrw.org/news/2009/09/16/israelgaza-implement-goldstone-recommendations-gaza

Human Rights Watch. "Newest 'Observer State' Should Act on Rights Treaties." November 29, 2012. https://www.hrw.org/node/248152/printable/print

Human Rights Watch. "ICC Should Open Formal Probe Impartial Justice Needed as Occupation Enters 50th Year." June 5, 2016. https://www.hrw.org/news/2016/06/05/palestine-icc-should-open-formal-probe

Human Rights Watch. "Human Rights Watch Denied Work Permit: Authorities Accuse Organization of Promoting 'Propaganda'." February 24, 2017. https://www.hrw.org/news/2017/02/24/israel-human-rights-watch-denied-work-permit#

Ignatieff, M. *Human Rights as Politics and Ideology*, 9. Princeton, NJ: Princeton University Press, 2001.

International Criminal Court. "#ICC Prosecutor #fatoubensouda & @kenroth, Executive Director of @hrw at #MSC2019 - #civilsociety Played an Important Role in the

Creation of the #ICC & Continues to Play an Indispensable Role in Promoting the Fight against #impunity for #atrocity Crimes #justicematters." February 17, 2019. https://twitter.com/IntlCrimCourt/status/1096921158123966464

Israel High Court of Justice. "Shawan Rateb Abdullah Jabarin Vs the Commander of IDF Forces in the West Bank." Case 5182/07. https://elyon1.court.gov.il/files/07/820/051/T02/07051820.t02.pdf

Israel Ministry of Foreign Affairs. "Israel's Reaction to the UN Secretary General's Report on Jenin." August 2002. http://www.israel.org/MFA/PressRoom/2002/Pages/Israel-s%20Reaction%20to%20the%20UN%20Secretary%20General-s%20Re.aspx

"Israel, Ministry of the Interior. Letter (Hebrew) from Moshe Nakash, Permit Division Director, to Adv. Emily Schaeffer Omer-Man." translated by Human Rights Watch. February 20, 2017. https://www.hrw.org/sites/default/files/supporting_resources/gl.2017.2.5.moi_denial_of_work_permit_letter_to_human_rights_watch.pdf

Keinon, H. 2019. "Human Rights Watch Head Claims Israel Interfering in UK Politics." *Jerusalem Post*, February 10. https://www.jpost.com/Israel-News/Human-Rights-Watch-head-claimsIsrael-is-interfering-in-UK-politics-580216

Kohn, D. 2017. "Human Rights Watch Tweet Exposes Decades-Old Anti Israel Bias." *Forward*, September 8. https://forward.com/opinion/382213/human-rights-watch-tweet-exposes-decades-old-anti-israel-bias/

Kredo, A. 2020. "'Missing a Tablespoon of Blood': Quincy Institute Scholar Laments Lack of Violence amid Corona Outbreak in Israel." *Washington Free Beacon*, March 16. https://freebeacon.com/national-security/missing-a-tablespoon-of-blood-quincy-institute-scholar-laments-lack-of-violence-amid-corona-outbreak-in-israel/

Kreiger, H. L. 2004. "We Don't Do Comparisons." *Jerusalem Post*, September 11. https://web.archive.org/web/20050920052627/http://www.jpost.com:80/servlet/Satellite?pagename=JPost/JPArticle/ShowFull&cid=1099543819705

Mearsheimer, J. J., and S. M. Walt. *The Israel Lobby and U.S. Foreign Policy*. New York: Macmillan, 2008.

Mirsky, Y. "Photo Is Disturbing, Yes. @kenroth Linking to Piece Casually Calling All Us Zionists Racists Is Foolish & Offensive." September 1, 2017. https://twitter.com/YehudahMirsky/status/903366978022277122?s=20

Muravchik, J. 2006. "Human Rights Watch Vs. Human Rights." *Weekly Standard*, September 9. 11 no. 48. http://www.weeklystandard.com/Content/Public/Articles/000/000/012/649efeoa.asp

Murray, L. 2018. "Human Rights Watch Director (And Former Lawyer) Ken Roth Clocks up 25 Years." *Australian Financial Review*, July 30.https://www.afr.com/work-and-careers/management/human-rights-crusader-ken-roth-clocks-up-25-years-on-the-front-line-20180716-h12r1t

National Public Radio. 2001 August 14. Cited by Bayefsky, Anne. "Human Rights Watch Coverup." *Jerusalem Post*. accessed April 13, 2004. https://web.archive.org/web/20040620103544/http://ngo-monitor.org/archives/op-eds/041304-1.htm

NGO Monitor. "Experts or Ideologues: Systematic Analysis of Human Rights Watch." September 2009. http://www.ngo-monitor.org/hrw.pdf

NGO Monitor. 2014. "Kenneth Roth Twitter Activity on Israel & Palestinian Authority." July 5. accessed September 12, 2014. https://docs.google.com/document/u/1/d/1Iie7Hp5zpQTHpPbqA3hbGCvmlq5-x5YHxf1pc2k1a8k/pub

Pompeo, M. R. "Identifying Organizations Engaged in Anti-Semitic BDS Activities." Press Statement, United States State Department. November 19, 2020. https://www.state.gov/identifying-organizations-engaged-in-anti-semitic-bds-activities/

Ron, J., and H. Ramos 2009. "Why are the United States and Israel at the Top of Human Rights Hit Lists?" *Foreign Policy*, November 3. https://foreignpolicy.com/2009/11/03/why-are-the-united-states-and-israel-at-the-top-of-human-rights-hit-lists/

Ron, J., H. Ramos, and K. Rodgers. "Transnational Information Politics: NGO Human Rights Reporting." *International Studies Quarterly* 49, no. 3 (2005): 557–587.

Roth, K. 1998. "We Need an International Court." Letters, *Wall Street Journal*, August 18. https://www.wsj.com/articles/SB903387750836620000

Roth, K. 1999. "An International Criminal Court." Letter to the editor. *Washington Post*, 7 July.

Roth, K. 2006a. "Getting It Straight." Letters to the Editor. *New York Sun*, July 31. http://www.nysun.com/opinion/letters-to-the-editor-2006-07-31/36984/

Roth, K. 2006b. "On Human Rights Watch, Etc." *Weekly Standard*, September 23. 12, No. 3 https://web.archive.org/web/20160103013226/http://www.weeklystandard.com/article/13863

Roth, K. 2009a. "The Incendiary IDF." *Forbes*, January 22. http://www.forbes.com/2009/01/22/israel-gaza-phosphorous-oped-cx_kr_0122roth.html

Roth, K. 2009b"Human Rights Watch Applies Same Standards to Israel, Hamas." *Haaretz*, October 26. https://www.hrw.org/news/2009/10/26/human-rights-watch-applies-same-standards-israel-hamas

Roth, K. 2011. "Gaza: The Stain Remains on Israel's War Record." *The Guardian*, April 5. https://www.theguardian.com/commentisfree/2011/apr/05/gaza-stain-remains-israel-war-record

Roth, K. 2012a. "#ICC Prosecutor Says #palestine Statehood Status Rests with UN General Assembly (Which Is Why #israel Is so Worried). April 3. http://icc-cpi.int/NR/rdonlyres/C6162BBF-FEB9-4FAF-AFA9-836106D2694A/284387/SituationinPalestine030412ENG.pdf." https://twitter.com/KenRoth/status/187186689075195904?s=20

Roth, K. 2012b. "Since #israel Insists It Doesn't Commit War Crimes, Why Not Call PA Bluff & Welcome #ICC to Deter Hamas Rocket Attacks?" November 29. https://twitter.com/KenRoth/status/274226886517854211?s=20

Roth, K. 2013. "Barack Obama: Dump These 8 Unsavory Allies." *Foreign Policy*, January 2. https://web.archive.org/web/20130105020724/https://foreignpolicy.com/articles/2013/01/02/the_second_coming?page=0,4

Roth, K. "Tunnels Used to Attack or Capture Civilians Is a Rights Violation. Tunnels Used to Attack or Capture Soldiers Isn't." July 30 2014a. https://twitter.com/KenRoth/status/494227604598452225?s=20

Roth, K. "Tunnels Used to Attack or Capture Civilians Is a Rights Violation. Tunnels Used to Attack or Capture Soldiers Isn't." July 30, 2014b. https://twitter.com/KenRoth/status/494227604598452225?s=20

Roth, K. "UN Commission of Inquiry Should Work to End the Impunity for War Crimes the Has Typified Both Israel and Hamas: @HRW. http://trib.al/dLrOaT0." March 24, 2015. https://twitter.com/KenRoth/status/580243972251107328?s=20

Roth, K. "No Endless ICC Preliminary Examination of Israel-Palestine. Time for Formal Investigation. http://bit.ly/24qF4k1." June 5, 2016. https://twitter.com/KenRoth/status/739459685380706304?s=20

Roth, K. "Israel Joins an Unsavory Group in Denying Access to an @HRW Researcher: Cuba, N Korea, Sudan, Uzbekistan, Venezuela. Https://hrw.org/news/2017/02/24/israel-human-rights-watch-denied-work-permit." February 24, 2017a. https://twitter.com/KenRoth/status/835042886722932736

Roth, K. "Many Rights Activists Condemn Israeli Abuse & anti-Semitism. Some White Supremacists Embrace Israel & anti-Semitism. http://bit.ly/2viVPIh."August 27, 2017b, https://twitter.com/KenRoth/status/901898833201954818?s=20

"Sarah Leah Whitson." 2020. *Wikipedia*, April 24. https://en.wikipedia.org/wiki/Sarah_Leah_Whitson#Early_life_and_education

Schwartz, A., and E. Wilf. *The War of Return: How Western Indulgence of the Palestinian Dream Has Obstructed the Path to Peace.* New York: St. Martin's Press, 2020.

Shakir, O. "Today at Human Rights Council, @hrw Called for Holding to Account Those Who Ordered Gaza Killings, Supporting UN Database of Settlement Businesses, Reversing Plans to Demolish Khan alAhmar & Resisting Israeli Efforts to Block Scrutiny of Its Rights Record. https://hrw.org/news/2018/07/02/gaza-killings-unabated-settlement-activity-underscore-need-international." July 2, 2018a. https://twitter.com/OmarSShakir/status/1013844013663899650.

Shakir, O. "History Will Remember Today as Day US/Israeli Officials Celebrated Embassy Move as Israeli Forces Fired on Unarmed Palestinians in Gaza, Who They've Kept Caged in for Decade, Occupied for Half Century & Blocked (Refugees) from Recognized Right to Return for 70 Years. Black Mark." May 14, 2018b. https://twitter.com/OmarSShakir/status/996511403354808320

Shakir, O. 2019. "Israel Wants to Deport Me for My Human Rights Work." *Washington Post*, April 18. https://www.washingtonpost.com/opinions/2019/04/18/israel-wants-deport-me-my-human-rights-work/

Steinberg, G. "From Durban to the Goldstone Report: The Centrality of Human Rights NGOs in the Political Dimension of the Arab-Israeli Conflict." *Israel Affairs* 18, no. 3 (2012a): 372–388.

Steinberg, G. "International NGOs, the Arab Upheaval, and Human Rights: Examining NGO Resource Allocation." *Northwestern Journal of International Human Rights* 11, no. 1 (2012b): 123–149.

Steinberg, G., A. Herzberg, and J. Berman. *Best Practices for Human Rights and Humanitarian NGO Fact-Finding.* Leiden: Nijhoff Brill, 2012.

Steinberg, G., and M. Rockland 2020. "Palestinian Activists at Human Rights Watch." Begin-Sadat Center for Strategic Studies, Bar-Ilan University, Policy Studies Paper #177. July. https://besacenter.org/mideast-security-and-policy-studies/human-rights-watch-activists/

Stork, J. "The American New Left and Palestine." *Journal of Palestine Studies* 2, no. 1 Autumn, (1972): 64–69.

Stroehlein, A. 2014 August 23. Retweeted by Kenneth Roth. https://twitter.com/astroehlein/status/503236540399906817

Toosi, N. 2020. "U.S. Weighs Labeling Leading Human Rights Groups 'Anti-semitic'. " *Politico*, October 21.

United Nations Human Rights Council. "Report of the Fact Finding Mission on the Gaza Conflict." Twelfth session Agenda item 7. September 23, 2009. https://www2.ohchr.org/english/bodies/hrcouncil/docs/12session/A-HRC-12-48_ADVANCE1.pdf

Vennesson, P., and N. M. Rajkovic. "The Transnational Politics of Warfare Accountability: Human Rights Watch versus the Israel Defense Forces." *International Relations* 26, no. 4 (2012): 409–429.

Watch, H. R. "Promoting Impunity: The Israeli Military's Failure to Investigate Wrongdoing." June 21, 2005. https://www.hrw.org/report/2005/06/21/promoting-impunity/israeli-militarys-failure-investigate-wrongdoing

Whitson, S. L. 2005. "The Middle East through the Looking Glass." *Wall Street Journal Europe*, January 18.

Whitson, S. L. 2009a. "Tripoli Spring." *Foreign Policy*, May. http://www.foreignpo
licy.com/story/cms.php?story_id=4949

Whitson, S. L. 2009b. "Israel's Settlements are on Shaky Ground." *Los Angeles Times*,
June 28. http://www.latimes.com/news/opinion/commentary/la-oe-whitson28
-2009jun28,0,2006530.story

Whitson, S. L. 2011. "A Matter of Civil Rights." *Huffington Post*, April 15.

Whitson, S. L. "@bbckimghattas @drovera @holocaustmuseum @bbcnewsus Should
Also Show Pics of Death and Destruction in #gaza." January 25, 2018. Tweet.
https://twitter.com/sarahleah1/status/560700886805389312

Israel in modern Jewish identity: an internal debate

Evyatar Friesel

ABSTRACT

Contemporary Jewry is burdened by a fierce debate about Zionism and Israel. A sizeable sector of Jewish academics, where leftists and self-declared liberals are strongly represented, criticises the Jewish state to the point of casting doubts regarding its very existence. Although their argumentation is frequently similar to the utterances of non-Jewish antisemites, what moves these Jewish Israel-critics is not so much Jews and Judaism but rather the Zionist idea. Such anti-Israel Jews are influenced by modern ideological trends and pressures that affect also, strangely enough, certain Israeli Jewish intellectuals. These developments happen on the background of an increasing pattern of Jew-hatred in non-Jewish society, a transformation of past antisemitism now expressed as anti-Israelism.

There is a growing tension in contemporary Jewry between supporters and critics of the Jewish state, its foundations, and its character. Recent years saw dozens of books written by Jews critical of Israel and Zionism, published in English, German and other languages,[1] not to mention recurrent lectures, interviews, or articles. Israeli academics constitute a significant presence among the critics.

The dynamics of the debate deserve attention. Its drive comes from the critics, and their tone is highly emotional. Many in Israel underrate that phenomenon and solve the issue by tagging those Jewish critics as antisemites or as self-hating Jews. Both labels are wrong and misleading. Antisemitism is an 'external' issue, a problem in the relationship between non-Jews and Jews. Jewish anti-Israel positions are an 'internal' issue, an expression of contemporary tensions between Jews. Nevertheless, many assumptions of the critics are similar to those of antisemites – a significant fact since it presupposes similar approaches to matters Jewish – even if the conclusions are not the same.[2]

Jewish anti-Israelism is an expression of the complexities of the modern Jewish identity, that was shaped and reshaped by two main factors: the acculturation, meaning the integration of Jews in non-Jewish surroundings, and the pressure of antisemitism in its various forms. The dynamics of Jewish modernisation differed from one place to another, and Jewish society divided into a variety of positions influenced by local social and spiritual dynamics not always clearly understood, even when elaborated positions were formulated. Personal and social profiles were never static. A Jew might find himself as religiously observant in one phase of his life, and less observant, or entirely secular, in a later stage. He might turn into a socialist or a Zionist, or a combination of both. The upheavals of the 1940s, the destruction of European Jewry and the creation of the Jewish state upset again, each event in its own way, the Jewish life. A recent factor is the development of the new Jewish society in Israel. In contemporary social experience, there is nothing comparable to what happened in the Jewish state: a meeting of Jews that for centuries had lived in lands all over the world, influenced by local cultures, speaking different languages, shaped by separate traditions, now brought together in a short time by the power of an idea, *shivat-Zion*, the Return to the Land of Israel. Inevitably, such a process produced tensions, positive and negative, pulling together and pushing apart. Sharp internal confrontations developed inside Jewry, where opposing concepts of Jewish religiosity or Jewish secularism clashed, diverse concepts were formulated concerning what it meant to be a Jew, how to define the Jews as a group, how to organise Jewish society in the framework of a state meant to be Jewish and democratic, how to understand and to shape the present and the future of world Jewry. The resulting discussions are frequently as acerb as the tensions between Jews and antisemites.

The internal Jewish debate of our time reflects the political and cultural tempests that have characterised Jewish life in the last century, exacerbated by the fact that so far, no calmness has emerged in Jewish life. Especially in Israel, these questions and tension encumber reality. Jewish critics of Israel concentrate on interrelated topics mixing historical and current public issues such as Israel and the Palestinians, antisemitism, and frequently, the circumstances of the creation of the Jewish state in 1947/48, a theme that, somewhat surprisingly, is still debated.

Antisemitism is an essential theme in the positioning of contemporary Israel critics, although mostly as a background factor of other trends in Jewish life. For example, antisemitism, according to Moshe Zuckermann, an Israeli professor of Sociology at Tel Aviv University, is a prejudice like any other, such as xenophobia, anti-Islamism, or discrimination against women or homosexuals.[3] 'Most anti-Semitic present-day utterances are related to rightwing white supremacist ideologies and not from leftist and liberal ideologies,' as he explains in an article of the Institute for National Security Studies of Tel Aviv University, published in Germany in 2019.[4] Moshe Zimmermann, an Israeli professor of history at the Hebrew University, maintains that views about the increase of antisemitism in Europe are based on subjective impressions stimulated and manipulated by the present right-wing Israeli government.[5] For Brian Klug, a Jewish philosophy professor at Oxford University, Zionism 'is the stepchild of antisemitism,'[6] meaning that the Zionist idea was a Jewish reaction to European Jew-hatred, a position shared by many Jewish academics.

The recent call of Israeli PM Netanyahu, that Jews who feel endangered by European antisemitism should come to Israel, is rejected by Micha Brumlik, a German-Jewish professor. 'Israel, I remain here! As German among Germans', he announced in a recent article. Jewish life in Israel is far from secure and the call to emigrate to Israel, so Brumlik, is an expression of a wish for a common death, a position that supposedly runs like a red thread through Jewish history, from the suicides at Massada two thousand years ago to the deaths in the Warsaw ghetto during WWII. Jewish immigration to Israel then, according to Brumlik, as an expression of a Jewish collective death-wish, not as assertion of Jewish vitality and continuity.[7]

Many Jewish (and non-Jewish) Israel critics claim that antisemitism was a significant factor in the creation of the Jewish state in 1947/48. Shocked by the Jewish tragedy in World War II, so runs the argument, the countries represented in the United Nations recommended in November 1947 the establishment of a Jewish state in Mandatory Palestine, on the understanding that only a Jewish state might avoid a repetition of the horrors of the 1940s. If so, argues the British-Jewish professor Jacqueline Rose, Palestine was taken from its rightful Arab inhabitants.[8]

A far-reaching denial about Israel is expressed by Shlomo Sand, an Israeli professor of history at Tel Aviv University: the whole Zionist project, the connection to Palestine, is nothing but an invention; there never was a Jewish people with historical roots in Palestine. Modern Jews are the descendants of Turkic inhabitants of the Khazar kingdom that existed in the early Middle Ages in the south-eastern part of present European Russia who converted to Judaism.[9]

An apocalyptic tone concerning Israel is typical of many utterances of these Jewish critics. For Jacqueline Rose, Zionism embodies a messianic aberration whose success, in the form of Jewish statehood, carries in itself the seeds of its destruction.[10] Or Shlomo Sand, in the concluding sentence of his book: since Jewish connection to the land is a 'myth,' the imaginations that were 'able to create Israeli society are now powerful forces helping to raise the possibility of its destruction.'

Since presently Israel seems unable to deal with her problems, the German government should 'come to the rescue' (*unter die Armen greifen*), to 'save' the democratic institutions of the state – as suggested by Moshe Zimmermann and Shimon Stein (a former Israeli ambassador to Germany), in an article in the prestigious German weekly *Die Zeit*.[11]

All together, these Jewish critics, among them also Israeli academics, justify their views with a variety of historical and political arguments about the foundation of the Jewish state, the significance of antisemitism, and the present policies of Israel that together represent an elaborated position. Do these views hold, when submitted to a historical examination?

They do not. Starting with the supposed connection between the Shoah and the creation of Israel: this is a myth not supported neither by historical fact nor by logical thinking. How possibly could the almost complete destruction of East European Jewry, the creative core of the Zionist movement, bring about the establishment of Israel? The view, held by many Jews and non-Jews, that sorrow and compassion with the tragedy of European Jewry during World War II brought the nations represented at the UN to support the creation of a Jewish state, is bizarre, to say the least. In history there never was an international decision based on pity – nations are moved by political interests, and so it happened also in the case of Palestine. The aim was to find a way to avoid the worsening conflict between Arabs and Jews. The solution adopted (in fact, a wobbling one, about which many members of the UN, the Americans included, soon had second thoughts) was to divide the country and to support the establishment of two states, a Jewish and an Arab one.[12] Once Israel was proclaimed in May 1948 and was able to affirm itself in the armed confrontation against the Arabs, a trickle of survivors of the Holocaust came to the country. More than half of the Jewish immigrants who settled in the young state were Jews from Arab countries. This had nothing to do with the Shoah; they were moved by Jewish religious and cultural values.

Then there is the understanding of antisemitism: To consider antisemitism as a prejudice like any other, or to compare it with xenophobia, or with anti-Islamism, or to bind it too much to racism is incorrect and shows lack of knowledge (unintentional or intentional) with mainstream historical research.[13] Antisemitism (anti-Judaism is a better term) is doctrine, Christian doctrine deeply embedded in Western culture, which turned secular and racist in modern times.

One of the illusions of our times, an understandable case of wishful thinking, is that the horrors of the Holocaust rattled Western societies and paved the way to an end to Jew-hatred. Sectors of Western society were indeed rattled, but a few decades of soul-searching proved insufficient to erase a millennia-old component of the Western spiritual heritage. Like a chameleon, Judaeophobia changed colours and leitmotifs over the centuries, and so it continues to do. In our days, Jew-hatred has reformulated itself and is directed against the Jewish state. Now it is Israel, the unequivocal symbol of present-day Jewish vitality, that is in the sights of Jew-haters. Non-Jews as Jews claim that such a view is but a fig-leaf of Israeli policies. Again, wrong. Israel or Israeli policies are criticised every day everywhere, including in Israel itself. However, to declare Israel as a danger for world peace or to demand the „abolition" of the Jewish state for the good of humanity is a Jew-hatred in new garb. Examples: 'Israel does not have a right to exist. Its establishment after the the 2nd world war was a major mistake, and rode roughshod over the human rights of the residents of Palestine ... Zionism has transformed from religious philosophy to an evil world view,' wrote a citizen in June 2011, to the Israel Embassy in London, in June 2011. Or, a German professor, who declared himself as a pacifist and a man who transmits humanistic values to his children, emailed to the Israel embassy in Berlin, in July 2012, that 'Israel is an anomaly and should be dissolved peacefully – for the sake of us all.'

Furthermore, the connection between antisemitism and Zionism is a tenue one. Zionism was an ideology built on traditional Jewish values (*shivat-Zion*, the yearning, or the return-to-Zion) influenced by modern European concepts and circumstances (such as nationalism). European factors such as antisemitism played a limited role, but the spark, the impelling thrust of Zionism, was the Jewish historical attachment to the Land of Israel. From a broader Jewish history perspective, the creation of Israel repeated a historical pattern: an adaptation by the Jews to possibilities and demands of the time, combined with the preservation of their specificity as a people. From this perspective, Shlomo Sand's theories of a non-connection of the Jews to Palestine, or that the Jewish people is an invention, are figments of his imagination.

A new characteristic of present Judaeophobia regards its ideological representatives, again a matter where many Jewish Israel critics miss the point, by describing it as a right-wing phenomenon. So it was in the nineteenth and twentieth centuries, when the ideological impulse of Jew-hatred originated mainly from the political right and from nationalist circles. Although Jew-hatred remains also presently a significant theme in the Right, the main ideological impulse of Judaeophobia comes now from the political Left and mostly relates to the Israel-Palestinian conflict. That changed attitude of the Left with regards to Israel represents an astonishing mutation. Until the second half of the 20th century, the Jewish settlement in Palestine, and especially its social creations, were consistently supported by progressive circles and Left parties.[14] The present view, which relates to the Israeli-Palestinian conflict in black-white colours (black for the Israelis, white for the Palestinians) carries all the hallmarks of classical anti-Jewish prejudice, now in the garb of anti-Israelism: a unique sensibility for the sufferings of the Palestinians, and a parallel indifference about the distress of the Israelis; the use of Nazi concepts and deeds, now transferred to the Israelis; an amazing indifference about the existing and repeated threats from Muslim quarters against the existence of the Jewish state.

As in the past, new Judeophobic patterns appear bound to political or ideological strains that outwardly seem unrelated to Jewish affairs. In our case, an apparent factor is a sense of guilt among Western intellectuals, and especially the leftists among them, for past wrong-doings, real or imaginary, towards the 'Orient.' It is an attitude that emerged in recent decades, one that was artfully described and explored by Edward Said and others.[15] There is a wish among contemporary Western liberals and leftists to build bridges of understanding and collaboration with Moslems. The problem is that both sides profoundly diverge in their social and political values: they disagree on such fundamental matters as democracy, secularism, women's rights, church-state separation, and many more issues. However, on one theme they do meet: against Israel. The opposition to

Israel provides a powerful theme of cooperation. Indeed, it is one of the few points of a political agreement between the two sides. Sizeable parts of what comes today under the general category of 'the Left' take a negative stance towards the Jewish state and that opposition is frequently characterised by an emotional level and a one-sidedness that strongly reminds antisemitic utterances of the not-far-away past. A political and moral picture of the conflict between the Arabs and the Israelis is presented that has surrealistic tones: the Middle East is depicted as a static landscape drafted in black and white, where no one plans, says or does anything or is responsible for anything – not the Arabs, nor the Palestinians, nor the Iranians, nobody. The only active and responsibility-bearing agents are the Israelis, and they, of course, are in the wrong, always, since ever. Catchwords from the leftist conceptual arsenal are hurled at Zionism and Jewish statehood: colonial enterprise, antisemitism response, imperialist venture, Holocaust reaction. This new Judeophobic instance fits into deeply-set anti-Jewish prejudices that are part of Western culture, and which are re-inventing themselves in a negative attitude towards what represents in our days a central focus of Jewish life, the state of Israel.

Since many Jewish academics, among them Israelis, support such views, the question arises: What drives the Jewish Israel critics? These are educated people, who in the regular walks of life are balanced in their views and utterances, relatively passive in their public behaviour – up to the point where the issue is Israel. Then the Zimmermanns and Brumliks, the Sands and Roses turn strident and apocalyptic: 'The Fate of Israel: How Zionism Pursues its Downfall' roars Moshe Zuckermann, in a book (in German) from 2014.[16] Such a doomsday view about the future of Israel, familiar to and shared by Jewish critics, deserves particular attention, since it mirrors well the state of mind of those Jewish academics. To see the Jewish state as a huge success, born under almost impossible circumstances, that step by step worked itself up to the status of a first world country, a democracy with a developed economy, a functioning multicultural society and vibrant culture – this seems unacceptable for those Jews, including the Israelis among them.

Yoav Gelber, a historian at Haifa University, along with other scholars observes that the Israel-critical Israeli academics 'are not a school and not even a coherent group sharing a worldview, program, or methodology. They are individuals who come from diverse backgrounds and hold distinctive stances and professional approaches.'[17] Which only sharpens the question: what ideological pressures lay behind the anti-Israel views of a whole sector of the contemporary Jewish *intelligentsia*?

A historical analysis offers an explanation: the major cultural trend shaping Jewry in modern times (indeed, up to our days) was and is the social, economic, and cultural acculturation in the Western world. It means that in the balance between Jewish and Western cultural factors in Jewish identity new profiles arose, with a tendency, especially among academics, towards the Western side. At present, most Jews are connected ideologically to the Western liberal and centre-left values that, along modern times, were the cultural and political anchor of modern Jewry and for which Jews do not see, with good reason, alternatives. Nevertheless, the anti-Israel attitudes that emerged in the recent decades in the centre-left and left camps have created a disturbing situation, since they come close to the new forms of antisemitism. One possible Jewish answer to such a development is to recognise the new reality as is and to try the make the best out of a problematic situation. Admittedly, in that case one may be left in an ideological no-land: cut-off from the spiritual companions of the past and pushed towards circles, mostly right-wing ones, with whom Jews have little in common. Another alternative, a disturbing one, is to go along, knowingly or unknowingly, with the negative attitude towards Israel that now prevails the Left – which is happening to many Jewish academics. The strains imbued in that situation are usually kept low-keyed. However, there is a minority among such Jews where a dormant Israel-critical inclination, frequently (but not necessarily) influenced by left-wing circles, gets transformed into an anti-Israeli platform. Surprisingly or unsurprisingly, among such Jews are also Israelis: although living in Israel, they are bound to the mentioned trends in Western society.

The intellectual ambiguities regarding modern Jewish realities among the centre and centre-left Jewish intellectuals (Israelis included) are expressed in the attitude towards the BDS (Boycott, Divestment, and Sanctions) movement. In a declaration from November 2019, subscribed by 240 academics and opposing a critical position approved by the German parliament against the BDS movement, they reject vehemently the assessment that the BDS movement is antisemitic.[18] 'The threat of antisemitism does not originate from Palestinian rights activists, but mainly from the extreme right and from Jihadist groups.' For them, the stated aims of BDS: 'the three main goals of BDS – ending the occupation, full equality to the Arab citizens of Israel and the right of return of Palestinian refugees – adhere to international law, even if the third goal is undoubtedly debatable.' Worth noting that 'the right of return of Palestinian refugees,' is nothing but a euphemism for the abolition of the Jewish state. Then they conclude, 'We are shocked that demands for equality and compliance with international law are considered anti-Semitic.' Among many Israelis, the position towards the BDS movement gets mixed with their antagonism against the Netanyahu government: 'this motion [against BDS] is driven by political interests and policies of Israel's most right-wing government in history.'

The opening of the declaration, claiming that it is supported by 'Jewish and Israeli scholars, many of whom specialized in antisemitism, Jewish history and history of the Holocaust,' states a situation known in Jewish academic circles but downplayed: a deep schism among Jewish intellectuals regarding issues that are decisive for the understanding of present Jewish life. Dismissing that many expressions of Israel-hatred are a contemporary incarnation of classical Jew-hatred, affirming there is no antisemitism raging in leftist circles, or ignoring the real meaning of 'the return of Palestinian refugees' indicates that some Jewish scholars, including Israeli ones, are incapable, obviously for ideological reasons, to recognise political realities. The condemnation of the Israeli government by these Israeli academics as the most right-wing government in Israel's history deserves attention as well since it suggests a very particular understanding of the democratic system. Whether one likes or does not like the present political alignments in Israel, the present Israeli government is the result of an electoral process that is recognised as free and open. A majority of the Israeli population has moved in an ideological and cultural direction that is different from the one preferred by the academics mentioned above. The unsolved and seemingly unsolvable Israel-Palestinian conflict may be a significant reason for this. There is a possibility that the average Israeli citizen has a more realistic understanding of the problems of Israel than many of the mentioned intellectuals.

As stated at the beginning, these Jewish Israel-critics are neither self-hating Jews nor Jewish antisemites, even if their argumentation is frequently similar to non-Jewish antisemites. Often, they embody a negative Jewish identity, and yet a phenomenon that belongs (possibly to the dismay of such Jews) to the sociological framework of modern Jewish life. Like all Jews, they bear the hallmark of the modern Jewish condition. For an Israeli to support an Israel-critical or Israel-denying position involves a reflection, a decision, and possibly a personal crisis. Many of these Jews blow shrill trumpets, but their message bears no hope, a vision of continued Jewish life they certainly do not offer. Nevertheless, we are faced with an ideological upheaval in modern-day Jewry that we shall have to live with.

Notes

1. See for example, literature for the years 2002–2017: Avishai, *The Tragedy of Zionism*; Beinart, *The Crisis of Zionism*; Braverman, *Planted Flags*; Brumlik, *Kritik des Zionismus*; Butler, *Parting Ways*; Carlstrom, *How Long Will Israel Survive?*; Gordon, *Israel's Occupation*; Greenstein, *Zionism and its Discontents*; Honig-Parnass, *False Prophets of Peace*; Karpf & Klug, *A Time to Speak Out*; Kovel, *Overcoming Zionism*; Loewenstein & Moor, *After Zionism*; Lerman, *The Making and Unmaking of a Zionist*; Melzer, *Merkel erwache! Israel vor Gericht*; Menuhin & Crispin Miller, *Not by Might, Nor by Power*; Neumann, *The Case Against Israel*; Pappe, *Ten Myths About Israel*; Rose, *The Myths of Zionism*; Sand, *The Invention of the Land of Israel*; Shatz, *Prophets Outcast*; Shlaim, *Israel and Palestine*); Svirsky, *After Israel*; Vattimo & Marder, *Deconstructing Zionism*; Verleger, *Israels Irrweg*; Viorst, *Zionism*; and Zuckermann, *Israels Schicksal*. The trend continues energically also in the present.
2. A semantic observation: applied to present-day realities, the term 'antisemitism' is incorrect. Jew-hatred is a spiritual phenomenon rooted in Western culture that has changed expressions over the centuries while keeping constant its negative attitude towards Jews. Antisemitism was an expression of this Jew-hatred from about the second half of the 19th. to about the middle of the 20th

centuries, mostly secular and strongly influenced by racial theories current at the time. However, since the term has become accepted coinage it will occasionally be used in the present essay. Incorrect also is the concept 'secondary antisemitism,' an unfortunate sociological formulation, which presupposes the existence of a scale-like antisemitism (primary, secondary, tertiary …) that does not exist.

3. See his article in a German periodical of Marxist tendency, *Neue Welt* (no. 34, 10 February 2017), entitled 'German Sensitivities' ('*Deutsche Befindlichkeiten*').
4. Yadlin, "Die fatale Dämonisierung."
5. Among other utterances, see his lecture on 06.02.2020 – https://youtu.be/d5zNRdYtiSo
6. "The State of Zionism."
7. Brumlik,"Israel."
8. Rose, "This Land."
9. Sand, *The Invention of the Jewish People.*
10. Rose, *The Question.*
11. Stein "Deutsch-israelische."
12. Friesel, "On the myth."
13. Poliakov, *Harvest*; Wistrich, *Antisemitism*; Nirenberg, *Anti-Judaism*; and Schwarz-Friesel, *Inside.*
14. Gorni, *The British.*
15. Said, *Orientalism.*
16. Zuckermann, *Israels Schicksal.*
17. Gelber, *The New Post-Zionist.*
18. "Call to the German Government." See also, in the same vein, a declaration of 35 Israeli scholars from 20 November 2018: "To Europe We Say."

Disclosure statement

No potential conflict of interest was reported by the author(s).

Bibliography

Avishai, B. *The Tragedy of Zionism: How Its Revolutionary past Haunts Israeli Democracy.* New York: Watson-Guptill Publications, 2002.
Beinart, P. *The Crisis of Zionism.* New York: Picador, 2013.
Braverman, I. *Planted Flags: Trees, Land, and Law in Israel/Palestine.* New York: Cambridge University Press, 2014.
Brumlik, M. *Kritik des Zionismus.* Hamburg: Europäische Va,2007.
Brumlik, M. "'Israel, ich bleibe!' Als Deutscher unter Deutschen." *Blätter für deutsche und internationale Politik* 4 (2015): 59–68.
Butler, J. *Parting Ways. Jewishness and the Critique of Zionism.* New York: Columbia University Press,2012.

"Call to the German Government by 240 Jewish and Israeli Scholars: Do Not Equate 'BDS' with Antisemitism," June 3, 2019. https://www.infosperber.ch/data/attache ments/Call%20by%20240%20Jewish%20and%20Israeli%20scholars%20to% 20German%20government%20on%20BDS%20and%20anti-Semitism.pdf

Carlstrom, G. *How Long Will Israel Survive? The Threat from Within*. New York: Oxford University Press, 2017.

Friesel, E. "On the Myth of the Connection between the Holocaust and the Creation of Israel." *Israel Affairs* 14, no. 3 (2008): 446–466.

Gelber, Y. *The New Post-Zionist Historians*. New York: American Jewish Committee, 2008.

Gordon, N. *Israel's Occupation*. Berkeley, CA: University of California Press, 2008.

Gorni, Y. *The British Labour Movement and Zionism, 1917-1948*. London: Frank Cass, 1983.

Greenstein, R. *Zionism and Its Discontents: A Century of Radical Dissent in Israel/ Palestine*. London: Pluto, 2014.

Honig-Parnass, T. *False Prophets of Peace: Liberal Zionism and the Struggle for Palestine*. Chicago: Haymarket Books, 2011.

Joffre, T. 2019. "240 Israeli, Jewish Academics Urge against Calling BDS Antisemitic." *Jerusalem Post*, June 12.

Karpf, A., and B. Klug. *A Time to Speak Out: Independent Jewish Voices on Israel, Zionism and Jewish Identity*. New York: Verso Book, 2008.

Klug, B. 2007 . "The State of Zionism." *The Nation*, June 18. https://www.thenation. com/article/archive/state-zionism/

Kovel, J. *Overcoming Zionism: Creating a Single Democratic State in Israel/Palestine*. London: Pluto, 2007.

Lerman, A. *The Making and Unmaking of a Zionist*. London: Pluto, 2012.

Loewenstein, A., and A. Moor. *After Zionism: One State for Israel and Palestine*. London: Saqi Books, 2012.

Melzer, A. *Merkel erwache! Israel vor Gericht: Essays eines antizionistischen Juden*. Frankfurt a.M: Zambon Verlag + Vertrieb, 2015.

Menuhin, M., and M. C. Miller. *"Not by Might, nor by Power": The Zionist Betrayal of Judaism*. New York: Open Road Media, 2017.

Neumann, M. *The Case Against Israel*. Oakland, CA: Counterpunch, 2005.

Nirenberg, D. *Anti-Judaism: The Western Tradition*. New York: W. W. Norton & Co., 2013.

Pappe, I. *Ten Myths About Israel*. New York: Verso Books, 2017.

Poliakov, L. *Harvest of Hate: The Nazi Program for the Destruction of the Jews of Europe*. New York: Holocaust Library, 1979.

Rose, J. 2002. "This Land Is Your Land." *The Observer*, August 18.

Rose, J. *The Question of Zion*. Princeton, NJ: Princeton University Press, 2005.

Rose, J. *The Myths of Zionism*. London: Pluto, 2004.

Said, E. W. *Orientalism*. New York: Pantheon Books, 1978.

Sand, S. *The Invention of the Jewish People*. London: Verso, 2010.

Sand, S. *The Invention of the Land of Israel: From Holy Land to Homeland*. Brooklin, NY: Verso, 2012.

Schwarz-Friesel, M., and J. Reinharz. *Inside the Antisemitic Mind: The Language of Jew-Hatred in Contemporary Germany*. Waltham, Mass: Brandeis University Press, 2016.

Shatz, A. *Prophets Outcast: A Century of Dissident Jewish Writing about Zionism and Israel*. Boston, Mass: Da Capo Press Inc, 2004.

Shlaim, A. *Israel and Palestine: Reappraisals, Revisions, Refutations.* London: Verso, 2010.

Stein, S., and M. Zimmermann. 2018. "Deutsch-israelische Beziehungen: Mehr Kritik wagen," Mehr Kritik wagen." *Die Zeit*, no. 20, May 8.

Svirsky, M. *After Israel: Towards Cultural Transformation.* London: Zed Books, 2014.

"To Europe We Say: Don't Conflate Criticism of Israel with Antisemitism." 2018. *Jewish Voice for Labor*, November 21.

Vattimo, G., and M. Marder. *Deconstructing Zionism: A Critique of Political Metaphysics.* New York: Bloomsbury, 2013.

Verleger, R. *Israels Irrweg: Eine jüdische Sicht.* Köln: PapyRose Verlag, 2010.

Viorst, M. *Zionism: The Birth and Transformation of an Ideal.* New York: Thomas Dunne Books, 2016.

Wistrich, R. *Antisemitism: The Longest Hatred.* Holocaust Library, New York: Pantheon, 1991.

Wistrich, R. *A Lethal Obsession.* New York: Random House, 2010.

Yadlin, A., and M. Hatuel-Radoshitzky. 2019. "Die fatale Dämonisierung des Staates Israel." *Die Welt*, September 26.

Zuckermann, M. *Israels Schicksal: Wie der Zionismus seinen Untergang betreibt.* Vienna: Promedia, 2014.

The Palestinian campaign against Israel at the United Nations Human Rights Council

Eytan Gilboa

ABSTRACT
This article scrutinises the Palestinian 'smart power' strategy of demonising Israel and diminishing its ability to defend itself against violence. The United Nations Human Rights Council (UNHRC) and the International Criminal Court (ICC) offered the best vehicles to execute this strategy. The article critically examines three Committees of Inquiry (COI) the UNHRC established to investigate alleged Israeli war crimes during confrontations with Hamas in Gaza. It demonstrates that the COIs biased mandates, selection of chairs and members, investigative methods, selection of evidence, and final reports were all deliberately designed to find Israel guilty of war crimes at the UNHRC and the ICC.

For decades, the Palestinian-Israeli conflict has received more scrutiny in international organisations than any other conflict in the world. Almost every event or development in the conflict prompts an avalanche of special and emergency sessions, resolutions, investigations, committees of inquiry and reports at the United Nations (UN) and its agencies. Israel has been the single most discriminated-against state at the UN. Of all the UN agencies, the United Nations Human Rights Council (UNHRC) has been the most politicised and anti-Israeli UN body. It has one agenda item dedicated solely to Israel and another for the rest of the world, and it has passed more resolutions condemning Israel than the rest of the world's countries combined. The UNHRC has employed biased special rapporteurs on the conflict, established one-sided Committees of Inquiry (COI) to investigate alleged Israeli war crimes, and published skewed and erroneous reports on military skirmishes and operations.

Much of the existing literature on the UNHRC posture towards Israel suffers from considerable deficiencies. First, much of the discussion has focused on issues of international humanitarian laws, laws of war, and legal procedures and norms. Legal scholars and jurists debate the nature, applicability, and ramifications of international law to the Palestinian-Israeli conflict. This approach, however, has overlooked the main political and strategic context of the UNHRC's actions against Israel. Since most of the UNHRC's activities are highly politicised in intents and effects, the more illuminating approach to investigate them must be via political analysis. Secondly, research has been carried out via case studies of individual events. This approach misses the overarching issues and long-term processes. This study attempts to address these shortcomings by exploring the UNHRC's activities over time and identifying a consistent pattern of political motivation, conduct, and consequences.

Any activity of the UNHRC must be placed within broad political and strategic contexts. These include the Palestinian strategy in the conflict with Israel, the tense relationship between the UN and Israel, and the decision-making mechanisms of the UN agencies. This work begins with a brief analysis of these contexts. The theoretical approach is based on a distinction among types of power: 'hard power' – uses of force and sanctions; 'soft power' – attracting and persuading peoples through values, policies and institutions; and 'smart power' – a combination of hard and soft power where each reinforces the other.[1] The Palestinians have moved from hard power to smart power and have exploited the UN in general and the UNHRC in particular to demonise Israel and curtail its ability to defend itself.

The Palestinian smart power strategy has been simple and straightforward, proceeding through a sequence of several interconnected steps. The first was to use violence and terrorism that would necessarily trigger an Israeli military reprisal. In this context, they cynically if not shrewdly sought to induce high injury and death counts among their own people, with a premium on women and children. This would in turn attract favourable and sympathetic media coverage, denunciations from world leaders and human rights organisations, one-sided UN condemnations, UNHRC resolutions, and COIs, all to culminate in indictments of Israelis at the International Criminal Court (ICC). Knowingly or unwittingly, high-level officials at the UNHRC and the ICC collaborated with this strategy of distortion and abuse of international law and the commandeering of international organisations. Following the section on contexts, the study offers a critical analysis of three COIs the UNHRC established to investigate alleged Israeli war crimes in confrontations with Hamas in Gaza. Since the COIs were designed to transfer the issue to the ICC for personal indictments, the last section analyses the ICC's handling of war crimes allegations against Israel.

Political contexts

Arab and Muslim countries, Russia, China, and the so-called Non-Aligned Movement (NAM) have used the UN as a forum for isolating and chastising Israel. NAM is a forum of 120 states that are ostensibly aligned with or against any major power bloc, however almost half of NAMS's members are Muslim countries. The Palestinians have enjoyed unqualified support from the anti-Israel bloc, and 'Palestine,' a non-existent entity, was admitted to NAM in 1976. Out of 193 members of the UN General Assembly (UNGA), the Palestinians benefit from an automatic majority of 120 members, a majority that is also reflected in the composition of many UN agencies.

Together, this large and powerful bloc has had little difficulty in passing numerous harsh anti-Israel resolutions, especially at the UNGA. Israel has been the most discriminated-against state at the UN and its agencies.[2] From 2012 through 2019, the UNGA had adopted a total of 202 resolutions criticising countries. Israel was the subject of 163 of those, accounting for 81% of all resolutions criticising countries.[3] The UNHRC has become the most biased and politicised forum of the UN.[4] It was established in 2006 to replace the UN Commission on Human Rights, which ran from 1947 to 2006. The Commission was dismantled because of overt politicisation and the inclusion as members many countries that have been among the greatest abusers of human rights in the world, such as Cuba, China, Russia, Iran, Libya, Sudan, Qatar, and Zimbabwe. The UNHRC has fared no better. These same and additional abusers were elected to the new body and its performance has been as ignominious as that of its predecessor.[5] The UNHRC's handling of Israel has been especially egregious.

The UNHRC has one agenda item dedicated solely to Israel and another for all other human rights issues around the world.[6] More than half of all resolutions this body adopts every year criticise Israel, are one-sided in content and false or inaccurate in substance.[7] In June 2018, The US left the UNHRC mainly due to the membership of the world's most inhumane regimes, which promote investigations of democratic countries in order to divert attention from their abuses. Successive UN Secretaries General have acknowledged the UN discrimination and bias against Israel. In March 1998, Kofi Annan denounced the resolutions exclusively blaming Israel only for violence in the region.[8] In December 2016, Ban Ki-Moon told the UNGA: 'Decades of political maneuvering have created a disproportionate number of resolutions, reports and committees against Israel.'[9] In April 2017, Antonio Guterres said, '[a]s secretary-general of the UN, I consider that the state of Israel needs to be treated as any other state.'[10]

Since the beginning of this century, the Palestinians have supplemented violence and terrorism with an aggressive disinformation, delegitimization and demonisation campaign against Israel, mostly at the UN and its agencies.[11] They portray Israel as a racist and apartheid state, the worst violator of human rights in the world – so vile that it is devoid of the right to defend itself and even to exist. The Palestinians employ the automatic majority they have at the UN to ostracise Israel and adopt radical and preposterous resolutions against Israel. This strategy was adopted after the 2001 UN Conference against Racism in

SOFT THREATS TO NATIONAL SECURITY

Durban, South Africa. The conference became an exhibition of bigotry against Israel and the Jewish people.[12] States and NGOs focused their indignation almost exclusively on Israel, defining it as a racist and apartheid state. They also accused Israel of committing war crimes and Nazi-like atrocities against defenceless, irreproachable Palestinians. Later, they recast limited Israeli defencive measures against Palestinian terrorism -especially from Gaza- as genocide, and the results a Holocaust.

The current Gaza predicament began in 2005 when Israel unilaterally dismantled all its settlements and evacuated all Israeli inhabitants and forces from Gaza. In the second -and last- elections to the Palestinian Legislative Council held in January 2006, Hamas, the extremist Islamic terrorist organisation, defeated the Fatah movement. In June 2007, it employed brutal force against Fatah's political and military presence in Gaza to take sole control of the area.

Instead of investing in economic development and infrastructure, Hamas spent hundreds of millions of dollars annually in producing rockets, digging attack tunnels and raising a significant military force. Iran's proxy in Gaza, the Islamic Jihad terrorist organisation, assumed an increasingly important role. In the years since wresting power, Hamas has frequently attacked Israeli cities and towns, primarily via rockets and mortar fire.[13] In deliberately firing rockets from civilian locations like schools, hospitals, and mosques, Hamas seeks to provoke an Israeli counterattack on such places, which would necessarily cause much collateral damage. Hamas consistently employs women and children as human shields, and subsequently uses their deaths and injuries for propaganda effects. Hamas anticipates that the world media will cover the damage sympathetically, and Israel will consequently be harshly condemned by the international community. Yet, every instance of firing from Palestinian civilian locations into civilian areas in Israel and of using civilians as human shields is a serious violation of the laws of wars.

Israel first responded to Hamas aggression with a limited siege to prevent smuggling of weapons into Gaza. Hamas claimed it needed weapons because of the Israeli blockade and 'attacks' on Gaza. This was patently false. The siege was the result of Hamas's aggression and violence, not the other way around. Israel subsequently initiated three large military operations to stop Hamas's incessant, increasingly-lethal attacks: Operation Cast Lead (27 December 2008–18 January 2009), Operation Pillar of Defence (14–21 November 2012), and Operation Protective Edge (8 July-26 August 2014).[14]

From March 2018 to December 2019, Hamas orchestrated violent riots along the Gaza border with Israel euphemised as the 'March of Return.' Hamas misrepresented them as peaceful demonstrations spontaneously initiated by suffering citizens to protest their awful economic and social conditions. This was not only false but the inverse of the truth. It was Hamas, not ordinary civilians, that initiated and organised the 'march.' Hamas evinced an indiscriminate intent to kill Israeli soldiers and civilians alike, interspersed its operatives among civilians, and deployed women and children as human shields. Hamas's objectives were again the win favourable media coverage, global sympathy, denunciation of Israel, condemnatory resolutions and criminal investigations.

The Palestinian strategy has succeeded, and they found in the UNHRC an excellent forum and accomplice to bring it to fruition. The UNHRC appointed three COIs to investigate alleged 'war crimes' by Israel in Gaza. All were highly biased and politicised, lacked basic standards of professional conduct, and were based mostly on distorted, false or fabricated evidence. The UNHRC commissioned them in order to undermine, limit, and deny Israel's right to self-Defence, and set the stage for prosecution of Israeli politicians and military officials at the ICC. No country in any other international conflict has ever been subjected to these types of systemically biased and unfounded investigations, nor been persecuted so vigorously and concomitantly by the many arms of the UN.

The Goldstone commission of inquiry

In April 2009, the UNHRC established a COI to investigate Operation Cast Lead. Its mandate was to 'investigate all violations of international human rights law and international humanitarian law by the occupying power, Israel, against the Palestinian people ... particularly in the occupied Gaza Strip, due to the current aggression.'[15] The mandate itself was prejudicial – completely eliding Hamas's aggression, which triggered the operation. It was also inaccurate as to the status of Gaza, being that Israel withdrew from Gaza in 2005, and the territory was ruled exclusively by Hamas during the timeframe being investigated.

Further, the individuals named to the COI each evinced some form of disqualifying animus regarding Israel, suggesting that their selection was due mainly to their conspicuous criticism of Israeli policy. The COI's head was Richard Goldstone, a Jewish South African judge who was a Human Rights Watch (HRW) board member at the time of his appointment (HRW has been a pervasive anti-Israel organisation). The other members were Christine Chinkin -who prior to her appointment had signed a public petition lambasting Israel's military campaign in Gaza as 'an act of aggression' and 'a war crime'[16] – as well as Hina Jilani and Desmond Travers. These latter two were co-signees, along with Goldstone, on an open letter to the UN Secretary General and the UN Security Council (UNSC) the month before their appointments decrying the 'gross violations' of the laws of war and international humanitarian law and the 'targeting of civilians' in the Gaza conflict.[17] These were all sufficient grounds to disqualify each member, yet they lacked the integrity and professionalism to recuse themselves. Israel refused to officially cooperate with the COI, citing its biased mandate, the prejudicial statements of its members, as well as the UNHRC's institutionalised anti-Israel posture.

In September 2009, the COI submitted the Goldstone Report. It determined that 'Israel had committed war crimes in Gaza, including the deliberate and premeditated targeting of civilians.'[18] The operations of the Israel Defence Forces (IDF) were 'to a large degree aimed at destroying or incapacitating civilian property and the means of subsistence of the civilian population.' The report claimed that Israel's military operation 'was a deliberately disproportionate attack designed to punish, humiliate and terrorize a civilian population.' The report concluded that the IDF was responsible for 'extensive destruction of property, not justified by military necessity and carried out unlawfully and wantonly. As grave breaches these acts give rise to individual criminal responsibility.'

The report dedicated a scant few paragraphs to Hamas's conduct in comparison, and where it was discussed, it was distinctly softer in tone and far more tentative in its language. Hamas's alleged crimes were described as passive omissions, as opposed to the imputing of active and criminal intent in Israel's case. Bell noted that the report at no point 'acknowledge[d] that Hamas is a terrorist organization ... Indeed, it claimed legal protection for terrorist organizations.'[19] Evans observed that the Report was created by 'a commission whose terms of reference were designed to excuse the aggressor, Hamas, and punish the defender, Israel.'[20] The discussion on Hamas thus appeared to be more of a perfunctory formality to establish the COI's ostensible bona fides and even-handedness.

Israel offered a point-by-point rebuttal of the report's fallacies and flaws, stating that it 'advances a narrative which ignores the threats to Israeli civilians .. . self-Defence finds no place.'[21] It accused the report of being a 'one-sided mandate, bending both facts and laws,' repeatedly adopting 'evidentiary double standards, attributing credibility to every anti-Israel allegation, and invariably dismissing evidence that indicates any wrongdoing by Hamas.' In January 2010, Israel released a report detailing the IDF internal investigation into charges of wrongdoing. Unlike Hamas or the PA, which never investigate allegations of war crimes, the IDF investigated 150 separate incidents, including 36 criminal investigations. The investigations led to indictments against several officers and soldiers.[22]

Many highly reputable legal scholars and strategic experts strongly challenged and repudiated the report, especially on the proportionality accusation.[23] Cotler argued that 'consistently applying discriminatory standards has the effect not only of demonizing Israel, but of undermining the integrity of the UN and the edifice of international law.'[24] Morgan concurred, stating that the report 'will undermine faith in the rule of international law.'[25] The Chatham House determined that 'Incidents ... are presented as factual narratives with little analysis. The titles appeared to disclose bias. There were hardly any documentary references.'[26] Blank found the report a 'flawed examination' that 'uses the incorrect legal standard' and 'applies the wrong law when more than one body of law applies.'[27] Berkowitz cited numerous examples of 'factual findings whose bases in fact are doubtful ... And the unreliability of the report's factual findings undercuts the validity of its legal findings.'[28]

In an unprecedented move, Goldstone himself retracted the report's claim that Israel deliberately targeted civilians.[29] He praised Israel's own investigation of incidents and criticised Hamas for failing to do the same. He insisted that 'our mission was in no way a judicial or even quasi-judicial proceeding.' His COI, however, saw it differently; the report detailed Israel's alleged failure to adhere to a variety of international laws, and also recommended referring 'the situation in Gaza to the ICC's Prosecutor.'[30] The Goldstone Report was biased, misleading, legally flawed, sloppy, and propagated on unethical grounds, and Goldstone's mea culpa was too little too late. It caused palpable damage to Israel and proved to the Palestinians that a smart power attack on Israel within the UN framework could be very beneficial, and further encouraged their employment of this strategy.

The Schabas-Davis investigation

In July 2014, two weeks into Israel's Operation Protective Edge -initiated in response to another intense round of Hamas rocket barrages from Gaza into Israel- the UNHRC established a COI to investigate all violations of international humanitarian law and international human rights law in the Occupied Palestinian Territory, including East Jerusalem, particularly in the occupied Gaza Strip, in the context of the military operations conducted since 13 June 2014 ... and to identify those responsible, to make recommendations, in particular on accountability measures.[31]

This statement implied that the COI would examine the conduct of both Israel and Hamas, but any doubt as to whether this investigation would seriously diverge from its predecessor was assuaged in the same resolution, when it pre-emptively concluded that the UNHRC 'condemns in the strongest terms the widespread, systematic and gross violations of international human rights and fundamental freedoms arising from the Israeli military operations carried out in the Occupied Palestinian Territory since 13 June 2014.' Weiler criticised this mandate, stating that '[i]t serves neither the interests of justice nor the credibility of the bodies charged in administering such to reach these categorical conclusions before the body set up.'[32]

The COI was originally chaired by William Schabas, a Jewish Canadian professor of international law, and included former New York Supreme Court Justice Mary McGowan Davis and Doudou Diène, a Senegalese expert on racism. Israel refused to cooperate with the COI and assailed Schabas's appointment due to his demonstrable history of anti-Israel bias. In a complaint to the UNHRC, Israel revealed that he did paid-consulting work for the Palestine Liberation Organisation (PLO) in 2012. He also strongly defended the Goldstone Report, participated in a panel in 2013 where he stated that he supported Israel's prosecution at the ICC for 'crimes against humanity, war crimes, and the crime of aggression.'[33]

Schabas expressed a singular hostility to Israeli PM Benjamin Netanyahu in the same speech when he stated that '[m]y favorite would be Netanyahu in the dock of the International Criminal Court.' When asked about this statement he explained that it was made in reference to the 2006 Israel-Hizballah war in Lebanon. Thus, aside from his bias, Schabas inadvertently revealed how poorly-informed he was on the topic – for the PM of Israel during that war was Ehud Olmert, not Netanyahu. Weiler argued that Schabas's pronouncement on Netanyahu was inconsistent with ensuring 'the appearance of impartiality' required of any COI member let alone a chair.[34]

The stark juxtaposition of Schabas's definitive and prejudicial position on Israel and his circumspect, judicious treatment of the Palestinians laid bare the absurdity of his placement on the COI. As a legal scholar, he displayed an astonishing lack of integrity, and a breach of ethics and professional conduct entirely unbecoming a chair of a UN investigation of war crimes. In February 2015, about a month before its report was due, Schabas resigned from the COI.[35] He revealed, however, that the COI had finished compiling evidence and had already begun drafting its report.

Schabas was replaced by Davis, and in June 2015 the COI released its report. It leaned heavily on distorted and false information provided by a bevy of anti-Israel NGOs – like B'Tselem, Breaking the Silence, Palestinian Centre for Human Rights and Al Mezan, many of which do not employ the methodological and procedural standards that would presumably be required for an UN-mandated investigation.[36] The report concluded that Israel committed violations with 'impunity ... both in Gaza and the West Bank.'[37] It also 'calls upon the international community ... to support actively the work of the ICC in relation to the Occupied Palestinian Territory; to exercise universal jurisdiction to try international crimes in national courts; and to comply with extradition requests pertaining to suspects of such crimes.'

Israel rejected the report and its findings, stating that 'this report was commissioned by a notoriously biased institution, given an obviously biased mandate, and initially headed by a grossly biased chairperson, William Schabas ... The commission of inquiry's mandate presumed Israel guilty from the start.'[38] The Palestinians welcomed the report because it served well their design to steer the matter to the ICC.

Davis said in reference to Israel, that 'the whole use of explosive weapons in densely populated neighborhoods is problematic and that the policy needs to change ... Because it is not OK to drop a one-ton bomb in the middle of a neighborhood.'[39] These comments revealed how little she understood the realities of Hamas's terrorism and low-intensity warfare. A group of military experts, the High-Level International Military Group (HLMG), observed that

'Hamas actively sought the death of its own civilians as an advantageous rein-forcement of its strategic concept aimed at the erosion of Israel's legitimacy.'[40] Lt. Gen. Martin Dempsey, then-chairman of the US Joint Chiefs of Staff, refuted the COI's charges that Israel used disproportionate force in Gaza: 'I actually do think that Israel went to extraordinary lengths to limit collateral damage and civilian casualties.'[41]

Wittes questioned the evidence gathered by the COI and noted the meagre reference to Hamas responsibility for the warfare and the casualties: 'There were 667 paragraphs in the commission's report, yet only 18 of them dealt with the use of civilian infrastructure by Hamas for military purposes.'[42] He also found that the COI, in direct contrast to its treatment of Israel, granted the benefit of the doubt to Hamas as a matter of course.

HLMG concluded that the Schabas-Davis Report contained 'stark, unwar-ranted condemnations of the IDF's conduct that do not accord with our own examination' and that 'the IDF not only met its obligations under the Law of Armed Conflict, but often exceeded them.'[43] Richard Kemp, former Commander of British Forces in Afghanistan blasted the report as lacking military expertise and stated that this rendered the Report meaningless, as it had no orientation nor benchmarks for assessing Israel's conduct.[44]

The Schabas-Davis investigation suffered from the same faults and deficien-cies as the Goldstone inquiry.[45] These include the COI's biased mandate, Schabas's selection to chair the committee, his own bias and ethical failure to disclose his prior relations with the PLO, and the COI's shoddy and unprofes-sional work. The UNHRC ignored the severe criticism of the Goldstone Report, including Goldstone's own retraction, his praise for Israel's investigation of war crimes, his criticism of Hamas's failure to do the same, and his criticism of the UNHRC's biased attitude towards Israel. The UNHRC failed to draw any lessons from the Goldstone episode. The next investigation wasn't better.

Gaza border riots inquiry

In May 2018, the UNHRC appointed yet another COI, this one to investigate Israel's alleged crimes in responding to the above-noted riots on the Gaza border that began in March 2018. These consisted of constant demonstra-tions in which crowds of protesters and rioters swarmed the border fence separating Gaza from Israel, hoping to overwhelm Israeli forces, break through the fence, attack Israeli soldiers and citizens, and thereafter reap the benefit of the negative publicity Israel would incur in containing the threat to its sovereignty and security.

The prejudicial nature of the COI was again manifest in its very mandate, which was cast as an investigation into 'the disproportionate and indiscriminate use of force by the Israeli occupying forces against Palestinian civilians ... in violation of international humanitarian law, international human rights law' and had already determined that the riots were 'peaceful protests.'[46] Ironically, the mandate of the highly biased and politicised UNHRC also highlighted 'the systematic failure by Israel to carry out genuine investigations in an impartial, independent, prompt and effective way,' implying the increasingly urgent need for an international tribunal to step in. Again, this COI wrongly defined the IDF as 'the occupying forces' of Gaza. The COI was chaired by Santiago Canton, a human rights expert and former aide to President Jimmy Carter (the most anti-Israel president in American history) and included Bangladeshi lawyer Sara Hossein and Kenyan human rights lawyer Kaari Betty Murungi. Israel, for the same reasons as those given in the previous inquiries, spurned the COI.

The report was released in February 2019 and covered the period from March 2018 through December 2018. The COI concluded that 'Israeli soldiers committed violations of international human rights and humanitarian law. Some of those violations may constitute war crimes or crimes against humanity.'[47] The COI also 'found reasonable grounds to believe that Israeli snipers shot at journalists, health workers, children and persons with disabilities, knowing they were clearly recognizable as such.' Additionally, the report determined that the IDF killed and wounded protestors 'who did not pose an imminent threat of death or serious injury to others.'[48]

The report merely 'took note' of the Israeli assertion that the protests were a guise for terrorist activities orchestrated by Hamas and other Palestinian terror organisations. Yet -despite ample proof to the contrary- the report discarded these contentions as quickly as it acknowledged them, concluding that the protests were 'civilian in nature,' and 'did not constitute combat or military campaigns.' Ignoring the overwhelming evidence of Hamas's active involvement in and sponsorship of Palestinian 'kite units,'[49] the report found 'no evidence to suggest that they were directed or coordinated by armed groups.' Rather, Hamas representatives merely 'encouraged or defended demonstrators use of indiscriminate incendiary kites and balloons.' Abstaining from assigning responsibility for these tactics to Hamas, the COI meekly settled for a soft rebuke with a passive voice, concluding that Hamas failed to 'prevent and stop the use of these indiscriminate devices.'

Importantly, the report stated that it would ensure that its findings would be made available 'to national and international justice mechanisms. The International Criminal Court is already concerned with this situation.' This revealed the underlying strategy – to get the report before the ICC so charges could be brought against senior Israeli political and military officials. To that end, the COI even compiled a dossier of 'those it deemed responsible for the violations' and authorised the UN's High Commissioner for Human Rights to convey this 'confidential file' to the ICC and national authorities to ensure accountability for alleged Israeli war crimes.

Israel rejected the report and its adoption by the UNHRC, stating: 'Dictatorships and hypocrites vote in favor of the singling-out, absurd pro-

Hamas pro-terror report ... We will not cooperate with this mockery and will keep protecting Israel and Israelis.'[50] The report was replete with fatal bias and procedural and substantive flaws, starting with the fact that its mandate predetermined the conclusions by focusing on investigating Israel's 'military assaults on ... civilian protests.' Like its predecessors, the report relied extensively -without confirmation or substantiation- on anti-Israeli radical and terrorist-associated NGOs.[51] Another concern, voiced by Kemp, was the shocking lack of both transparency and military expertise, which is a fundamental problem when '[t]he events under investigation involve terrorism, military operations, and the laws of armed conflict.'[52]

On its face, the characterisation of the riots as 'civilian protests' is patently false and disingenuous. Muhammad Shahada for example, admitted at the time that 'Hamas firmly controls the march planning and mobilization from behind the scene ... the local media and TV channels, the social media and newspapers are all filled with calls to join the protest.'[53]

The COI did not need to be dispatched to uncover the motivations and intent of the leaders of the riots. In March 2018, Hamas leader Yahya Al-Senawar stated that '[t]he March of Return will continue ... until we remove this transient border.'[54] In May, Mahmoud al-Zahar, another Hamas leader, declared that 'when we talk about "peaceful resistance," we are deceiving the public. This is a peaceful resistance bolstered by a military force and by security agencies and enjoying tremendous popular support.'[55]

As for the report's conclusion that the IDF used 'disproportionate and indiscriminate' force against 'civilian demonstrations' and 'peaceful protests' the facts tell a different story. In the period from the start of the demonstrations up to May 15 (3 days before the UNHRC resolution establishing the COI), of the 183 Palestinian fatalities ... 83% were known terrorist operatives.[56] On 14 May 2018, when approximately 60 Palestinians were killed in the course of violent riots, Hamas announced that 50 were Hamas 'martyrs.'[57] Israel argued that Hamas purposefully interspersed fighters among the general crowd, in order to provide cover and induce Israel to kill civilians – essentially employing their own people as human shields.

Furthermore, over a dozen clear, incontrovertible examples of the Palestinians' cynical use of children on the frontlines of the march were documented; including for the purposes of launching incendiary balloons, cutting the border fence, and serving as human shields and decoys. Corn and Margulies observed that '[b]y omitting from the UNHRC inquiry reports of the use of human shields by Hamas, the report incentivizes these terror tactics in the future, and the risk posed to the civilian population of Gaza is exacerbated.'[58]

In addition, the report consistently downplayed the concerns of the IDF for its soldiers and Israeli civilians, mainly because the COI honoured its mandate by focusing on and presuming Israel's guilt, leaving the assessment of Palestinian conduct and potential crimes cursory and shallow. With regard to Palestinians' use of incendiary kites and balloons, border infiltration, Molotov cocktails, and grenades, the report sufficed with stating that 'the Commission is aware of [such] claims' and dismissed most of them as not posing 'an imminent threat to life or serious bodily harm to IDF soldiers or Israeli citizens.'[59] But Israeli soldiers were killed and injured.[60] The COI ignored all of the incriminating and publicly available evidence of nefarious Palestinian intent and actions and relied on fabricated information from dubious sources in order to conform to the UNHRC's fundamental anti-Israel platform and arrive at the conclusions embedded in its mandate.

From the UNHRC to the ICC

The COIs' reports invariably concluded with recommendations for further actions by the ICC. The Court is one of the few international institutions that has an enforcement mechanism, albeit putative and controversial, in prosecuting and punishing individuals for genocide, war crimes, and crimes against humanity. The ICC was established in 2002 by the Rome Statute and currently has 123 members. The US and Israel are among those not members, out of concern that it would be exploited to dispense politicised and biased judgements. Those concerns turn out to have been justified.

The ICC is not an ordinary court that adheres to standardised rules of judicial evidence and procedure. It selectively employs rules from both common and civil law at a given Judge's discretion. Predictably, this creates internal contradictions and inconsistencies. It is also not an independent body, as it depends entirely on the UNGA for its budget and operations. The Court also utilises resolutions, reports, and recommendations produced by UN agencies for its evidentiary materials. Thus, the ICC is another highly politicised UN body driven by a prejudiced political agenda.

In December 2019, Fatou Bensouda, the chief prosecutor of the ICC announced: 'I am satisfied that war crimes have been or are being committed in the West Bank, East Jerusalem and the Gaza Strip.'[61] Among the crimes committed, she referred to Operation Protective Edge and Israel's response to Hamas's violent 'March of Return.' She mentioned war crimes committed by Hamas and other Palestinian 'armed groups,' but like the UNHRC reports upon which she relied, this was a feint intended to create the impression of neutrality. The object of her case – to prosecute and demonise Israel – was reflected in the enthusiastic praise she received for her decision from the Palestinians.

Israel, having refused to join the ICC, would presumably not be subject to the ICC's exercise of jurisdiction. But in a highly controversial move, the ICC had admitted Palestine as a member in 2015. Bensouda thus claimed jurisdiction on the basis that crimes were committed by Israelis on the territory of a member of the ICC – Palestine. She further determined that Palestine is a 'state' and that there was no jurisdictional bar for her opening a full criminal investigation. However, she also requested that the ICC Pretrial Chamber confirm her determination of Palestinian statehood.

In February 2020, the Pretrial Chamber granted the request of around 50 countries, NGOs, and experts to file amicus curiae briefs to offer insights and appraisals on whether the ICC has authority to prosecute Israelis. Eight countries from all continents except Asia – Germany, Austria, Hungary, Brazil, Australia, Uganda, the Czech Republic, and Canada – delivered formal objections to Bensouda's prosecution plan. Germany's objection is especially important because Berlin is considered one of the strongest supporters of the ICC. In April 2020 Bensouda tendered her response to the amicus curiae submissions, reiterating her determination that Palestine can be considered a state over which the ICC could exercise jurisdiction.

Bensouda's opinion has been roundly criticised by legal experts. Kontorovich put it succinctly, stating that Bensouda 'has come to the absurd decision that a non-country can sue a non-member of the ICC for a non-crime that nobody has ever been prosecuted for.'[62] On a fundamental level, the mere fact that Bensouda is pursuing prosecution, having to warp and distort legal principles just to bring the case before the ICC, while neglecting flagrant cases of war crimes, is the most damning confirmation of the heavily biased and agenda-driven focus on Israel. Apparently, the ICC does not see the crimes committed by Russia in Chechnya and the Ukraine, by China on its Uighur population, and by Syria and Iran for pursuing a bloody civil war as warranting charges, yet Israel is indeed singled out.

Bensouda cited UNGA's resolutions to claim that Palestine is a 'state.' However, these sources can also be marshalled to negate her point. In November 2012, the UNGA upgraded Palestine only from 'observer status' to 'non-member state.'[63] Still Bensouda advocated for elasticity in using such concepts, and that 'these criteria can also be less restrictively applied to Palestine for the sole purposes of the exercise of the Court's jurisdiction.'[64]

Another legal criterion Bensouda obfuscates is the ICC's principle of 'complementarity.'[65] The ICC can only investigate and prosecute crimes of individuals that states are 'unwilling or unable to prosecute.' The Israeli case doesn't meet this fundamental condition. Israel is a democracy with a robust, independent, and active judiciary, and has consistently engaged in independent inquiries. As Dershowitz stated: 'If it were to be ruled that the Israeli legal system doesn't provide the required complementarity to deny the ICC institution jurisdiction as "a court of last resort," then no nation would pass that test.'[66]

Further, the Rome Statute states that '[n]either the Prosecutor nor a Deputy Prosecutor shall participate in any matter in which their impartiality might reasonably be doubted on any ground.'[67] Kittrie concluded that Bensouda's partiality was apparent before she even decided to prosecute, when in August 2014 she wrote in an article that 'Palestine could now join the Rome statute' as a state.[68] He added, '[i]t was surprising, and perhaps inappropriate, for the ICC prosecutor to pronounce on such an issue prior to being formally presented with it.' In addition, Rose and Hirsch noted that: "Journalists report that the prosecutor maintains close liaison with figures in the PA ... Saeb Erekat disclosed that he chairs the liaison committee and that it includes representatives of Hamas and the Popular Front for the Liberation of Palestine.'[69] Moreover, Rose and Hirsch stated, '[a]mple evidence of prosecutorial bias can be found in the prosecutor's actual request to the pre-trial chamber. Its citations of academic literature are partial: they cite anti-Zionist academics while conspicuously omitting authoritative scholarly literature.'

The substantive framework within which Bensouda works are the reports, documents, and information provided by the UNGA, UNHRC, and the NGOs customarily utilised by both bodies. As demonstrated above, both the UNGA and UNHRC have been hijacked by non-democratic and authoritarian regimes, some of which are among the greatest abusers of human rights on earth; both bodies have evinced a particularly vicious bias towards and a fanatical preoccupation with Israel. Thus, the material on which Bensouda relies is entirely compromised, politicised, and discredited.

The Israeli case is playing out against the backdrop of Bensouda's pursuit of war crimes charges against US officials. Her conduct and that of the US government on the issue is instructive. In November 2017, Bensouda announced that she would open an investigation into alleged US war crimes in Afghanistan. She also asked a Pretrial Chamber to authorise the investigation. The US criticised her strongly, cancelled her visa to the US, and threatened to prosecute her -as well all those who might be involved in the case, including her staff and even ICC judges- in a US court.[70]

In April 2019, a Pretrial Chamber rejected Bensouda's request to open an investigation against the US. She appealed this decision, and in March 2020 an appeals panel reversed the decision of the Pretrial Chamber and authorised Bensouda to investigate the US. Secretary of State Mike Pompeo responded with a blistering attack on the ICC, stating: 'The United States is not a party to the ICC, and we will take all necessary measures to protect our citizens from this renegade, so-called court.'[71] On 11 June 2020, US President Donald Trump imposed severe travel and financial sanctions on ICC personnel, citing bias and abuses of international law against both the US and Israel.[72] Bensouda's respective prosecution plans do not meet any of the criteria required to open an investigation against democracies like Israel or the US at the ICC.

Conclusion

During the last twenty years, the Palestinians have effectively employed a smart power strategy against Israel. Despite peace agreements that established the PA in the West Bank and Gaza, and the complete Israeli withdrawal from Gaza, the

Palestinians have never ceased using violence and terrorism against Israel. Their strategic goal has remained to eliminate Israel as a Jewish state. Its smart power goals have been both 'hard' – to significantly limit Israel's ability to defend itself against violence; and 'soft' – to demonise Israel as a serial violator of human rights and international law. The combination of actions at the UNHRC and the ICC has been the most effective and the most promising vehicle to achieve these strategic goals.

The evidence presented in this article clearly shows a consistent pattern of systemic discrimination, politicisation and double-standard in UNHRC resolutions and actions concerning the Palestinian-Israeli conflict. The UNHRC appointed three COIs to investigate alleged Israeli war crimes in Gaza, yet bias and prejudice were embedded in each of their mandates, predetermining Israel guilt before the investigations even began. The formulations of these mandates were unethical and unconscionable for two reasons: first, they drew the conclusions that the COIs were expected to arrive at, and secondly, they compromised the investigators' independence by unduly pressuring them to reach these conclusions.

The selection of the COIs' chairs and members raised serious questions of fairness and integrity. Two of the chairs were Jews known for their critical views of Israel's policies and conduct. Undoubtedly, the UNHRC selected them because it presumed that they would deliver harsh condemnations of Israel, and that such condemnations coming from Jews would be more credible and have added effect. The assumption of readers, even professionals, would be that if a Jew arrived at an unfavourable judgement on the Jewish state, it must be true.

Officials and organisations involved in legal and judicial processes should be impartial, professional, ethical, and beyond reproach regarding motivations and political orientation. The UNHRC, the COIs' chairs, and its members failed this fundamental test of institutional and personal integrity. Prior to their appointment, COI members criticised Israel, then lacked integrity in failing to disqualify themselves. Schabas was forced to resign only after Israel revealed his association with the PLO. Bensouda violated the ICC's rules by advising the Palestinians on how to join the Court and consulted with them about her plan to investigate Israel.

The UNHRC and the COIs displayed total ignorance of low-intensity warfare and terrorism. They treated Hamas as a legitimate actor, ignored its extreme ideology and strategy, and minimised its responsibly for the hostilities, the casualties, and the destruction in Gaza. The UNHRC and the ICC systematically ignored Israel's arguments, complaints, and evidence, as well as the evaluations of senior military experts from several countries who possessed substantial combat experience. All UNHRC's reports, resolutions, and COIs were driven by hostility to Israel, not by a genuine concern for justice and human rights. The ICC has been similarly blighted. The Israeli case casts dishonour on and undercuts the ability of these UN bodies to combat human rights abuses and war crimes. The

UNHRC's predecessor was dismantled for its virulent politicisation and moral bankruptcy. Since it bears the same deficiencies, it is time for the UN to dismantle its current incarnation, along with the dysfunctional ICC, and rebuild both so they can ethically and professionally fulfil the noble missions for which they were conceived.

Notes

1. Gilboa, "Sharp Power."
2. Muravchik, "The UN."
3. UN Watch, "The UN and Israel"; and UN Watch, "2019–2020 General Assembly Resolutions."
4. Calamur, "The UN Human Rights."
5. Freedom House Perspectives, *With New Members.*
6. Hunt, "The UN Human Rights Council Ignored."
7. See note 3 above.
8. Epstein, "Annan."
9. Bulman, "Ban Ki-moon."
10. "UN Chief Vows."
11. Gilboa, "Israel: Countering Brandjacking."
12. Schoenberg, "Demonization.in Durban."
13. Kuperwasser, and Fischberger, *The War of Many Rounds.*
14. Dershowitz, *Terror Tunnels.*
15. UNHRC *The Grave Violations.*
16. "Israel's Bombardment of Gaza."
17. Amnesty International, "Gaza Investigators."
18. UNHRC, *Human Rights in Palestine.*
19. Bell, "Critique."
20. Evans, "A Moral Atrocity."
21. Israel Ministry of Foreign Affairs, *Initial Response.*
22. Israel Ministry of Foreign Affairs, "IDF Military Advocate General."
23. E.g. Walzer, "The Gaza War"; and Samson, "Necessity."
24. Cotler, "The Goldstone Mission."
25. Morgan, "Goldstone Report."
26. Chatham House, "Report."
27. Blank, "Finding Facts."
28. Berkowitz, "The Goldstone Report."
29. Goldstone, "Reconsidering."
30. See note 18 above.
31. UNHRC, *Ensuring Respect.*
32. Weiler, "After Gaza."
33. William Schabas, YouTube Video.
34. See note 32 above.
35. "Head of UN War Crimes Inquiry."
36. NGO Monitor, *Filling in the Blanks.*
37. UNHRC, *Report of the Detailed Findings.*
38. Israel Ministry of Foreign Affairs, "Israeli Response."
39. Ravid, "Head of UN Gaza Probe."
40. High Level Military Group, *An Assessment.*

41. Berman, "Top US General."
42. Wittes, "Israeli Targeting Procedures."
43. See note 41 above.
44. Kemp, 'The U.N.'s Gaza Report."
45. Baruch, "The Report of the Human Rights' Council."
46. UNHRC, *Violations of International Law.*
47. United Nations. "UN Independent Commission."
48. UNHRC, *Report of the Detailed Finding – Protests.*
49. Meir Amit Intelligence and Terrorism Information Centre, "Arson Terrorism."
50. Nahshon, Twitter Post.
51. NGO Monitor, *Submission to the UNHRC.*
52. High Level Military Group, *Submission on the 2018 Protests.*
53. Shehada, "The Full Story."
54. Abu Toameh, "Hamas Head."
55. "Hamas Co-founder Admits."
56. See note 50 above.
57. Gross, "Hamas Official."
58. Corn, and Margulies, "Framing Israel."
59. See note 49 above.
60. "IDF Believes Gaza Snipers."
61. International Criminal Court, "Statement of ICC Prosecutor."
62. Kasnett, "Legal Experts Argue."
63. Baker, *The Failure.*
64. International Criminal Court, *Situation in the State of Palestine.*
65. International Criminal Court *Rome Statute.*
66. Dershowitz, "The Case against ICC's Investigation."
67. Ibid.
68. Kittrie, *Lawfare*, 211.
69. Rose, and Hirsch, "Rule or Ruse of Law."
70. Kahn, "National Security Adviser."
71. Pompeo, "ICC Decision on Afghanistan."
72. Hansler, "Trump Authorizes Sanctions."

Acknowledgments

Research for this study was supported by the BESA Center for Strategic Studies at Bar-Ilan University. The author thanks Raphael Harkham for his valuable research assistance.

Disclosure statement

No potential conflict of interest was reported by the author(s).

Bibliography

Abu Toameh, K. "Hamas Head Sinwar Says Gaza Protests Will Continue." *Times of Israel*, March 30, 2018. https://www.timesofisrael.com/hamas-head-sinwar-says-gaza-protests-will-continue-until-border-erased/

Amnesty International. "Gaza Investigators Call for War Crimes Inquiry." March 16, 2009. https://web.archive.org/web/20160408011126/http://www.amnesty.org.au/news/comments/20572/

Baker, A. *The Failure of the International Criminal Court.* November 18, 2019. https://jcpa.org/article/the-failure-of-the-international-criminal-court-icc/

Baruch, P. "The Report of the Human Rights' Council COI on the 2014 Operation in the Gaza Strip: A Critical Analysis." *Israel Yearbook on Human Rights* 46 (2016): 29–102.

Bell, A. "Critique of the Goldstone Report and Its Treatment of International Humanitarian Law." *Proceedings of the American Society of International Law* 104 (2010): 79–86.

Berkowitz, P. "The Goldstone Report and International Law." *Policy Review* 162 (2010): 13–35.

Berman, L. "Top US General: Israel Protected Civilian Lives in Gaza." *Times of Israel*, November 7, 2014. https://www.timesofisrael.com/top-us-general-israel-protected-civilian-lives-in-gaza/

Blank, L. R. "Finding Facts but Missing the Law: The Goldstone Report, Gaza and Lawfare." *Case Western Reserve Journal of International Law* 43, nos. 1–2 (2011): 279–305.

Bulman, M. "Ban Ki-moon Says UN Has 'Disproportionate' Focus on Israel." *Independent*, December 18, 2016. https://www.independent.co.uk/news/world/middle-east/ban-ki-moon-united-nations-disproportionate-israel-focus-resolutions-palestinians-human-rights-danny-a7481961.html

Calamur, K. "The UN Human Rights Council Is a Deeply Flawed Body." *The Atlantic*, June 20, 2018. https://www.theatlantic.com/international/archive/2018/06/us-un-human-rights/563276/

Chatham House. "Report of an Expert Meeting." December 14, 2009. https://www.chathamhouse.org/publications/papers/view/109211

Corn, J., and P. Margulies. "Framing Israel: The U.N. Commission of Inquiry on the Spring 2018 Gaza Border Confrontations." *Lawfare*, March 18, 2019.

Cotler, I. "The Goldstone Mission - Tainted to the Core (II)." *Jerusalem Post*, August 18, 2009. https://www.jpost.com/Opinion/Op-Ed-Contributors/The-Goldstone-Mission-Tainted-to-the-core-II

Dershowitz, A. *Terror Tunnels: The Case for Israel's Just War against Hamas.* New York, NY: Rosetta Books, 2014.

Dershowitz, A. "The Case against ICC's Investigation of Israel." *Jerusalem Post*, January 24, 2015. https://www.jpost.com/Opinion/Special-to-JPost-Alan-Dershowitz-makes-case-against-ICCs-investigation-of-Israel-388782

Epstein, E. "Annan Made the Nations a Little Less United against Israel." *Forward*, December 22, 2006. https://forward.com/opinion/9702/annan-made-the-nations-a-little-less-united-agains/

Evans, H. "A Moral Atrocity." *The Guardian*, October 20, 2009. http://www.theguardian.com/commentisfree/2009/oct/20/israel-goldstone-palestine-gaza-un

Freedom House Perspectives. *With New Members, the UN Human Rights Council Goes from Bad to Worse.* November 19, 2018. https://freedomhouse.org/article/new-members-un-human-rights-council-goes-bad-worse

Gilboa, E. "Sharp Power: Hamas's Dirty War against Israel." *BESA Center Perspectives* no. 800, April 17, 2018. https://besacenter.org/perspectives-papers/hamas-dirty-war/

Gilboa, E. "Israel: Countering Brandjacking." In *Handbook of Public Diplomacy*, edited by N. Snow and N. Cull, 331–341. London: Routledge, 2020.

Goldstone, R. "Reconsidering the Goldstone Report on Israel and War Crimes." *The Washington Post*, April 1, 2011. https://www.washingtonpost.com/opinions/reconsidering-the-goldstone-report-on-israel-and-war-crimes/2011/04/01/AFg111JC_story.html

Gross, J., "Hamas Official: 50 Of The 62 Gazans Killed In Border Violence Were Our Members." *Times of Israel*, May 16, 2018. https://www.timesofisrael.com/hamas-official-50-of-the-people-killed-in-gaza-riots-were-members

"Hamas Co-founder Admits We are Deceiving the Public about Peaceful Protests." *Times of Israel*, May 17, 2018. https://www.timesofisrael.com/hamas-co-founder-admits-we-are-deceiving-the-public-about-peaceful-protests/

Hansler, J. "Trump Authorizes Sanctions Against International Criminal Court Officials." *CNN.com*, June 11, 2020. https://edition.cnn.com/2020/06/11/politics/icc-executive-order/index.html

"Head of UN War Crimes Inquiry Resigns after Israel Accuses Him of pro-Gaza Bias." *The Guardian*, February 3, 2015. https://www.theguardian.com/world/2015/feb/02/un-war-crimes-inquiry-resigns-israel-gaza-palestine

High Level Military Group. *An Assessment of the 2014 Gaza Conflict*. October 2015. http://www.high-level-military-group.org/pdf/hlmg-assessment-2014-gaza-conflict.pdf

High Level Military Group. *Submission on the 2018 Protests*. February 28, 2019. http://high-level-military-group.org/pdf/hlmg-unhrc-col-richard-kemp-2.pdf

Hunt, J. "The UN Human Rights Council Ignored Our Concerns on Its Israel Approach. Now We Must Act." *The Jewish Chronicle*, March 21, 2019. https://www.thejc.com/comment/comment/jeremy-hunt-un-human-rights-council-ignored-our-concerns-on-its-israel-approach-now-we-must-act-1.481829

"IDF Believes Gaza Snipers Used Iranian Armor-Piercing Rifle to Kill Soldier." *Times of Israel*, July 22, 2018. https://www.timesofisrael.com/idf-believes-gaza-snipers-used-iranian-armor-piercing-rifle-to-kill-soldier/

International Criminal Court. *Rome Statute of the International Criminal Court*. The Hague: United Nations, 1998.

International Criminal Court. "Statement of ICC Prosecutor, Fatou Bensouda." December 20, 2019. https://www.icc-cpi.int/Pages/item.aspx?name=20191220-otp-statement-palestine

International Criminal Court. *Situation in the State of Palestine: Prosecution Response to the Observations of Amici Curiae*. The Hague: United Nations, 2020.

Israel Ministry of Foreign Affairs. *Initial Response to Report of the Fact-Finding Mission on Gaza*. September 24, 2009. https://mfa.gov.il/MFA_Graphics/MFA%20Gallery/Documents/GoldstoneReportInitialResponse240909.pdf

Israel Ministry of Foreign Affairs. "IDF Military Advocate General Indicts Soldiers for Incidents during Operation Cast Lead." July 6, 2010. https://mfa.gov.il/MFA/AboutIsrael/State/Law/Pages/Military_Advocate_General_indicts_IDF_soldiers_Operation_Cast_Lead_6_Jul_2010.aspx

Israel Ministry of Foreign Affairs. "Israeli Response to the UNHRC Commission of Inquiry." June 22, 2015. https://mfa.gov.il/MFA/PressRoom/2015/Pages/Israeli-response-to-the-UNHRC-Commission-of-Inquiry-22-Jun-2015.aspx

"Israel's Bombardment of Gaza Is Not Self-Defence – It's a War Crime." *Sunday Times*, January 11, 2009. https://web.archive.org/web/20090319105413/http://www.timesonline.co.uk/tol/comment/letters/article5488380.ece

Kahn, M. "National Security Adviser John Bolton Remarks to Federalist Society." *Lawfare*, September 10, 2018. https://www.lawfareblog.com/national-security-adviser-john-bolton-remarks-federalist-society

Kasnett, I. "Legal Experts Argue Impartiality, Point to ICC Bias." *JNS.org*, May 11, 2020. https://www.jns.org/legal-experts-question-impartiality-decry-bias-of-icc-in-alleged-israeli-war-crimes-case/

Kemp, R. "The U.N.'s Gaza Report Is Flawed and Dangerous." *New York Times*, June 25, 2015. https://www.nytimes.com/2015/06/26/opinion/the-uns-gaza-report-is-flawed-and-dangerous.html?_r=0

Kittrie, O. *Lawfare: Law as a Weapon of War*. New York, NY: Oxford University Press, 2016.

Kuperwasser, Y., and E. Fischberger. *The War of Many Rounds in Gaza: Hamas/Islamic Jihad Vs. Israel*. Jerusalem: The Jerusalem Center for Public Affairs, 2019.

Meir Amit Intelligence and Terrorism Information Center. "Arson Terrorism." June 19, 2018. https://www.terrorism-info.org.il/en/arson-terrorism-a-new-method-devised-by-hamas-during-the-return-marches-to-attack-the-communities-near-the-gaza-strip-and-disrupt-their-daily-lives/

Morgan, E. "Goldstone Report Undermines Faith in International Law." *Toronto Star*, October 22, 2009. http://www.thestar.com/comment/article/713921.

Muravchik, J. "The UN and Israel: A History of Discrimination." *World Affairs* 176 (2013): 35–46.

Nahshon, E. Twitter Post. March 22, 2019, 11:46 PM. https://twitter.com/emmanuel nahshon/status/1109028620436193280

NGO Monitor. *Filling in the Blanks*. July 12, 2015. https://www.ngo-monitor.org/2014_Gaza_Conflict.pdf

NGO Monitor. *Submission to the UNHRC Commission of Inquiry on the 2018 Protest*. November 15, 2018. https://www.ngo-monitor.org/nm/wp-content/uploads/2018/11/2018-Gaza-COI-Submission-FINAL.pdf

Pompeo, M. "ICC Decision on Afghanistan." *U.S. Department of State*, March 5, 2020. https://www.state.gov/icc-decision-on-afghanistan/

Ravid, B. "Head of UN Gaza Probe." *Haaretz*, June 23, 2015. https://www.haaretz.com/.premium-head-of-un-s-gaza-report-in-interview-with-haaretz-1.5373798

Rose, G., and M. Hirsch. "Rule or Ruse of Law." *Australian Institute of International Affairs*, May 6, 2020. http://www.internationalaffairs.org.au/australianoutlook/rule-or-ruse-of-law-in-the-un-international-criminal-court/

Samson, E. "Necessity, Proportionality, and Distinction in Nontraditional Conflicts: The Unfortunate Case Study of the Goldstone Report." In *Rethinking the Law of Armed Conflict in an Age of Terrorism*, edited by C. A. Ford and A. Cohen, 195–214. Lanham, MD: Lexington, 2012.

Schoenberg, H. "Demonization in Durban: The World Conference against Racism." *The American Jewish Yearbook* 102 (2002): 85–111.

Shehada, M. "The Full Story behind the 'March of Return.'" *YnetNews*, March 30, 2018. https://www.ynetnews.com/articles/0,7340,L-5210084,00.html

"UN Chief Vows to Stand up against Anti-Israel Bias, Anti-Semitism." *Times of Israel*, April 24, 2017. https://www.timesofisrael.com/un-chief-vows-to-stand-up-against-anti-israel-bias-anti-semitism/

UN Watch. "The UN and Israel: Key Statistics." August 23, 2016. https://unwatch. org/un-israel-key-statistics/

UN Watch, "2019–2020 General Assembly Resolutions Singling Out Israel." November 19, 2019. https://unwatch.org/2019-un-general-assembly-resolutions-singling-out-israel-texts-votes-analysis/

UNHRC. *Human Rights in Palestine and Other Occupied Arab Territories.* Report of the United Nations Fact-Finding Mission on the Gaza Conflict. New York, NY: United Nations, 2009.

UNHRC. *The Grave Violations of Human Rights in the Occupied Palestinian Territory, Particularly Due to the Recent Israeli Military Attacks against the Occupied Gaza Strip.* Resolution S-9/1. New York, NY: United Nations, 2009.

UNHRC. *Ensuring Respect for International Law in the Occupied Palestinian Territory.* Resolution S-21/1. New York, NY: United Nations, 2014.

UNHRC. *Report of the Detailed Findings of the Independent Commission of Inquiry Established Pursuant to Human Rights Council Resolution S-21/1.* New York, NY: United Nations, 2015.

UNHRC. *Violations of International Law in the Context of Large-Scale Civilian Protests.* Resolution S-28/1. New York, NY: United Nations, 2018.

UNHRC. *Report of the Detailed Findings of the Independent International Commission of Inquiry on the Protests.* New York, NY: United Nations, 2019.

United Nations. "UN Independent Commission of Inquiry on Protests in Gaza Presents Its Findings." February 28, 2019. https://www.un.org/unispal/docu ment/un-independent-commission-of-inquiry-on-protests-in-gaza-presents-its-findings-press-release/

Walzer, M. "The Gaza War and Proportionality." *Dissent*, January 8, 2009. https:// www.dissentmagazine.org/online_articles/the-gaza-war-and-proportionality

Weiler, J. "After Gaza 2014: Schabas." *Blog of the European Journal of International Law*, November 4, 2014. https://www.ejiltalk.org/after-gaza-2014-schabas/comment-page -1/#comment-222487

William Schabas. "YouTube Video, 30: 36. Posted by the Russell Tribunal on Palestine." October 7, 2012. https://youtu.be/Vm_WhxIGytk

Winer, S. "UN Gaza Probe Head Says He's Not Anti-Israel, Will Be Impartial." *Times of Israel*, August 12, 2014. https://www.timesofisrael.com/un-gaza-probe-head-says-hes-not-anti-israel-will-be-impartial/

Wittes, B. "Israeli Targeting Procedures and the Concept of Proportionality." *Lawfare*, December 15, 2015. https://www.lawfareblog.com/israeli-targeting-procedures-and-concept-proportionality

Birds of a feather vote together? EU and Arab League UNGA Israel voting

Leah Mandler and Carmela Lutmar

ABSTRACT
UN General Assembly (UNGA) voting is non-binding, unlike voting in the Security Council (UNSC), yet is considered to reflect states' interests. This article attempts to explore, compare, and explain patterns in UNGA voting of two regional organisations (ROs) on Israel-related resolutions, and/or issues that are of importance to Israel. Israel has been a unique case when it comes to the UN, which has shown pervasive hostility towards the Jewish state over the past decades (e.g. 83 of the 97 UNGA resolutions criticising countries in 2012–15 [or 86%] were directed against Israel). While most researchers agree that ROs differ in the level of their group vote uniformity, this article argues that states' voting on resolutions related to Israel also varies within ROs and over time. As such, it sheds light on internal changes within the examined ROs (the Arab League and the EU) and shows important differences among members of these organisations.

These days, states are required to simultaneously coordinate their foreign policies due to overlapping membership in regional and international organisations. Multiple memberships affect state behaviour in international arenas; instead of voicing a single, national position, states also articulate positions of their Regional Organisations (ROs).[1] In an effort to influence international politics and/or promote a particular agenda, states can (and some may even say, should) coordinate with fellow RO members in order to speak with a single voice in International Organisations (IO) negotiations.[2] Therefore, member states can and do initiate resolutions on behalf of their regional group and speak up on behalf of their ROs during negotiations. More importantly, IR scholars tend to agree that ROs seek to foster and sustain high levels of coherency among their members in UNGA voting as well.[3]

Previous analysis of the voting patterns among RO members revealed that in most cases EU states have a common position and vote uniformly, though the more politicised an issue of the vote is the smaller the chances that a common EU position will be reached. Since Israel-related topics may be seen as highly politicised due to the Israeli-Palestinian conflict, we decided to examine whether that uniformity also characterises EU voting in UNGA on resolutions related to Israel.

General Assembly voting

Voting at the UN General Assembly (UNGA) is just one determinant of states' foreign policy behaviour as it is considered to signal foreign policy preferences, even if voting is non-binding. Whereas diplomatic bonds represent a vague factor as they symbolise a more 'external' manifestation of bilateral relationships. States might have economic ties and cooperate on security issues and not have official ties for various reasons such as appeasing a third party. For example, Israel had economic relations and vast security cooperation on many projects with China and India before establishing diplomatic relations. This was during the Cold War era and considerations of great power politics played a major role in foreign policy decision-making.

The study of foreign policy behaviour and its determinants has mostly focused on North-South relations and the relationships between foreign aid and foreign policy compliance. Some studies probed the process by which the foreign policy behaviour of weak states comes to reflect the preferences of more powerful nations.

Moon contrasts two models – the bargaining model and the dependency model. The bargaining model regards the policymaking process of weak states as relatively autonomous. We say 'relatively autonomous' because the bargaining model recognises that weak states are influenced by reward/ punishment actions of a more powerful state. Those actions are thought to condition the weaker state's policies. By contrast, the dependency model stresses the long-term character of the influence exerted by stronger states on weaker states and the indirect path through which such influence occurs. It regards the decision-making process as embedded in a social/political structure, which is itself distorted by the dependency relationship.

Moon relies on UN voting data and measures of the relations between the US and 88 less-developed states, and uses a cross-section time-series analysis to show that the explanatory power of the bargaining model is relatively limited and that the dependency model is a more appropriate conception. He also finds through a cross-sectional analysis, that in both models, compliant behaviour is rewarded (with aid). Moreover, the dependency-indicating transactions (e.g. treaties, trade, arms sales, IGO memberships, consultations, etc.) exhibit correlations with voting behaviour. By using longitudinal analysis, he exposes much greater stability in voting behaviour over time –

SOFT THREATS TO NATIONAL SECURITY

and much less correlation with aid-giving – than one would expect if bargaining were present.[4]

In more recent studies on UN voting, Dreher and Jensen empirically investigate changes in voting in the United Nations General Assembly (UNGA) following leader turnovers during the period 1985–2008, and find evidence that governments with new leaders are more supportive of the United States on important votes.[5] Mattes, Leeds, and Carroll examine the effect of domestic political change on UNGA voting, and argue that foreign policy change is most likely when a new leader – one who relies on different societal groups for support than one's predecessor – comes to power.[6] Smith links leadership turnover, regime type, and changes in UNGA voting. He argues that leader turnover, especially in less democratic systems, increases the likelihood of policy realignment. Dictators who are accountable and dependent for the purpose of staying in power on only a small proportion of the population represent the foreign policy interests of their small number of supporters. So, when there is a leadership turnover, the interests represented often shift too and this results in an increased volatility and regression towards a neutral position of a state's alignment at the United Nations vis-a-vis the United States.[7]

These studies show clearly two parallel, though contradictory, features of UN voting in the General Assembly – on the one hand the voting is non-binding, hence one would think states would not take voting there as indicative of foreign policy preferences, whereas on the other, the alignments in voting patterns in the General Assembly change following leadership turnovers, and vary in different regime types.

UNGA voting on Israel

Israel, as a small state, does not consider UN voting to be a true indicator of political interests' alignment or of states' support of Israel. Though a disproportionate number of UNGA resolutions deal with Israel every year, their main purpose is to delegitimise the Jewish state. In 65% of instances in which a member state is criticised in a UNGA resolution, that state is Israel, with no other member state criticised in more than 10% of resolutions.[8] Therefore, anti-Israeli resolutions are perceived more as expressive than decisive not only by Israeli government officials but also by the states voting on these resolutions.[9] As argued earlier, the voting in the UN General Assembly is non-binding, so it is hardly surprising, and certainly not unique to Israel to hold such positions. Mandler and Lutmar argue that instead, Israel defines specific bilateral foreign policy goals, and pursues them by providing foreign aid to the countries it deems as crucial to advancing those goals. They find that Israel provides aid disproportionally to its size, and though one would think, and expect, that this is done primarily in order to promote interests in foreign policy through voting in the UNGA, the empirical findings present a significant rebuttal to this assumption, which is interesting, counterintuitive, and warrant a second thought as to the usefulness of this strategy.[10]

In November 2012, the UNGA granted the Palestinians non-member observer state status after their failed UNSC bid to gain full statehood. Though the empirics do not provide evidence of any significant change in overall UNGA voting on Israel after 2012 (see below), Israeli behaviour vis-a-vis the Palestinians has been repeatedly singled out in the UNGA as an issue of racism, human rights and international law violations throughout the researched period.[11]

Regional Organisations (ROs) and UN voting

One of the first studies to investigate the role of regional organisations in the UN has been Haas and Rowe in which they explore phenomenon of externalisation: they want to use the voting behaviour in the UN General Assembly of members of regional organisations as an indicator for determining whether and to what extent these regional players have succeeded in translating their regional concerns into cohesive behaviour towards third parties organised globally. Their findings show a significant variation in levels of externalisation of specific regional organisations. They also found poor correspondence between the general performance of regional organisations and their conduct at the UN. The main conclusion to be drawn from the study is that there is a gap between the way governments act in their regional groupings and the way they behave in the United Nations, depending on how they view the issues involved and what they expect to gain.[12]

Recent research on ROs behaviour at the UN found that not only are they becoming increasingly important in international politics,[13] but that nowadays almost every regional organisation is investing significant efforts to actively coordinate its votes at the UNGA.[14] However, since in parallel to their membership in regional organisations states retain their sovereignty in regard to foreign policy, a RO member cannot be forced to agree to the position of the regional group and is not bound by other RO members' positions. Therefore, RO officials in New York usually invest huge efforts to coordinate the positions of member states before each UNGA session. The more their national interests overlap, the more likely it is for RO members to agree on the RO's preferred vote.

Among the factors that may influence RO's coordination capabilities and the level of uniformity among the RO members' UNGA voting, scholars mention several factors, such as the size of the RO, its policy scope and age of the organisation.[15] Despite all efforts invested by RO officials, Panke, Lang and Wiedemann claim that most ROs lack the ability, opportunity, and willingness to coordinate their positions within the UNGA. They claim that member states have the incentive to only adhere to those RO positions that align most closely with their already existing national preferences.[16]

Empirics and methods

The articles explored 21 Arab League members[17] and 28 EU members and their UNGA voting. Voting data was obtained from UNGA Voting Records Online Database,[18] by first compiling the list of all GA resolutions dealing with Israel and/or Israeli territories. The list includes 148 UNGA resolutions against Israel in 1996–2017.[19] Since all resolutions are characterised by negative actions against Israel (e.g. condemnations, criticism, etc.), each vote was coded in relation to a 'level of resistance' to the resolution, i.e. level of support for Israel. Thus, if the state voted against the (anti-Israel) resolution, it was graded as providing the highest level of support (0.5) for Israel. If the state voted 'yes' (in favour of an anti-Israel resolution) it received the lowest level of support (0). It is important to emphasise that the coding of voting patterns on UN resolutions against Israel is in accord with criteria suggested by Voeten.[20] Since abstentions require physical presence while openly expressing some level of resistance to the proposed resolution while absences in many cases have other non-related causes, abstentions were coded as (0.3) and absences as (0.2). Voting data was aggregated annually, so each state is given an annual grade which expresses its 'level of support' for Israel. Since in most resolutions examined, most states aligned with UNGA's majority anti-Israeli vote, the numbers are very close to 0.

Results

Israel-related resolutions and EU

The EU was the first Regional Organisation to gain a formal observer status at the UN in 2011. However, to make an effective use of its observer status, the EU must bring its members to exhibit a joint position in UNGA voting. While EU members maintain close contact and meet in New York before every UNGA resolution,[21] coordinating a joint position is not always easy. This has become even more evident in recent years when EU members have disagreed quite often on foreign policy issues.

Greater agreement among EU members on issues of foreign policy did follow the Treaty of Lisbon after 2009. However, Jin and Hosli found that although EU voting coherence has gradually increased over time, its voting cohesion still varies across issue areas, making it not the most cohesive actor in comparison to other ROs in the UN.[22] They also found that the EU's coherence (in terms of UNGA voting behaviour) was not influenced by the organisation's recent enlargements. In contrast to their findings, Burmester and Jankowski claim that while EU member states' UNGA vote record may seem to be surprisingly incoherent, its relative ability to coordinate contested votes proves a more successful vote coordination than other ROs.[23]

Since the end of the 1990s, the EU and Israel have increasingly differed on the topic of Israeli localities in the West Bank and East Jerusalem.[24] The findings below clarify that these may be more of a declarative EU statement against Israel than a true indicator of increasing rifts between Israel and the EU.

Variance among EU members

Figure 1 shows the average level of support for Israel among the examined 28 EU states, measured annually in the period between 1996 and 2017, as expressed by their voting on UNGA resolutions regarding Israel.

As shown in Figure 1, the two most supportive EU members in the research period were Bulgaria and Romania, while the two EU members that showed lowest levels of support for Israel in their voting patterns were Cyprus and Malta. Though Romania and Bulgaria, which joined the EU in 2007, have the highest average annual levels of support, it is important to note that the main reason for that is not active abstention but instead absence from voting. Bulgaria was absent from 33 votes (out of 148) and Romania from 31, which are more than 20% of votes on anti-Israeli resolutions.

Actually, the only EU member state that actively showed its support during the research period by abstention was Greece (5 resolutions), while

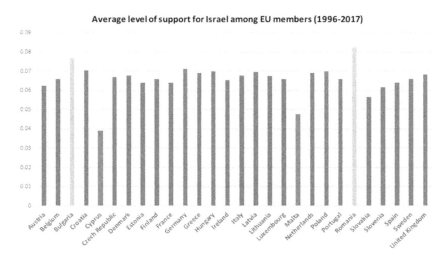

Figure 1. Average annual level of support (EU).

Romania, Croatia, Poland and Ireland, which exhibited seemingly relatively high levels of support, abstained only once each. If we assume that absences from voting can also be an indication of support, albeit a less definitive one, then Croatia, Germany, Latvia and Lithuania may also be considered relatively more supportive of Israel than other EU members. Interestingly, Cyprus also abstained from anti-Israeli vote once (in 2015), though it exhibited very low level of support for Israel overall. These findings contradict the claims made by Jin and Hosli mentioned above, since 'old' and 'new' EU members do exhibit significantly different levels of support for Israel.

Variance over time

When we examine the level of EU support for Israel in the UNGA over time, it is interesting to note that the late 1990s and early 2000s were characterised by a relatively higher level of support for Israel than the period after 2010 (see Figure 2).

Of the ten abstentions in the whole research period, only two occurred in the post-2010 period – one by Cyprus, the other by Ireland. However, it is important to note that the two least supportive members mentioned above, Cyprus and Malta, joined the EU in 2004. Since Romania and Bulgaria, the two most supportive EU members, joined only in 2007, it is interesting to examine whether the relative change in the overall level of support for Israel in the second decade of the research period is the result of EU enlargement. Figure 3 shows the level of support exhibited by the original 15 EU members, present in the EU from 1996 to 2017.

As can be seen, the most Israel-supportive constant EU members were Greece and Germany, and the least supportive among them was Austria.

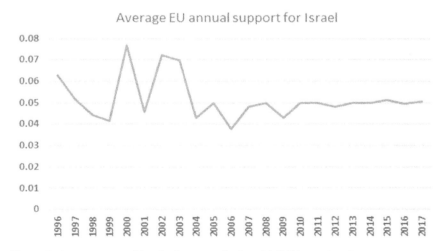

Figure 2. Average annual level of support for Israel (all EU members).

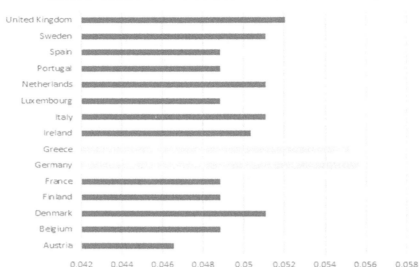

Figure 3. Average level of support for Israel (15 EU members only).

Also, when comparing the average annual vote of original 15 members with the vote of all EU members, including all member states that joined during the 2000s, it can be seen that the addition has changed the vote slightly in favour of Israel (See Figure 4).

While the average annual vote of all members has been higher throughout the whole time, it can be seen that the differences were more significant at the

Figure 4. Comparison between all EU members and 'old' EU members.

beginning of the research period, and as it seems, may be starting to be significant again at its end (though not necessarily according to the same division lines). It seems that after 2010, EU members exhibit greater uniformity of vote than before as well as lower overall support for Israel, while internal politics may be the reason why states such as Ireland and Cyprus voted differently in 2015 and 2016 than other members.

Israel-related resolutions and Arab League

The Arab League (AL) is one of the oldest regional groupings in the UN setting, having been present already at the 1945 San Francisco Conference. Though lacking the official observer status the EU possesses, Arab League Secretary-General was invited to attend sessions of the General Assembly since 1950.[25]

Previous research found the Arab League is one of the most cohesive groups at the UNGA.[26] Since the Palestinian question concerns roughly a third of all resolutions voted at each UNGA session – unanimity against Israel (and US) is considered to be the dominant cohesive factor in this RO. Our findings confirm the assumption that most Arab League members stand firmly against Israel throughout the research period. However, this stance is not unanimous and the reasons for outlier behaviour are further discussed clarified in the next section.

Variance among members

Figure 5 shows the average level of support among AL members in the researched period. While 11 members (52%) voted in favour of all anti-Israeli resolutions examined, thus maintaining the average 0 vote, several states do stand out. Somalia, Comoros, Iraq and Mauritania voted differently than the majority of AL members.

Variance over time

The only 'Nay' vote was made by Mauritania on applicability of the Geneva Convention relative to the Protection of Civilian Persons in Time of War to the 'Occupied Palestinian Territory', including East Jerusalem, and other Arab territories occupied by Israel in 1967 (Resolution 59/122; 10 December 2004). On all other 147 resolutions, Arab League member states either voted in favour or abstained. It is interesting to note that Somalia abstained on all votes in 1996–2001, and then again in 2007–9 and 2015–17. Interestingly, Iraq abstained on all anti-Israeli resolutions in 1996–2003, but since 2005 voted against Israel on all relevant resolutions.

To notice changes over time, we first analysed how the annual level of support of AL as a whole changed between 1996 and 2017, taking into account all AL members (including the states that constantly voted against

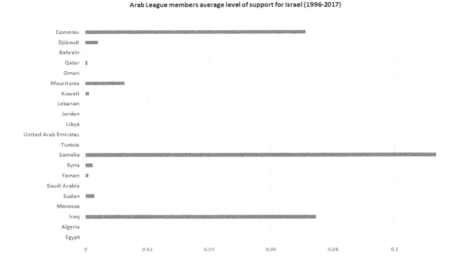

Figure 5. Average level of support for Israel among Arab League members.

Israel). As Figure 6 shows, the overall level of support was much lower at the end of the research period than at its beginning.

Secondly, we looked in greater detail into voting patterns of AL members that did not vote against Israel on all resolutions.[27] As can be seen in Figure 7, Iraq and Mauritania changed their voting after 2005 and voted against Israel ever since. Sudan, Syria and Djibouti voted periodically in favour of Israel in 1996–2009 but started complying with the majority of Arab League members

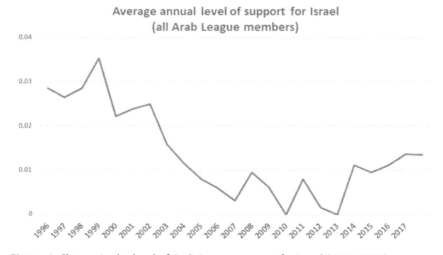

Figure 6. Change in the level of Arab League support for Israel (1996–2017).

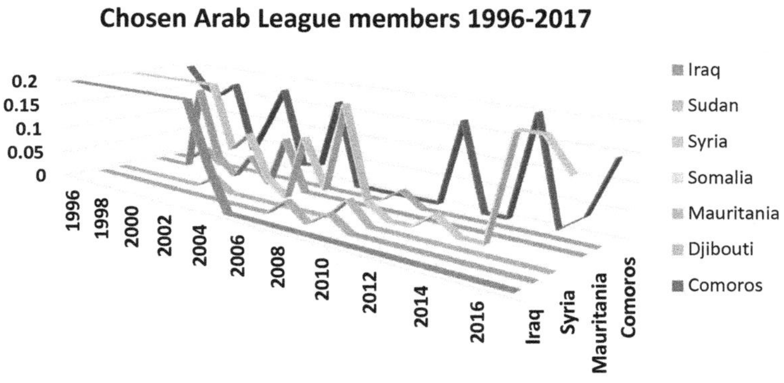

Chosen Arab League members 1996-2017

Figure 7. Level of support for Israel – chosen Arab League members only (1996–2017).

since 2010. Comoros has been among the most Israel-supportive AL member along the research period but voted against Israel in 2006–11. Somalia, the most Israel-supportive state in the League, voted against Israel more often in 2009–15, but abstained from voting in favour of anti-Israel resolutions in the rest of the period.

The data shows decrease in the pro-Israeli vote, i.e. greater compliance with the voting patterns of the AL majority from 2005 onwards, with the exceptions of Somalia and Comoros, which will be explained in greater details below. Higher voting uniformity within the Arab League in the second period may have to do with the fact that in January 2005 its members signed an internal free trade agreement. It may also be related to the Lebanese-Syrian crisis, during which the League intervened to diffuse tensions between the rival Lebanese factions, between Lebanon and Syria, and between Syria and the international community.[28]

Discussion

Outliers explained – Somalia and Comoros

Though Arab League members, both Comoros and Somalia are considered quintessential 'failed states'. Both states joined the Arab League under pressure from their Arab counterparts due to 'historical ties', but both also 'owe' their internal instability and nation-building failure to foreign intervention, mostly by Iran.

Internal political and military crises in Comoros and Somalia have been either highly neglected or inefficiently treated by the Arab League.[29] For example, the AL does not even have an office in Comoros, nor has the Comorian issue ever been seriously discussed or listed as a priority on the League's agenda. Occasionally, the League issues invitations to conflicting parties to meet and negotiate, but so far it has not allocated any significant resources for conflict resolution. Meanwhile, Iran successfully extended its influence in Comoros, especially through financial and material support to the controversial president Sambi, to whom Iran provides security consultants and personal bodyguards.[30]

Furthermore, despite the AL's economic embargo on Israel, and regardless of non-existent official diplomatic ties with the Jewish state, Comoros and Israel engage in mutual trade. Israel does report to the World Trade Organisation about its imports from Comoros (albeit not annually), but there is no reported record of bilateral trade with Israel on behalf of Comoros.[31] Considering Iran's extensive involvement in Comoros, it is perhaps obvious why in parallel to its relatively pro-Israel voting at the UNGA and bilateral trade Comoros had to be the one to bring a complaint against Israel to the International Criminal Court in 2013 regarding the Israeli takeover of the Mavi Marmara flotilla.

Somalia faces similar political and military challenges as Comoros and shares its (silent) dissatisfaction with Arab League attempts to solve its internal problems. Tehran exploits its relations with the al-Shabab terrorist organisation to move arms to regional proxies in Lebanon, Gaza, and Yemen, to threaten international navigation with piracy and to gain control over several uranium mines in Somalia for its nuclear activities. All these pushed the Somali government to join Saudi Arabia and close Gulf allies like the UAE and Bahrain towards an unofficial strategic rapprochement with Israel mainly in the field of military intelligence.[32] Therefore, as the article's findings show, despite the pervasive 'rally around the flag' that League members increasingly exhibited since 2005, Somalia's covert security-related collaboration with Israel, Comoros's economic interests and both countries' strategic threat from Iran were more crucial to the regimes' survival and successful counterinsurgency than anything that Arab League membership could offer.[33]

Conclusions

Both ROs explored here underwent important changes during the research period. Both also seem to be struggling to create a more unified voice, and the votes of their members seem to have grown more uniform over time. While differences among EU members may be related to old and new memberships in the Union, the differences among AL members are more long term. These patterns raise questions about the role regional organisations play in shaping foreign policy preferences, and in influencing policy outcomes. Moreover, it raises theoretical questions about coordination between international organisations – is it possible, and if so, under what conditions?

Traditionally, regional organisations in general, and their voting patterns in particular, have been relatively understudied. Furthermore, the angle analysed in this article, namely comparison of two regional organisations' voting behaviour in relation to a single issue, is unique in its attempt to find and explain variations within members of each RO, while also finding common features between the two. One of its most intriguing findings that remains to be explored in greater detail is the fact that while the EU is largely considered more pro-Israeli oriented than the Arab League, it is the League member that voted against anti-Israeli resolution in the period when no EU member voted against, not even once. We believe that our findings open the door to further studies that will explore voting behaviour of these and other ROs members at the UN General Assembly in an effort to translate voting patterns into foreign policy preferences of their members.

Notes

1. Panke et al., *State and regional actors in complex governance systems*, 92.
2. Panke et al., *Regional actors in the United Nations*, 438.
3. Panke, *Regional power revisited*, 267.
4. Moon, *Trade Dependence and Foreign Policy Compliance*.
5. Dreher and Jensen, *Country or leader?*
6. Mattes et al., *Leadership Turnover and Foreign Policy Change*.
7. Smith, *Leader Turnover, Institutions, and Voting*.
8. Becker et al., *The preoccupation of the United Nations with Israel*, 414.
9. Schifter, *The United Nations and Israel*, 34.
10. Mandler and Lutmar, *Israel's foreign Assistance*.
11. Cohen et al., *The Delegitimization of Israel*, 30.
12. Haas and Rowe, *Regional organisations in the United Nations*.
13. Björn and Söderbaum, *The UN and Regional Organisations in Global Security*, 229.
14. Panke, *Regional power revisited*, 289.
15. Burmester and Jankowski, *Reassessing the European Union*, 1492.
16. Panke et al., *State and regional actors in complex governance systems*.
17. Though 'Palestine' is a member of the Arab League, according to 'Status of Palestine in the UN – Non-member observer State status – SecGen report,' it does not have a voting right.
18. General Assembly Voting Records, http://www.un.org/en/ga/documents/voting.asp.
19. Resolutions discussing 'the Palestinian territories' only, with no direct regard to Israeli authorities were not included.
20. Voeten, *Data and Analyses of Voting in the United Nations General Assembly*, 80–92.
21. Panke, *Speaking with one voice*, 29.
22. Jin and Hosli, *Pre-and post-Lisbon*.
23. Burmester and Jankowski, *Reassessing the European Union*.
24. Marzano, *The loneliness of Israel*, 98.

25. Johansson-Nogués, *The Organisation of Islamic Cooperation and the Arab League*, 98.
26. Beauguitte, *European Union Cohesiveness at the UNGA*.
27. While Yemen and Kuwait did not vote against Israel on all resolutions, they abstained only once in the research period and were thus not included in Figure 7.
28. Secretary-General Amr Moussa conducted a series of talks with Lebanese, Syrian and Arab leaders. According to Moussa's Chief of Staff Hesham Youssef, such shuttle diplomacy was ongoing from 2005 to the conclusion of the Doha Agreement in 2008. Dakhlallah, *The Arab League in Lebanon*, 62.
29. Hassan, *The Comoros and the Crisis of Building a National state*, 230.
30. Massey and Baker, *Comoros*, 26.
31. World Trade Organisation, *International Trade Statistics Database*, https://data.wto.org/.
32. Shahvar, *Iran's global reach*, 55.
33. Faisal, *Somalia and Israel*.

Disclosure statement

No potential conflict of interest was reported by the author(s).

Funding

This research was supported by the Israel Science Foundation (grant No. 2716/19).

Bibliography

Beauguitte, L. "European Union Cohesiveness at the UNGA: A Comparative and Critical Approach." In *Networks of Global Governance: International Organisations and European Integration in a Historical Perspective*, edited by L. Mechi, G. Migani, and F. Petrini, 309–324. Cambridge, UK: Cambridge Scholars Publishing, 2014.

Brazys, S., and D. Panke. "Why Do States Change Positions in the United Nations General Assembly?" *International Political Science Review* 38, no. 1 (2017): 70–84. doi:10.1177/0192512115616540.

Burmester, N., and M. Jankowski. "Reassessing the European Union in the United Nations General Assembly." *Journal of European Public Policy* 21, no. 10 (2014): 1491–1508. doi:10.1080/13501763.2014.919833.

Cohen, M. S., and C. D. Freilich. "The Delegitimization of Israel: Diplomatic Warfare, Sanctions, and Lawfare." *Israel Journal of Foreign Affairs* 9, no. 1 (2015): 29–48. doi:10.1080/23739770.2015.1015095.

Dakhlallah, F. "The Arab League in Lebanon: 2005–2008." *Cambridge Review of International Affairs* 25, no. 1 (2012): 53–74. doi:10.1080/09557571.2011.646241.

Dixon, W. J. "Reciprocity in United States-soviet Relations: Multiple Symmetry or Issue Linkage?" *American Journal of Political Science* 30, no. 2 (1986): 421–445. doi:10.2307/2111103.

Dixon, W. J., and B. Moon. "Political Similarity and American Foreign Trade Patterns." *Political Research Quarterly* 46, no. 1 (1993): 5–25. doi:10.1177/106591299304600102.

Dreher, A., and N. M. Jensen. "Country or Leader? Political Change and UN General Assembly Voting." *European Journal of Political Economy* 29, no. 1 (2013): 183–196. doi:10.1016/j.ejpoleco.2012.10.002.

Faisal, A. "Somalia and Israel: Do All Roads Lead to Tel Aviv?" *Medium*, March 30, 2019. https://medium.com/@fromadic92/somalia-and-israel-do-all-roads-lead-to-tel-aviv-b94efd52aba7

Haas, E. B., and E. T. Rowe. "Regional Organizations in the United Nations: Is There Externalization?" *International Studies Quarterly* 17, no. 1 (1973): 3–54. doi:10.2307/3013462.

Hagan, J. D. "Domestic Political Regime Changes and Foreign Policy Restructuring in Western Europe: A Conceptual Framework and Initial Empirical Analysis." *Cooperation and Conflict* 24, no. 3 (1989): 141–162. doi:10.1177/001083678902400303.

Hassan, H. A. "The Comoros and the Crisis of Building a National State." *Contemporary Arab Affairs* 2, no. 2 (2009): 229–239. doi:10.1080/17550910802589059.

Hey, J. "Foreign Policy Options under Dependence: A Theoretical Evaluation with Evidence from Ecuador." *Journal of Latin American Studies* 25, no. 3 (1993): 543–574. doi:10.1017/S0022216X00006660.

Jin, X., and M. O. Hosli. "Pre-and post-Lisbon: European Union Voting in the United Nations General Assembly." *West European Politics* 36, no. 6 (2013): 1274–1291. doi:10.1080/01402382.2013.826032.

Johansson-Nogués, E. "The Organization of Islamic Cooperation and the Arab League." In *Group Politics in UN Multilateralism*, edited by K. Smith and K. Laatikainen, 97–114. Brill, Leiden: the Netherlands, 2020.

Mandler, L., and C. Lutmar. "Israel's Foreign Assistance and UN Voting – Does It Pay?" *Israel Studies* 25, no. 1 (2020): 99–121. doi:10.2979/israelstudies.25.1.05. Spring.

Marzano, A. "The Loneliness of Israel. The Jewish State's Status in International Relations." *The International Spectator* 48, no. 2 (2013): 96–113. doi:10.1080/03932729.2013.787829.

Mattes, M., B. A. Leeds, and R. Carroll. "Leadership Turnover and Foreign Policy Change: Societal Interests, Domestic Institutions, and Voting in the United Nations." *International Studies Quarterly* 59, no. 2 (2015): 280–290. doi:10.1111/isqu.12175.

Moon, B. "Trade Dependence and Foreign Policy Compliance: A Longitudinal Analysis." *International Studies Quarterly* 24, no. 2 (1980): 191–222.

Moon, B. "The Foreign Policy of the Dependent State." *International Studies Quarterly* 27, no. 3 (1983): 315–340. doi:10.2307/2600686.

Moon, B. "Consensus or Compliance? Foreign Policy Change and External Dependence." *International Organization* 39, no. 2 (1985): 297–329. doi:10.1017/S0020818300026989.

Moon, B., and W. Dixon. "Political Similarity and American Foreign Trade Patterns." *Political Research Quarterly* 46 (1982): 1–21.

Panke, D. "Regional Power Revisited: How to Explain Differences in Coherency and Success of Regional Organizations in the United Nations General Assembly." *International Negotiation* 18, no. 2 (2013): 265–291. doi:10.1163/15718069-12341256.

Panke, D. "Speaking with One Voice: Easier Said than Done? The EU in the UNGA." In *The EU in UN Politics*, edited by S. Blavoukos and D. Bourantonis, 27–46. London: Palgrave Macmillan, 2017.

Panke, D., S. Lang, and A. Wiedemann. "State and Regional Actors in Complex Governance Systems: Exploring Dynamics of International Negotiations." *The British Journal of Politics and International Relations* 19, no. 1 (2017): 91–112. doi:10.1177/1369148116669904.

Panke, D., S. Lang, and A. Wiedemann. "Regional Organisations in the UNGA: Who Is Most Active and Why?" *Journal of International Relations and Development* 22, no. 3 (2019): 744–785. doi:10.1057/s41268-017-0119-8.

Richardson, N. *Foreign Policy and Economic Dependence*. Austin: University of Texas Press, 1978.

Richardson, N. R., and C. W. Kegley Jr. "Trade Dependence and Foreign Policy Compliance: A Longitudinal Analysis." *International Studies Quarterly* 24, no. 2 (1980): 191–222. doi:10.2307/2600200.

Roeder, P. G. "The Ties that Bind: Aid, Trade, and Political Compliance in Soviet-third World Relations." *International Studies Quarterly* 29, no. 2 (1985): 191–216. doi:10.2307/2600506.

Schifter, R. "The United Nations and Israel." *Israel Journal of Foreign Affairs* 1, no. 1 (2006): 33–34. doi:10.1080/23739770.2006.11446237.

Shahvar, S. "Iran's Global Reach: The Islamic Republic of Iran's Policy, Involvement, and Activity in Africa." *Digest of Middle East Studies* 29, no. 1 (2020): 53–75. doi:10.1111/dome.12202.

Smith, A. "Leader Turnover, Institutions, and Voting at the UN General Assembly." *Journal of Conflict Resolution* 60, no. 1 (2016): 143–163. doi:10.1177/0022002714532689.

Voeten, E. "Data and Analyses of Voting in the United Nations General Assembly." In *Routledge Handbook of International Organization*, edited by B. Reinalda, 80–92. 2013.

World Trade Organization. "International Trade Statistics Database." https://data.wto.org/

The ICC's Prosecutor in the service of Palestinian Lawfare

Assaf Derri

ABSTRACT

The International Criminal Court has been recently called upon by the Court's Prosecutor to decide a highly unusual application, to approve its jurisdiction over the State of Israel which has not acceded to its Statute. The Prosecutor asks the Court to apply to Israel a special legal standard, openly discriminating it in comparison with other states. The Prosecutor's submission consciously deviates from established theories on the Israeli-Palestinian conflict in favour of unfounded contentions which were discussed and rejected by mainstream scholarship, supporting her tautological arguments with references to vague, unauthoritative sources. This article demonstrates that the accumulative weight of all these factors points to the conclusion that the Prosecutor's submission constitutes in fact a sophisticated action in the service of Palestinian Lawfare against Israel rather than a *bona fide* legal motion. The consequences of this project, should it be endorsed by the Court, might prove devastative to international law and the present world order.

The International Criminal Court (ICC) is a permanent international tribunal that was established through and operates by the Rome Statue of the International Criminal Court (the Rome Statute). The ICC's primary goal is to adjudicate 'the most serious crimes of international concern' and serve as a complementary to national criminal jurisdictions.[1] The Rome Statute provides for several preconditions to the exercise of the Court's jurisdiction. Generally, a state that becomes a party to the Rome Statute accepts thereby the Court's jurisdiction.[2] The preconditions for the ICC's jurisdiction over a specific crime are that (1) the alleged crime occurred in the territory of a state Party or on a vessel or an aircraft thereof; or that (2) the person accused of the crime is a national of a State Party.[3]

Though Israel has not acceded to the Rome Statute, and it exercises exclusive effective control over the territory it conquered in the 1967 Six

Day War, the ICC Prosecutor (the Office of the Prosecutor, or OTP) has demonstrated an exceptional determination to conduct a criminal investigation against the Jewish state for alleged acts perpetrated in the above territory. To this end, the OTP has recently submitted an application with the ICC Pre-Trial Chamber seeking a ruling on the ICC's territorial jurisdiction over this territory (the Submission),[4] thereby accepting a referral made by the Palestinian National Authority.[5]

As will be shown below, the Submission is anything but a *bona fide* legal procedural action in the normal course of events. Rather it is a sophisticated, well-disguised politically-driven action in the service of the Palestinian 'Lawfare' campaign against Israel. Keen on pursuing her partisan pro-Palestinian agenda, the current ICC Prosecutor, Ms Fatou Bensouda, has neglected to note the grave general ramifications ensuing from the Submission, which amount to nothing short of overturning basic principles of international law and world order.

Under the current state of affairs, a People seeking independence must firstly secure exclusive control over a piece of territory and only then seek legal status of a State. Under the revolutionary paradigm advanced by the OTP, an international tribunal may be called upon to declare the existence of a new State that does not in fact exist, and prescribe legal ratification for this pseudo-State's claim for a territory over which it has no effective – let alone exclusive – control. The rest of the world will be then presumably obliged to implement this legal ruling. In other words, the Submission envisions a world in which political controversies and international relations are regulated by courts of law instead of by nations, peoples and states. The main problem with this ambitious project is that it has very little to do with the way the real subjects of international law – i.e. states – act in the real world. International law, more than any other type of law, is not only supposed to reflect the way its subjects are normally behaving but it is, by definition, shaped by the common practice of states.[6]

Bensouda has been repeatedly (and justly) criticised for her insistence to focus her efforts – and consequently, the ICC's attention – on democracies such as Israel and the United States, while at the same time turning a blind eye to widely known, large-scale and amply documented grave war crimes such as were recently perpetrated by the Assad regime in Syria. By contrast, the present article focuses not on a comparative review of the OTP's policy but on an intrinsic analysis of her position on the Israeli-Palestinian conflict as reflected in the recent Submission. It shows that the OTP's treatment of the conflict is steeped in a strong anti-Israeli bias, an attitude highly inappropriate for a senior officer of a distinguished international tribunal. The OTP's pro-Palestinian political agenda permeates every single argument raised in the Submission, making it a political pamphlet rather than a balanced legal motion. The Submission is not merely legally unfounded but constructed in a way that points to a self-conscious political endeavour to advance the Palestinian cause, an integral part of the declared Palestinian 'Lawfare' campaign against Israel. It would not be farfetched to assume that Bensouda is aware of the threadbare nature of her arguments and of the Submission's scanty chances of being actually granted by the ICC. The OTP's decision to move forward with this high-profile but legally unsound motion gives rise to the suspicion that the Submission was never meant to function as an ordinary prosecutorial action but rather as a tactical move aimed at scoring a PR victory for the Palestinians while marring and wrongly implicating Israel.

This would not be the first time for Bensouda to compile a legally moot but publicly damaging document against Israel. The previous instance was her superfluous and eventually sterile treatment of the 2010 Gaza Flotilla incident, in which she saw fit to raise severe, unsubstantiated allegations of war crimes against Israel but declined to accompany them with operative measures, thus leaving the accusations to hang on-record, unanswered.

The OTP's dubious submission

All too often the Submission resorts to misuse of definitions and concepts in order to create the impression that a certain state of affairs should be taken as given or unequivocal. This stands out mostly in the insistence on referring to the territories captured by Israel in the 1967 war (i.e. the West Bank and the Gaza Strip) as 'Occupied Palestinian Territories' (or OPT). This biased definition creates the misleading impression that Israel seized these territories from the Palestinians while they were actually taken from Jordan and Egypt, which had occupied them illegally during their war of aggression against the nascent State of Israel in 1948/49 and continued to retain them unlawfully thereafter, with Jordan even annexing the West Bank to its territory in 1950.[7] Yet while only Britain and Pakistan acknowledged the unlawful Jordanian annexation, between 1948 and 1967 the Palestinians didn't claim it was impeding the fulfilment of their right to national self-determination.

In contrast to the illegality of the Jordanian occupation of the West Bank, Israel's capture of this territory was arguably legal as it amounted to conquering a non-regularised territory (of which the title was previously undefined, and to which Israel held a valid claim) during a lawful defensive campaign,[8] while a string of Israeli prime ministers – from Shimon Peres, to Ehud Barak, to Ariel Sharon, to Ehud Olmert, to Benjamin Netanyahu – accepted the creation of an independent Palestinian entity within the two-state solution framework.

Be that as it may, it is abundantly clear that a legal analysis with pretensions for objectivity needs to adopt a careful approach towards definitions and concepts. Hence the West Bank and Gaza will be referred to in this article as 'the 1967 Territories'.

'Case-specific' application of the law

Keenly aware that a normal, objective mode of application of the law will not yield the desired result of establishing the ICC's jurisdiction over Israel and the 1967 Territories, Bensouda claims that Israel should be treated differently from other states, alluding to this improper singular treatment as 'case-specific application' of the law.[9] This discriminatory treatment is justified in the Submission with the observation that 'the situation in Palestine is unique and therefore not comparable to other entities'.[10] A careful reading shows that the supposed uniqueness is in fact the most ordinary situation typical to every dispute of self-determination: a stateless people seeks independence on a territory under the possession of an established state. The main justification the OTP provides for her disparate treatment of Israel is 'the detrimental impact of the ongoing breaches of international law on Palestine's effective authority over the Occupied Palestinian Territories and on the realisation of the right to self-determination of its people'.[11] In other words, the fact that Israel allegedly refuses to bestow on the Palestinians the recognition of independence and the territory they desire – serves as justification to view the Palestinians as eligible to these benefits, and to bend the law to that effect.

The supposed 'ongoing breaches of international law' that are brought up to justify Israel's discriminatory treatment are, as a matter of fact, inseparable from the ongoing political controversy between Israel and the Palestinians that Bensouda simultaneously deems as a matter beyond the ICC's competence and as something that the ICC would be nevertheless permitted to establish its opinion on relying '*as a matter of fact*, on the prevalent views of the international community with respect to the negative impact of certain State practices which have clearly and unequivocally been deemed contrary to international law'.[12] By 'certain State practices' the OTP obviously refers to Israel's post-1967 civilian neighbourhoods in the West Bank and East Jerusalem, as the main thrust of the Submission is indicting Israel for these localities. It is indeed unfortunate that a senior legal officer of an international court of law opts to dispose of her duty to conduct serious legal analysis of the issues in the centre of her discussion, and instead rely and ask the Court to establish its opinion on something both vague and legally unauthoritative as 'the prevalent views of the international community'.

In her historical overview of the conflict, Bensouda briefly mentions but utterly fails to discuss the consequences of the main events of the conflict that would shed light on the problem of the Israeli settlements. Such is the case with the causes and the circumstances surrounding the outbreak of armed hostilities between Jews and Arabs in 1947 and the armed attack of the neighbouring Arab States on Israel upon its establishment in 1948. While the OTP acknowledges that violence initially broke as an organised act of 'local Palestinians' in response to the UN's partition resolution which they opposed,[13] and that shortly afterwards the neighbouring Arab states invaded the newly proclaimed State of Israel,[14] she fails to pronounce the immediate and undisputed legal implications of such acts that are distinctly defined in modern international law as aggression and are strictly prohibited by the UN Charter as well as customary international law.[15] Not only does she avoid stating the unlawfulness of this aggressive conduct, but she also refrains from further elaborating on its consequences, namely the illegality of the Jordanian occupation of the West Bank and East Jerusalem, though these consequences are very meaningful for any discussion of the status of Israel's post-1967 settlements.

Deviations from mainstream international law scholarship

The 'case-specific' treatment the OTP wishes to apply reflects a relaxed application of the Montevideo criteria of statehood to 'Palestine'.[16] Arguably, the most important element of statehood is exclusive, uninterrupted effective government on the territory.[17] As this element is obviously lacking in the case of 'Palestine', the OTP advances an argument that has been thoroughly discussed and expressly rejected by mainstream scholarship: that Palestinian independence is impeded by Israeli actions, such as the Israeli civilian settlements and the security barrier constructed to prevent Palestinian terrorist attacks.[18] Even if these allegations could be accepted at face value – which, to be sure, they cannot – the scholarly consensus against Palestinian statehood remains unaltered.[19] Crawford calls this theory 'prefiguring' of a state and rejects it altogether.[20]

In an attempt to substantiate her ambitious claim, Bensouda lingers on the two modern theories of statehood law, the declaratory and the constitutive.[21] But her description of the current balance between the two theories is highly inaccurate and heavily tilting towards the constitutive theory that was unanimously discredited by legal scholars. In Bensouda's description:

> Although preference has been shown for the declaratory theory (with emphasis on the criterion of 'independence'), the constitutive theory (that is, international recognition) still remains a relevant consideration, and even determinative, in certain cases'.[22]

This is simply a false description. A quick glance at the references cited in the OTP's own footnotes on this paragraph – presumably the best she could find to support her argument – suffices to see that all mainstream legal scholars are in full agreement that the declaratory theory prevails in modern international law – and no honest critic would describe this as a mere 'preference'.

It is further untrue to argue that the constitutive theory remains a relevant consideration, *a fortiori* not determinative. All the references clearly reflect that other states' recognition, at the most, may have an evidentiary value, which means that it can never be said to contribute directly to the creation of a new state, but only to serve as a proof in a factual controversy. A handful of scholars leaning towards recognition raise the possibility of considering it 'to some degree' (Saltzman),[23] or allowing it – as a secondary factor – some function in 'the application and appreciation of the Montevideo criteria' (Cerone).[24] These views, however, are not in the scholarly consensus and are a far cry from the power the OTP attributes to recognition.

Finally, Bensouda's surprising argument that recognition may be determinative 'in certain cases' calls for an investigation into these 'certain cases'. Her footnote (469) shows that she refers to the case of Bosnia/Herzegovina and Croatia which were given overwhelming international recognition even before they could demonstrate full effective government of their respective territories. The major, decisive difference, however, between these cases and the case of 'Palestine' is that these Balkan states were already established states, previously federated within the former Socialist Federal Republic of Yugoslavia. The difference between existing states and a non-state entity seeking recognition is surely familiar to the OTP. An existing, established state remains a state even if it is incorporated within a federative arrangement and then secedes from it. It remains a state even if it loses effective control altogether over its entire territory (as happened with many European states in WWII). This is not a simple mistake. It is at best a clear misconception of the law, at worst – a deliberate misrepresentation. It facially seems, albeit hard to believe, that Bensouda's failure to correctly represent the scholarly consensus on the status of these two theories flows from a genuine misunderstanding of the subject matter. As this seems very unlikely, given that precisely such issues are supposed to be within the OTP's expertise, the inevitable conclusion is that this gross misrepresentation of the law is attributable to the partisan nature of the entire project.

In the same vein, Bensouda erroneously applies self-determination law's rules of decolonisation to the Israeli-Palestinian conflict. It is important to note that legal scholarship has traditionally differentiated and applied a different set of rules to the category of decolonisation, with a much more relaxed standard of application of the usually rigorous statehood criteria. The Israeli-Palestinian conflict is quite obviously not a case of decolonisation under international law. No serious mainstream scholar treats it as such (Crawford, for example,

SOFT THREATS TO NATIONAL SECURITY

categorises the Israeli-Palestinian conflict as a case of secession). Even the Arab position on the legal classification of the conflict was never premised on a theory of decolonisation and it still isn't.[25] Bensodua is well aware of this state of affairs and therefore refrains in the body of her submission from bringing up decolonisation arguments, while disingenuously referencing irrelevant decolonisation discussions in a footnote.

Tautologies and other logical fallacies

Bensouda's solution to the impasse of 'Palestine's' indisputable lack of effective control over the 1967 Territories is simply ignoring it. In her theory the legal, so to speak, is exempt from its most rudimentary function of relating to the factual situation. If the Palestinians cannot establish a real state in the territories due to Israeli-caused impediments – the ICC should discard with the facts and statehood criteria in their case and accredit 'Palestine' with fictive recognition of authority over the self-same territory over which it admittedly does not exercise effective government as a matter of fact.

In this rather bizarre construct, the legal does not flow from the factual but is rather supposed to replace it. Legal fiction is called upon to play the part of a desired yet non-existent reality. This argumentative methodology amounts to a reversal of the normal course of affairs in the real world: in reality, almost every national group with aspirations of independence faces opposition from an established state. Nevertheless, such groups are expected to establish and be able to demonstrate exclusive, uninterrupted control of a piece of territory **before** and as a prerequisite for demanding recognition as a state. On the OTP's theory, things go the other way around: a national group may appeal to an international tribunal and claim that since its aspirations are viewed as 'just' by 'the international community' it is entitled to demand that political reality be adjusted in accordance with what it considers to be legally proper.

The Submission is abundant with tautologies and other logical fallacies, notably that of assuming the conclusion as a given (*petitio principii*). Unfortunately, these fallacies are located at the most crucial junctures of the Submission. A typical example can be found in section 101, which reads as follows:

> Further, the Prosecution considers that Palestine is the 'State on the territory of which the conduct in question occurred' (under article 12(2)(a) because of its status as an ICC State Party.[26]

The problem with this statement is that 'Palestine's' status as a state is precisely what is in question in these proceedings. The initial reason underlying the Submission is precisely the need for the ICC to rule on whether 'Palestine' may be considered a state capable of delegating its alleged jurisdiction to the ICC. Obviously, saying that 'Palestine' must be considered 'the state' etc. because of its status as a state, amounts to sheer circular reasoning. It is impossible for a legal argument to pull itself up by its own bootstraps.

Furthermore, the Submission is premised on the assumption that the Fourth Geneva Convention applies to the 1967 Territories while at the same time ignoring the basic principle of the same Convention – the Occupying Power's exclusive authority over the territory. The assumption that the Fourth Geneva Convention applies to the 1967 Territories seems plausible, albeit it has no bearing whatsoever on the permanent status of the territories.[27] From this Convention Bensouda purports to derive her main accusation against Israel, namely the crime of unlawfully transferring parts of its population into the Occupied Territory.[28]

However, in relying on the Fourth Geneva Convention the Submission stumbles into a self-contradictory pit, for the same Convention also vests the Occupying Power with an exclusive authority and jurisdiction over the Occupied Territory, thus dealing a fatal blow to the OTP's theory that 'Palestine' could be taken for the power vested with authority and capable of delegating jurisdiction. It should be noted that under Geneva Law, the comprehensive, exclusive jurisdiction entrusted with the Occupying Power is not a privilege but an obligation – the Occupying Power is obliged to establish orderly, well-functioning military rule over the Occupied Territory in order to maintain law and order and to prevent chaos and anarchy until the cessation of hostilities and the permanent status of the Occupied Territory be determined. If Geneva Law applies to the 1967 Territories – then the Palestinians have no jurisdiction whatsoever and cannot delegate to the ICC powers they themselves do not possess *(nemo dat quod non habet)*.

Unauthoritative authorities

It was demonstrated above how the Submission refers to such vague and abstract pseudo-authorities as the 'prevalent views of the international community' which, even if better identified, they certainly do not make the law. This habit of referring to unidentified, vague sources is complemented by a similar tendency to refer to unauthoritative sources such as the United Nations General Assembly (UNGA). Though it is common knowledge among international law scholars that UNGA is a political body that is not vested with legal authority whatsoever, Bensouda nevertheless opines that the jurisdiction of 'Palestine' extends to the 1967 Territories, explicitly rely-ing 'on the views of the international community as expressed primarily by the UN General Assembly.'[29]

Apart from its unauthoritative nature, the grave inconsistency of the UNGA's position vis-à-vis the 1967 Territories demonstrates its inadequacy to serve as a source of authority. This is vividly illustrated by two UNGA declarations, the first defined 'all non-Israeli Palestinians as legal refugees' whereas the second (taken from UNGA Resolution 2535 of 1969) is described by the OTP as shifting the former characterisation by 'recognising Palestinians for the first time as a people with a national identity and collective rights'. Indeed, the UNGA's position is not only a purely political stance, devoid of legal authority, but it also lacks the consistency the OTP attributes to it. It is quite obvious that the theory of a clearly defined Palestinian People with an inalienable right to self-determination within a delimited territory is a belated invention that was only brought forth well after 1967 and has powerfully advanced since. This analysis is supported by the blunt fact that between the 1949 armistice and the end of the 1967 Six Day War no demand was directed at Jordan and Egypt by the UNGA, to withdraw their armed forces from the West Bank and Gaza and desist from impeding the realisation of the inalienable right of the Palestinian people to self-determination, though the Jordanian and Egyptian occupation of these territories was indisputably a foreign occupation and the result of unlawful aggression. It was only the post-1967 reality that drove the UNGA to shift its characterisation of the situation and recognise for the first time the Palestinians as a People with national identity and collective rights. All this does not mean that the Palestinian claim for peoplehood is false or artificial or without merit. It does mean, however, that the theory about a consistent, almost 'natural' linkage between the Arab-Palestinian People and the 1967 Territories to which the OTP constantly alludes as 'Occupied Palestinian Territories' is totally unfounded from a legal point of view. The Palestinian claim to the 1967 Territories is a political, not a legal, claim, and as such it must be decided in the way political claims are being decided in our world, i.e. in peaceful negotiations or on the battlefield. It cannot be adjudicated by a court of law.

The dubious linkage between self-determination and the 'OPT'

Bensouda strongly believes in the existence of a linkage between the Palestinians' right to self-determination and their right to the 1967 Territories.[30] This notion comprises two distinct yet intertwined errors – a legal misconception of the nature of the right to national self-determination and a factual misrepresentation of the roots of the Palestinian-Israeli conflict:

- The legal scholarship on national self-determination distinguishes between a principled right to self-determination and its modes of implementation, most of all the territory on which the right may be exercised. More specifically, while the Palestinians may well have a strong claim to self-determination, its precise contents and modes of application remain to be decided. In that respect, their status is similar to many stateless peoples', for example the Catalonians. Contrary to Bensouda's erroneous presumption, a right to a specific piece of territory cannot be derived from the right to self-determination. If the law would be different, then the Catalonians could sue Spain for impeding the fulfilment of their right to self-determination on the Spanish territory densely populated with Spanish nationals of Catalonian descent.

The 1967 Territories, to which Bensouda persistently refers to as 'the Occupied Palestinian Territories' or OPT, are in fact unregulated territories to which there are conflicting claims, the Israeli case being no weaker than the Palestinian. One may – if unencumbered by the burden of objectivity which senior international legal functionaries are supposed to carry – side with Israel or with the Palestinians in this controversy as a matter of political preference. However, presenting this political question as a legally established right, is misconceived.

Accordingly, even if one were to grant Bensouda's presumption that 'Palestine' should be regarded a state, her conclusion of an automatic link between this quasi-state and a delimited territory (the so-called OPT) is not borne by its premise. If 'Palestine' is to be exempted from the territorial element of statehood, then the outcome must be that, at best, it could be recognised as a state with no territory. If this seems absurd, the blame for the absurdity lies with Bensouda's insistence of treating a non-state as a state, the facts of the ground notwithstanding. The alternative, to be sure, is much more absurd, as it involves pretending that the statehood-aspiring entity that doesn't control any territory (and for this reason gets an exemption from the territorial criterion) would be artificially viewed as controlling the territory it does not in fact control. When one calls for a 'case-specific' application of the law, one must be ready to face the 'case-specific' consequences that necessarily flow from this move.

- The second error in this regard relates to the gross misrepresentation of the relevant historic facts. At the beginning of the sub-section entitled 'Brief overview of contextual and historical background,'[31] Bensouda refers to Britain's commitment to the establishment of a 'national home for the Jewish people' in Palestine (the Balfour Declaration) then argues that concurrently Britain 'had also provided assurances of Arab independence in the region'. This statement, especially the use of the vague term 'the region', creates the erroneous impression that Britain gave contradictory assurances to both parties – Jews and Arabs – with regard to the same territory. This is far from being the case. It is common knowledge that Britain's pledge of a national home for the Jews in Palestine was **not** accompanied by a similar pledge to local Arabs who were only assured that their 'civil and religious right' would not be 'prejudiced' by the establishment of the Jewish national home.[32] Nor was there a contradiction between the promises made by the British (or rather the High Commissioner for Egypt, Sir Henry McMahon) to Sharif Hussein of Mecca, perpetrator of the so-called 'Great Arab Revolt', and the British government's pledge to the Zionist movement (i.e. the Balfour Declaration) as Palestine was specifically excluded by McMahon from the territory of the prospective Arab state.[33]

But whatever the supposed contradictions in Britain's WWI promises to Arab and Jews, they were wholly irrelevant for the simple fact that the Balfour Declaration was incorporated into the League of Nations' July 1922 Palestine Mandate. In other words, it was not Britain but the post-WWI world organisation and the United Nation's predecessor – in its capacity as the official representative of the will of the international community – which acknowledged 'the historical connection of the Jewish people with Palestine' as 'the grounds for reconstituting their national home in the country' and tasked Britain with implementing this goal.[34]

Bensouda's total obliviousness to the League's crucial role in Palestine's modern history at a time when she lays such a heavy emphasis (however misconceived) on the supposed importance of its UN successor to the country's future amounts at best to fundamental ignorance of the most rudimentary essentials of the Palestinian-Israeli conflict, at worst – to a deliberate attempt at historical and legal misrepresentation.

Having demonstrated how the UNGA's position in regard to the 1967 Territories has shifted after the 1967 war and how this shift has passed unnoticed by the OTP, this article will turn to yet another, perhaps even more important, blind spot of the OTP, namely the Palestinian opportunistic, instrumental position in regard to the 1967 Territories.

Bensouda subscribes to the notion that for the Palestinian, the 1967 Territories have always been 'the territory where the Palestinian people are entitled to exercise their right to self-determination and to an independent and sovereign State'.[35] However, Like the UNGA, the Palestinians themselves demonstrate a remarkable inconsistency on this issue, which seems fatal to their current pleading. As Bensouda notes, in 1988 the Palestinian National Council (PNC, the PLO's 'parliament') proclaimed 'the establishment of the State of Palestine in the land of Palestine with its capital at Jerusalem'.[36] This proclamation, its legal invalidity notwithstanding, does not refer to the 1967 Territories (including East Jerusalem) but rather to the entire territory of Mandatory Palestine and to the entire city of Jerusalem, thus implying the destruction of the State of Israel. As such, this proclamation serves as clear evidence for the non-existence of a linkage between the Palestinians and the 1967 Territories. The Palestinians themselves, as late as 1988 and later, were not of the opinion that such a legal linkage existed.

They are allowed, of course, to alter and calibrate their political expectations at will, however this alteration must bear upon the evaluation of their legal case.

Perhaps the OTP's disregard for the bad-faith shift in the Palestinian position in regard to the 1967 Territories should be explained differently. Surprisingly, the pro-Palestinian Submission reflects a strange tendency to deny the Palestinians the right to shape their own destiny and to substantiate their right to self-determination. This phenomenon is evidenced where international legal instruments which were signed by the Palestinians' representatives stand in the way of the OTP's theories. When this happens the OTP ventures to take the highly unusual stance that as a matter of principle, these Palestinian representatives are devoid of legal competence to negotiate on behalf of their people and commit to terms which in her view constitute a derogation from the Palestinian People's right to self-determination. This questionable attitude is demonstrated in the OTP's discussion of the Oslo Accords and the possible difficulty they pose for the theory on the Palestinians' competence to delegate jurisdiction to the ICC. The OTP holds that: 'To the extent that certain provisions of the Oslo Accords could be considered to violate the right of the Palestinian people to self-determination, these could not be determinative for the Court'.[37]

In other words, the ICC is invited to disregard and allow no weight to legally binding contracts that the Palestinians saw fit to enter into – in the name of respecting the Palestinians right to self-determination. Not only that, but the OTP further maintains that the Palestinians must be deemed wholly incompetent to enter into legally binding agreements due to their current status as 'protected persons under occupation [who] are not in a sufficiently independent and objective state of mind to fully appreciate the implication of their rights under the [Fourth Geneva] Convention'.[38]

Put in simple terms, what this extraordinary statement means is that the Palestinians should be regarded incompetent to evaluate correctly their position and to shape their future and that others (e.g., the OTP) know better which is the best way to substantiate their right to self-determination. Presumably, this also explains why we are expected to brush-off the recent statement of the Palestinian Authority prime minister, who declared in very clear terms that 'Palestine will declare its statehood over all of the West Bank and Gaza, with Jerusalem as its capital, and push for global recognition if Israel goes ahead with plans to annex land it occupies'.[39]

This attitude of the OTP is implausible and it detracts from, rather than advances, the right to self-determination in that it denies stateless peoples of the competence to negotiate and reach agreements with rival states on independence, autonomy or any other substantiation of their right to self-determination. According to Bensouda's theory, nothing short of what foreign observers deem a just fulfilment of a people's right to self-determination would suffice, and any other agreement would be considered void. Perhaps de-colonisation theories should be invited to the discussion after all.

Conclusion

The fundamental construct of statehood law involves a non-state entity securing its political independence by acquiring – violently or peacefully – exclusive effective domination over a piece of territory inhabited by its people. Only after it has attained sufficient measure of stable, uninterrupted domination would the newly formed state appeal to other subjects of international law, other states and international organisations and institutions, to recognise it as a full-fledged state. Ordinarily, an examination would then ensue aimed at evaluating the newly formed state's compliance with common legal criteria of statehood. Under this traditional construct – the legal follows the factual and the political.

The Submission aims at nothing less than turning this universally-accepted construct on its head and substituting it with a new paradigm that would amount to an all-embracing radical revision of statehood law, indeed to a genuine upheaval of the existing legal world order. This ambitious project may be roughly sketched thus: first, a judgement may be rendered that a non-state entity should – as a matter of justice, the factual situation on the ground notwithstanding – be recognised as a state. Then, this pseudo-state would be acknowledged as eligible to practice control over a delimited piece of territory on which it does not actually have any measure of control. Then, the state that actually exercises effective control over this territory would be accused of interfering with and breaching the legal rights of the non-existent state, thus coerced by a legal tribunal into making political concessions in favour of the non-state. In this brave new world turned upside down the factual and the political follow the legal, and judges would shape the destinies of peoples rather than the peoples themselves.

This revolutionary paradigm further imperils the important principle of state responsibility to territories under its effective control. Modern international law is hostile to the idea of 'vacuum of sovereignty', a territory to which no government is responsible and accountable. This rationale is the driving force behind, for example, the Fourth Geneva Convention. Naturally, responsibility must be accompanied with recognition of authority and jurisdiction: we cannot seriously expect a state to enforce law and order and secure basic human rights on a territory and at the same time deny recognition of the state's exclusive authority and jurisdiction over the territory. The Submission's underlying legal construct advances the idea that a non-state entity should be fictively taken not only as eligible to but as actually exercising legal authority over a piece of territory which it admittedly does not in fact control. Consequently, the state that does control the territory must be viewed as devoid of legal authority but at the same time is not allowed to disencumber itself from the legal responsibility attached to the territory.

It seems inconceivable that peoples who cannot back up their claims for political independence with a proven ability to exercise effective control over a territory would artificially be granted a court-initiated licence to this territory, upon abstract arguments of entitlement. It is hard to imagine a situation in which an international tribunal would order Spain to grant independence to the Catalonians on a piece of Spanish territory. Somehow, in the case of Israel, some people show a greater tendency towards imaginative thinking on international law.

Notes

1. Article 1 of the Rome Statute.
2. Article 12(1) of the Rome Statute. A non-member State may also accept the ICC's jurisdiction ad-hoc with respect to a specific crime (Article 12(3) of the Rome Statute).
3. Article 12(2) of the Rome Statute.
4. The original submission was made by the OTP on 20 December 2019, entitled 'Prosecution request pursuant to article 19(3) for a ruling on the Court's territorial jurisdiction in Palestine', marked ICC-01/18-9. Following the ICC's decision of 21 January 2020 in which the Court reproached the OTP for exceeding the set page-limit for such a request (albeit granting her request for an extension) the OTP has re-filed her Submission on 22 January 2020, which resembles in all essential aspects the original submission. Therefore, in order to allow for a complete analysis of the OTP's argumentation which is in the centre of the present study's interest, I shall refer hereafter to the original 20 December 2019 submission.
5. The Palestinian reference was made on 22 May 2018, pursuant to articles 13(a) and 14 of the Rome Statute, in regard to 'the situation in Palestine since 13 June 2014'.
6. Shaw, *International Law*, 57.
7. For practical reasons, the discussion in this article focuses on the West Bank and East Jerusalem as Gaza has been separate from both Israel and the West Bank and ruled by Hamas since 2007.
8. Dinstein, *War, Aggression*, 39–40.
9. OTP, 75.
10. Ibid., 79.
11. Ibid., 75.
12. Ibid., 7.
13. Ibid., 24.
14. Ibid., 25.
15. Article 2(4) of the Charter of the United Nations strictly prohibits the threat or use of armed force between UN Member States. The general prohibition on aggressive use of force is considered as customary rule of international law,

bearing universal applicability. See, for example, the decision of the International Court of Justice in ICJ, *Nicaragua Case*, 100.

16. OTP, 75.
17. This 'independence' test is considered by mainstream scholarship as the best indicator for deciding on statehood. Crawford, *Creation of States*, 62.
18. OTP, 7.
19. Crawford, *Creation of States*, 435, 438–40.
20. Ibid., 435.
21. The difference between the two theories may be summarised thus: whereas according to the constitutive theory recognition by other states is constitutive of statehood, the declaratory theory favours the combined factual-legal independence test and allows recognition a much more modest role mostly as an evidentiary instrument.
22. OTP, 76.
23. Ibid., 77, FN 468.
24. Ibid.
25. The Palestinians have not purported to argue to the applicability of decolonisation law, either in their pleadings in the case of the security barrier before the International Court of Justice or in the present proceedings. It is also interesting to note that as early as 1948, when the Arab states were called upon to justify their invasion of Israel, they argued that the state was in a legal status of *terra nullius* open for foreign invasion and occupation. Crawford, *Creation of States*, 432–3.
26. OTP, 55.
27. The Fourth Geneva Convention's main rationale is to afford maximal protection for civilians under military rule of a state that is not their state of nationality. This important IHL instrument was never intended to resolve or affect disputes on the permanent status or title on territories. Israel has traditionally maintained that from a legal point of view, as far as IHL is considered, the 1967 Territories do not constitute 'occupied territory' *stricto sensu* since it was never forcibly taken from a state that held legal sovereign title to them but rather liberated from a foreign invader.
28. Geneva Convention, Article 49. It should be noted, however, that both the rationale underlying the Geneva rule of non-transfer and its language support the interpretation that it was meant to apply to situations of forced transfer of civilians that are far removed from the situation of the Israeli neighbourhoods in the post-1967 territories, which are populated willingly by Jews returning to historic parts of their ancestral homeland.
29. OTP, 7.
30. For example, OTP, 9.
31. OTP, 22.
32. For the Balfour Declaration see Laqueur, *The Arab-Israeli Reader*, 36.
33. Karsh and Karsh, *Empires of the Sand*, 236–43; and Schneer, *Balfour Declaration*, 64–5.
34. Avalon Project, 'The Palestine Mandate,' Preamble.
35. OTP, 74.
36. Ibid., 31.
37. Ibid., 101.
38. Ibid.

39. https://www.theguardian.com/world/2020/jun/09/palestine-says-it-will-declare-statehood-if-israel-annexes-west-bank. This statement demonstrates, of course, that in his view Palestinian statehood is currently an envisaged rather than an existing state of affairs.

Disclosure statement

No potential conflict of interest was reported by the author(s).

Bibliography

Avalon Project. "The Palestine Mandate." 24 July 1922. https://avalon.law.yale.edu/20th_century/palmanda.asp.
Crawford, J. *The Creation of States in International Law.* Oxford: Oxford UP, 2006.
Derri, A. "Until They Say 'I Shall'? Hamas-Gaza and the Putative Right for non-Self Determination." *The Journal for Interdisciplinary Middle Eastern Studies* 6, no. 1 (2020): 35–59 [In Hebrew].
Dinstein, Y. *War, Aggression and Self Defence.* Cambridge: Cambridge UP, 2011.
Geneva Convention Relative to the Protection of Civilian Persons in Times of War, 12 August 1949.
The Guardian. English newspaper, London.
International Court of Justice. *Case Considering Military and Paramilitary Activities in and against Nicaragua [Nicaragua v. United States of America],* Judgment of 27 June 1986.
International Criminal Court, Office of the Prosecutor. *Prosecution request pursuant to article 19 (3)for a ruling on the Court's territorial jurisdiction in Palestine,* ICC-01/18-9, 20 December 2019.
Karsh, E., and I. Karsh. *Empires of the Sand: The Struggle for Mastery in the Middle East, 1789–1923.* Cambridge, MA: Harvard University Press, 1999.
Laqueur, W. *The Arab-Israeli Reader.* Penguin: Harmondsworth, 1970.
The Rome Statute of the International Criminal Court, 17 July 1998.
Schneer, J. *The Balfour Declaration: The Origins of the Arab-Israeli Conflict.* New-York: Random House, 2010.
Shaw, M. N. *International Law.* Cambridge: Cambridge UP, 1997.

The Negev Bedouin as a de-legitimization tool

Havatzelet Yahel

ABSTRACT
This article explores the evolution of Bedouin international advocacy and discourse within UN human rights bodies, starting with the first in 1998 to present. It demonstrates that during the last two decades, Bedouin international advocacy in UN bodies was carried out by various NGOs with differing agendas. The discourse on Bedouin issues was co-opted by national and foreign NGOs, some of which possessed clear anti-Israeli views. Parallel to the increasing volume of Bedouin international involvement, their issues became an asset in the overall efforts to de-legitimise Israel. The Bedouin's harsh living conditions and ongoing land conflict with the state assisted in portraying Israel as an apartheid state.

On 19 December 2019, the Israel-based Legal Centre for Arab Minority Rights in Israel, or Adalah (Justice in Arabic) as commonly known, proudly announced that it helped achieve 'historical dimensions' in which '[f]or the first time, Israel is defined by a United Nations expert committee as a regime that exercises apartheid practices against Palestinians on both sides of the Green Line.'[1] Adalah referred to the latest Concluding Observations (CO) given by the Human Rights Committee on the Elimination of Racial Discrimination (CERD), a treaty-based committee that began overseeing Israel since it signed the treaty in 1979. In the same announcement, Adalah stressed its successful joint effort with the Negev Coexistence Forum (NCF) that made the CERD request Israel submit a special report 'on its forced displacement and eviction of Palestinian Bedouin citizens of Israel living in the Naqab [Negev], the demolition of their homes, and other violations of their land and property rights.'[2]

Adalah's announcement is the beginning and the end of a journey to explore the connection between the Negev Bedouin and the international de-legitimisation process. In what follows, it will be argued that over the past two decades, the Negev Bedouin hardships have occupied a central place in international human rights arenas. Within that process, a more radical and anti-Israel agenda was added to the Bedouin discourse. Gradually, the Negev Bedouin became an asset in the ongoing efforts to de-legitimise and demonise Israel and present it as an apartheid entity.

Much has been written on the complex relations between the Negev Bedouin and the State of Israel. Most studies criticise various aspects of Israel's policy, presenting disputes over land, settlements, and house demolitions, as well as inadequate personal safety and problematic accessibility to welfare, education, environment, and health. There are also studies on Bedouin representation.[3] This article sheds light on the less-explored aspect of the internationalisation of Bedouin human rights advocacy and the association it developed to Israel de-legitimisation.[4]

There is no clear definition of the term 'de-legitimisation.' It is difficult to delimit and distinguish de-legitimisation from legitimate criticism. As the Jewish American diplomat Dennis Ross explained, '[m]ost of the attacks on Israel's legitimacy are carried out from a legitimate or ostensibly legitimate space ... but in a manner that crosses an abstruse line into de-legitimisation ... with an emphasis on the demonisation of Israel.'[5]

Generally, Israel's de-legitimisation can be described as a propagated campaign that includes activities designed to negate the legitimacy of Israel's establishment and existence by presenting it as a colonialist project originating in historical sin and wrongdoing towards the local indigenous population. It is a global campaign that consists of separate moves aimed at staining Israel's positive name and its foreign relations, including its unique connection with Diaspora Jews.[6] The various activities are presented as a liberal campaign for the protection of human rights against a brutal and immoral settler state. In order to obtain a moral façade, an emphasis is placed on associating the campaign with human rights organisations, particularly the UN.[7] Special significance is also given to the legal arena and the use of the justice systems.[8] Thus, the campaign intends is to portray Israel as a systematic violator of international law.[9]

The preliminary assumption is that efforts to change Israeli policies regarding the Bedouin are legitimate, welcome, may bring about better solutions and contribute to the public welfare. It also assumes that the initial motivation of the call for such changes, in both Israel and the international arena, did not necessarily include a broader agenda of Israel de-legitimisation. However, whenexamining Adalah's charges of Israeli apartheid, and others that will be discussed below, it appears that over time the initial good intentions gave way to the de-legitimisation agenda.

The article is based on a large body of primary archival materials, including hundreds of international records from UN human rights archives, NGOs, government documents, reports and pamphlets, as well as a collection of numerous papers written by individuals and organisations on Bedouin rights and several interviews.

The documents were mapped and analysed mainly in chronological order focusing on the bodies that submitted reports and the changes in terminology, especially terms connected to Bedouin identity (e.g. Palestinian, Arab, indigenous, and the English name of the region 'Negev' or 'Naqab'). Studies have shown that the renaming of places is often connected to geopolitical disputes, with examples given from regional, national and international arenas.[10] In Israel, the topic of renaming places has been explored extensively revealing the centrality of the phenomenon within the Arab-Jewish national dispute.[11] Themain results of the analysis are presented consecutively in several periods. In each period, indications are given to themost important documents that contribute to understanding the process. Analysis of the data and broader perspectives are included in the discussion section.

The purpose of the article is to highlight a phenomenon, explore the development of the discourse, and indicate changes and trends rather than investigate the Negev Bedouin situation or factual and legal errors in NGO reports. Other studies can shed further light on these issues.[12]

The Negev Bedouin

The Negev Bedouin are a population of approximately 270,000 Israeli Muslim citizens.[13] They are decedents of former nomadic tribes that took over the region from other tribes mainly in the late 18th and 19th century. Like many other countries with former nomadic populations, Israel promoted plans for their settlement.[14] Over the past 50 years, the majority of the Negev Bedouin have become primarily urbanised, with 70% living in 18 settlements and the rest residing in more than 1,000 scattered clusters, known as 'unrecognised villages'. The residents of these clusters suffer from harsh living conditions but prefer to remain in place while rejecting the state's offer of free land plots elsewhere. The process of settling former nomads who follow customary strict traditions and do not always comply with state laws is a great challenge, experienced by many modern states.[15] The main disputes with the Israeli Bedouin are linked to their former nomadic traditions. For example, they have different concepts of land ownership and a different view on settlement. Moreover, the state is obliged to provide the Bedouin similar conditions as the rest of its citizens, but de-facto there are still gaps that need to be filled, mainly in issues of health, welfare, education, and personal safety. State obligations are continuously monitored by Israeli courts, which intervene when needed.

Since the establishment of Israel, numerous plans have been promoted to address the Bedouin's needs.[16] In 2003, the government, headed by Ariel Sharon, promoted a comprehensive action plan (Sharon Plan). The goals of the plan included expanding and developing new Bedouin localities, thus terminating the land dispute via a mechanism of compromises or court litigations. In 2007, the Commission to Suggest Policy to the Settlement of Bedouin in the Negev, headed by former Supreme Court Justice Eliezer Goldberg, was appointed; it included two Bedouin representatives. The committee conducted an extensive public hearing and drew up a report that was adopted by the government.[17]

Among the Goldberg Committee's recommendations was the promotion of legislation for the settlement of the Bedouin. The framing of the legislation was put in the hands of a team headed by Udi Prawer from the PM office. The team's report that was submitted in 2011 provided a much higher compensation for Bedouin land claimants and a gradual process of recognition of new localities, yet it generated massive opposition.[18] One of the central arguments was that the Bedouin were not heard by the team. Therefore, the government decided to conduct public consultations and appointed Minister Binyamin Ze'ev Begin to the task.[19] The outcome was articulated in Begin's report and a Bill draft, known as the 'Begin-Prawer Bill,' which contained favourable terms for the Bedouin.[20] Still, the Bill was denounced by Bedouin activists who complained that it did not accept all their claims, while right-wing critics argued that it was too generous. Protests and demonstrations spread in the Negev and the governmentchose to shelve the Bill. Parallel to the Bill, the government promoted development plans, which invested unprecedented sums on employment, economic growth, education, health and social welfare for the Bedouin.[21] Overall, these plans are comparatively the largest and most comprehensive plans promoted in Israel in the past years for any community. However, the actual implementation of the plans is highly dependent on the leadership and cooperation of the Bedouin community. It is common that local and tribal disputes prevent development plans from being materialised.

Bedouin activities in UN human rights forums

International law was developed in Europe as of the seventeenth century to regulate relations among sovereign entities without addressing domestic issues.[22] The 1945 United Nations Charter followed the same path.[23] It was only in 1948, upon the Universal Declaration of Human Rights, that this situation changed and individual Human Rights (HR) came under international protection.[24] Over the years, international protection of HR has evolved through a collection of conventions subject to UN oversight. Israel is currently a member of seven major conventions and two human rights protocols.[25] As such, Negev Bedouin issues were mostly discussed within three international conventions: the Convention on the Elimination of All Forms of Racial Discrimination, monitored by the CERD; the Convention on

Economic, Social and Cultural Rights, monitored by the Committee of Economic, Social and Cultural Rights (CESCR) and the International Convention on Civil and Political Rights monitored by the Human Rights Committee (CCPR-HRC).[26] Though these conventions 'lack almost entirely a formal domestic legal status,'[27] they have an impact on the international public opinion towards Israel.[28] Generally, the UN conventions include a mechanism of periodic supervision over state compliance by a committee of appointed human rights experts. The standard modus operandi of these three committees include (not necessarily in this order): state reports, information from civil society (mainly NGOs) in the form of shadow reports, a list of issues or the like, an oral session with discussion and the committee's Concluding Observations (CO). NGOs can gain status as a Special Consultative (SC) to the Economic and Social Council, which gives them extra standing regarding reports, participation and presentation of their issues.[29]

Aside from individual HR forums, since the 1970s, an additional international platform was developed to address indigenous groups' rights. This was formalised in 2007 as the UN Declaration on the Rights of Indigenous Peoples (DRIP).[30] Israel did not sign the DRIP nor take part in any indigenous forums. However, Bedouin representatives became involved in indigenous UN forums. The development of the indigenous concept was already explored elsewhere; hence it will only be briefly addressed by this article.[31]

In what follows, the more significant events in the development of the Bedouin discourse within CERD, CESCR, CCPR-HRC will be discussed in chronological order. The description will include basic information about the more prominent NGOs and indications to the changes in their focus and position, as indicated in their reports.

First period: 1998-2004

While Israel's active involvement in CERD dates back to 1980, only in 1998 did Bedouin issues become a part of the agenda, and that was in CESCR and CCPR-HRC. Israel was the first to bring the Bedouin issues as part of its initial reports.[32] According to the documentation, no NGO gave CESCR a report regarding the Bedouin. It did receive information from Adalah, but this was on Israel's supposed violation of the rights of the 'Arab citizens' and the 'Arab minority' with no mention of the Bedouin.[33] This can be explained by the initial aim of Adalah, registered just a year earlier in Haifa with the purpose of '[p]romoting the issue of the rights of the Arab minority in Israel through litigation before the various courts. Promoting the issue of Arab minority rights in Israel in the educational and public spheres.'[34] Based on Israel's report and CESCR's own enquiry,[35] the CO expressed 'its grave concern about the situation of the Bedouin Palestinians settled in Israel' and urges Israel 'to recognize the existing Arab Bedouin villages, the land rights of the inhabitants and their right to basic services, including water.'[36]

CCPR-HRC received information regarding the Bedouin from Israel's initial report,[37] and from a shadow report that was submitted by the Association for Civil Rights in Israel (ACRI) and B'Tselem – The Israel Information Centre for Human Rights in the Occupied Territories.[38] It was noted that B'Tselem was involved only in 'Occupied Territories' issues.

ACRI is a national NGO that was established in 1983 in Jerusalem to 'promote the protection of human and civil rights in Israel.' Its mission was expanded later to include all territories that are under Israel's control.[39] They claim to be Israel's oldest, largest human rights organisation and the only one dealing with the entire spectrum of rights and civil liberties.[40] The shadow report included several sections on the Bedouin while presenting a detailed argument on the Bedouin's lack of infrastructure and services, a discriminatory allocation of land, poor planning and other Israeli discriminatory policies that needed to be changed. Bedouin issues were discussed separately from those in the West Bank and the Gaza Strip (hereafter: 'Territories').

In its CO, CCPR adopted some of the arguments presented by ACRI:

> [T]he discrimination faced by Bedouins, many of whom have expressed a desire to continue to live in settlements in the Negev which are not recognized by the Israeli Government and which are not provided with basic infrastructure and essential services. The Committee recommends that members of Bedouin communities should be given equality of treatment with Jewish settlements in the same region ....[41]

As for CERD - although the CERD mechanism was the first to be implemented in 1980, Bedouin issues were discussed much later. Adalah did submit a report to CERD, but like in the report for CESCR, they did not discuss the Negev Bedouin issues.[42] In its CO, CERD did not mention the term Bedouin, but raised concerns 'upon what are known as "unrecognized" Arab villages.'[43]

The first application of a local Bedouin NGO to one of these human rights forums was in 2003. In CESCR, Maha Qupty, the head of the Regional Council for Unrecognised Villages in the Negev (RCUV) presented a report on behalf of RCUV and the Arab Association for Human Rights (AHR).[44] Their report stressed Israel's alleged plans of segregation and concentration of the 'Palestinian Bedouins' through laws while restricting their movement in the Negev. He argued that these policies are discriminatory and inhumane.[45] Throughout the report and presentation, they used the word 'Negev'.

RCUV was a grassroots initiative established by local Bedouin activists in 1997 with the declared aim to promote the state's recognition in 45 Bedouin residential villages that had no official recognition.[46] It was never formally incorporated under that name. It claimed to represent the entire Bedouin community in those places, but that claim has not been ascertained.

AHR is a national organisation, founded in 1988 in the northern city of Nazareth to promote minority rights. In its reports, the situation of the Negev Bedouin was explained with emphasis given on the claim that Israel was using segregation and concentration, executing transfer and denying services, as well as implementing criminalisation of the Palestinian Bedouin. They also claimed that Israeli actions were 'a declaration of war' against the Bedouin minority in the Negev.

In their CO, CESCR repeated the Bedouin arguments and stated that it 'continues to be concerned about the situation of Bedouins residing in Israel, and in particular those living in villages that are still unrecognized.' They also stated that 'Bedouins continue to be subjected on a regular basis to land confiscations, house demolitions, fines for building "illegally," destruction of agricultural crops, fields and trees, and systematic harassment and persecution by the Green Patrol, in order to force them to resettle in "townships."'[47]

In CCPR's 2003 parallel session, unlike CESCR, no NGO mentioned Bedouin issues. Adalah submitted a report that included an argument of 'gross violation' of human rights against 'Palestinian citizens of Israel.'[48] In their CO, CCPR mentioned the Bedouin only once, to appreciate 'the efforts to increase the level of education for the Arab, Druze and Bedouin communities in Israel.'[49]

Second period: 2005-2008

The next period in the development of Bedouin issues at the UN started in 2005 when the Negev Coexistence Forum (NCF) submitted to the UN Working Group on Indigenous Populations (UNWGIP) the indigeneity claim.[50] This was the first time such a claim was raised in an international forum. NCF claimed that the Bedouin are indigenous people, and similar to other indigenous people, they also suffer from dispossession and HR violations. It was also stressed that Negev Bedouin 'are ethnically distinct from the Jewish majority and socially distinct from the Palestinian Arab minority living in Israel.' The report called on UNWGIP to 'publicize the plight of the Negev Bedouins and increase international pressure [on Israel] as well.'[51] The indigenous discourse assisted in the demonisation of Israel because it negates the Jewish narrative of historical connection to the Land of Israel as their ancestral homeland – specifically recognised by the League of Nations Palestine Mandate of July 1922.[52] Instead, it regards Israel as a new colonial regime that resembles the dispossession acts of the European settler.

NCF is a local organisation that was founded in 1997 in the Negev locality of Omer. It was formally registered in 1999 with a stated mission of 'deepening the connection and understanding between Jews and Arabs in the Negev. Creating a framework for Jewish and Arab activities in the Negev to address problems that the residents of the area share. Education for tolerance and activities for equal rights between Jews and Arabs.'[53] Although its mission seems to be directed towards local Jews and Bedouins from the Negev region, much of its activities and publicity efforts have been directed towards national and international audiences.[54] Since its first interaction with the UN in 2005, the NCF is regularly sending reports and representatives to UNWGIP meetings and has become the leading Israeli NGO in the indigenous forums.[55]

In December 2005, Adalah included for the first time a discussion of Bedouin affairs in its report to CERD and in that year gained SC status.[56] This happened when the Sharon Plan was being implemented, and anger arose. The term indigenous was mentioned only once in their report and it was not in relation to the Bedouin but to stress Palestinian indigeneity vs the Jewish state.[57] The report referred to the Sharon Plan's implementation as the 'new generation' of policies that aim to 'dispossess and displace.'[58] The report mentioned several times the phrase: 'Palestinian Arab Bedouin in the Naqab.'[59] This marked the beginning of the English use of the Arabic word 'Naqab' instead of the Hebrew 'Negev'. Along with the change in the region's name, the term 'Palestinian' was added to the Bedouin.

A year later, in 2006, Adalah also included the Bedouin in its statement to CESCR. The document continued the same line of argumentation while using the term 'Naqab' and 'Palestinian Bedouin'.[60] In the final paragraph, Adalah called on CESCR to 'issue a resolution condemning Israel's discriminatory policies.'

The same year, ACRI submitted a shadow report to CERD in which it included a chapter on 'Racial Discrimination against the Arab Bedouin Residents of the Unrecognized Villages in the Negev in the Areas of Housing and Health Rights'.[61] ACRI adopted the indigenous terminology and were more critical than before. They referred to the Israeli 'transfer policy [which] is tainted by racial discrimination that has its roots in a government resolution of March 2003 [Sharon Plan].'

NCF in collaboration with RCUV and others also submitted CERD a report. From now on they use the terms 'Naqab', 'Negev-Naqab' or 'Naqab–Negev'.[62]

The efforts of the NGO's in CERD to promote Bedouin issues proved rewarding. CERD's CO that ended the session in 2007 were extensive while adopting the term 'Negev/Naqab':

> The Committee recommends that the State party enquire into possible alternatives to the relocation of inhabitants of unrecognized Bedouin villages in the Negev/Naqab to planned towns, in particular through the recognition of these

SOFT THREATS TO NATIONAL SECURITY

villages and the recognition of the rights of the Bedouins to own, develop, control and use their communal lands, territories and resources traditionally owned or otherwise inhabited or used by them. It recommends that the State party enhance its efforts to consult with the inhabitants of the villages and notes that it should in any case obtain the free and informed consent of affected communities prior to such relocation.[63]

Third period: 2009-2016

The subsequent period in the internationalisation of Bedouin issues started around 2009. The Goldberg Report had just been accepted by the government, and Israel's periodic report to CCPR-HRC elaborated on the new plans.[64] CCPR-HRC received reports from NCF, Adalah and two other non-Israeli NGOs that joined the Bedouin discourse for the first time; namely, the Centre on Housing Rights and Evictions (COHRE) – a Swiss-based NGO, and the Resource Centre for Palestinian Residency and Refugee Rights-called Badil. Badil was established in 1998, registered as an NGO in the Palestinian Authority and gained SC status in 2006. Through its network, Badil promotes 'a unified strategy and vision for Palestinian campaigning and advocacy, and tries to unify the discourse and analyses the root-causes of the ongoing displacement of Palestinians, and the mechanisms for challenging the Israeli regime of occupation, colonisation and apartheid.'[65] Badil openly supports the BDS Movement and claims that there is '[a]partheid across the Green Line and Boundaries.'[66]

NCF's shadow report was devoted to the Bedouin titled 'The Bedouin-Arabs in the Negev-Naqab Desert in Israel.'[67] It continued to promote the claim for Bedouin indigeneity. The two main issues were Bedouin land ownership rights and the lack of recognition of the unrecognised villages. In June 2010, NCF submitted a supplementary report that, among other things, protested against afforestation activities which were tagged as acts of dispossession.[68] A month later, Khalil Alamour, a board member of NCF, gave a statement at a CCPR-HRC session expressing a more radical view, claiming that Israel 'denied all public services' and implemented 'gross violation of our rights as indigenous people.'[69]

Adalah's contributions to CCPR-HRC included two papers that promoted the claim of HR violations of the 'Palestinian Bedouin population in the Naqab.' It argued that Israel is seeking to evacuate the Bedouin's unrecognised villages and to concentrate the Bedouin into 'over-crowded and impoverished townships, and to allocate the remaining land to Jewish citizens in order to ensure a Jewish demographic majority in the Naqab.'[70] Bear in mind that in both papers, the term indigenous was not used.[71]

The reports of COHRE and Badil made use of NCF's data. One of Badil's papers described Israeli actions as a sequence of waves that since 1948 were aiming for Palestinian's 'dispossession and displacement.' It also argued that 'the Bedouin communities face imminent threat of forcible displacement.' The term indigenous did appear in the report but in a way where they incorporated the Bedouin within the Palestinian indigeneity: 'Bedouin in Israel are part of the indigenous Palestinian people.'[72]

In its CO, CCPR-HRC adopted the narrative of the Bedouin's 'right to their ancestral land and their traditional livelihood based on agriculture.'[73] Their critics were moderate while raising concerns regarding Bedouin access to services and the eviction with inadequate consideration. The term Naqab was not used.

Multiple organisations included in their reports to CESCR a discussion on Bedouin issues. Namely: NCF, Adalah, ACRI and Habitat International Coalition (HIC) together with Land Research Centre (LRC) and RCUV. Habitat is an international global network that supports rights in relation to housing and land.[74] According to their website, LRC was founded in 1986 in Jerusalem as part of the Arab Studies Society and was registered in the Palestinian territories.[75] Its mission is '[p]rotection, consolidation, and development of Palestinians and their lands, habitats, life styles, and capacities in standing up against the Israeli plan of forcible displacement.'

Both NCF and Adalah continued separately in their previous narrative against the new plans.[76] The ACRI submitted two papers that incorporated Bedouin issues as part of their general arguments regarding Israel's violation of Arab rights.[77] The second paper, in October 2011, continued with the Bedouin indigeneity argument which they adopted before; still, the 'Negev' remained the name of the region.[78] This was the last time ACRI included reports that discussed Negev Bedouin issues.

Similar to CCPR-HRC, the CO of CESCR adopted the Bedouin argument that refers to 'the rights of the Arab Bedouin people to their traditional and ancestral lands.' However, CESCR's criticism was much more detailed than that of CCPR-HRC. Referring to the newly adopted plan by the Israeli government in 2011, it recommended that 'any eviction should be based on free, prior and informed consent and that those relocated are offered adequate levels of compensation ... '; it also called on the state to 'officially regulate the unrecognized villages, cease the demolition of buildings in those villages, and ensure the enjoyment of the right to adequate housing.'[79]

CERD had started its session with the Israeli 2010 report which included extensive data on the development plans regarding the Negev Bedouin. Reports were sent by the same four groups that contribute to CESCR and included similar narratives. The Mossawa Centre, a Haifa based NGO that was established in the year 2000 to promote the equal rights of Arab citizens in Israel also sent a report.[80] The report included a lengthy chapter that was titled: 'The Naqab as a Case Study in Extreme Racial Discrimination.'[81]

For the first time, CERD adopted in its CO the term indigenous and called the newly proposed bill a discriminatory one that 'would legalize the ongoing policy of home demolitions and forced displacement of the indigenous Bedouin communities.'[82]

This period ends with CCPR-HRC 2013 session. This session took place at the same timeas the Bedouin were protesting against the Begin-Prawer Bill. The committee received complaints on Bedouin issues from six NGOs.[83] As mentioned before, the most radical voice was that of Badil with the waves of expulsion narrative. In the first joint report of Adalah and NCF submitted to CCPR in 2014, there was an attempt to navigate between the narratives stating that:

> The indigenous Bedouin community is part of the Palestinian Arab minority in Israel, a national minority ... who remained on their lands after the establishment of the State of Israel in 1948. The Palestinian minority in Israel has been the target of the state's ongoing policy of displacement, dispossession and concentration; today, the Israeli government aims to legitimize this policy against the Bedouin in the Naqab through the discriminatory Prawer Plan.

For the first and only time, Amnesty International also contributed to the Bedouin discussion. Its papers had a specific aim at halting what is called 'arbitrary and discriminatory' legislation on the 'Palestinian Bedouin citizens of Israel in the Negev/Naqab.'[84]

Amnesty's involvement was notable since they were among the first acknowledged human rights bodies in the UN.[85] It was also the first and only time that Bimkom – Planners for Planning Rights, submitted a report on Bedouin to any UN forums.[86] Bimkom was formally established in Jerusalem in 1999 with an initial mission of '[p]resenting professional-ethical- social positions regarding projects and planning procedures initiated by the establishment. Development of a methodology for community civic engagement in planning.'[87] Their report dealt with planning solutions and joined the call to halt the Begin-Prawer Bill. They also called for recognition of the 'Bedouin's historical connection to their land.' Unlike most of the other NGO reports in the session, they used the term 'Negev' and did not refer to the Bedouin as 'Palestinian' or 'indigenous.'

The CCPR-HRC adopted in their CO a highly critical narrative against Israel. It called for halting the Begin-Prawer legislation and stated many HR violations and incompliances. Furthermore, CCPR-HRC did not only raise 'concerns' as usualin the CO but gave direct orders. Israel was ordered to '[d]esist from any actions that may facilitate or result in forced displacement and dispossession of Bedouins residing in the Negev ... and withdraw the discriminatory Bill for the Regulation of the Bedouin Settlement in the Negev (the Prawer-Begin Bill)'.[88] It did not use the term indigenous but mixed and integrated Bedouin issues with Palestinians in the territories.

In 2015 it was already clear that the government was no longer promoting any legislation similar to the Begin-Prawer Bill.

Fourth period: 2017-2020

In 2017, the submission for the recent sessions in CERD started with an Israeli report that contained updated information on the Bedouin. The number of NGOs that were involved in Bedouin discussions was the highest.

NCF and Adalah continued their collaboration and submitted joint reports to all three committees. Their reports put great emphasis on claims of Israeli transfer and displacement of the Bedouin, but they also added arguments in regards to racist incitements against the Bedouin. In an additional report, they criticised the decision of the Planning Committee to approve the establishment of sites for temporary residency. They titled the action as one to '[f]acilitate Permanent Expulsion' for 'forced transfer and dispossession of their ancestral lands.'[89]

Bedouin issues were also discussed in a joint report of Badil NGO's that have pronounced an anti-Israeli agenda, Al-Haq – Law in the Service of Man, Addameer Prisoner Support and Human Rights Association, Civic Coalition for Palestinian Rights in Jerusalem, Habitat International Coalition – Housing and Land Rights Network (Cairo) and Cairo Institute for Human Rights Studies. The report reached a new level of accusations against Israel. The historical narrative of 'forced internal displacement' mentioned in Badil's 2009 report, transitioned into being an 'ethnic cleansing of the Naqab region.'[90] They rejected Israeli 'constructed fragments' of the Palestinian people. The report called for 'cumulative recognition of Israeli apartheid' while eliminating the differences between the Palestinians in the territories and Israeli citizens.

CERD was highly critical against Israel. From their CO it can be understood that they embraced, to some extent, the position that looks at the Palestinian on both sides of the Green Line, as people who suffer from Israeli apartheid.[91] As presented in the opening to the current study – Adalah was highly pleased with that perspective.

Actions among foreign states and the EU

The following part will discuss several actions aimed at reaching foreign states, including ambassadors, to convince them of Israel's supposed violations of human rights. Similar to the tours conducted by human rights organisations in Hebron seeking to reveal Israel's alleged violations , parallel tours are held for foreign ambassadors and others in the Negev. For instance, NCF holds 'Alternative Naqab Tours to Embassies'.[92]

In its website, NCF states that during the tours '[w]e will learn about the violation of the Bedouin's human rights.'[93] Adalah also offers similar tours. It was published that in 2011 it had conducted 34 tours together with RCUV and other Arab NGOs.[94] In 2012, at Adalah's invitation, 'more than 10 deputy heads of mission and political counselors from European and Latin American embassies in Israel visited.'[95] According to Adalah, in the tours '[t]he speakers also emphasized the role of the Jewish National Fund in Arab land confiscation.'[96]

In 2017 the NCF submitted a report to the US State Department referring to the violation of human rights by Israel.[97] According to the State Department's report, much of the data and findings were based on information received from NCF.[98]

The activities towards the EU were promoted by Adalah with collaboration from AHR through EuroMed Rights. EuroMed was founded in 1997 as a network of human rights organisations and activists from 30 different countries. They promote cooperation and dialogue around the Mediterranean Sea area[99] and support the BDS movement.[100] The Arab Association for Human Rights (HRA) was founded in 1988; it is an Israeli NGO with a goal tointernationally promote the protection of the Palestinian Arab minority rights in Israel.[101]

In 2011, EuroMed, Adalah and AHR published a joint publication on the 'Palestinian Arab Minority'; they called for the EU to make full use of their means to put pressure on Israel, including conditionality, declaratory diplomacy and more. They argued that the Israeli-Palestinian conflict was too 'narrowly defined'.[102] A photo of Bedouin children from the 'Naqab' was posted on the front cover to demonstrate the centrality of their issue. The report refers to 'the displacement and dispossession of lands from the Arab Bedouin in the unrecognized villages in the Naqab (Negev).'[103] In its publication, Adalah gave recognition to its achievement in hindering EU-Israel relations.[104]

Direct activities of de-legitimisation and boycott call

While the main focus of this article is activities at the UN, EU and foreign states, there are other frameworks in which Bedouin issues are framed and associated with Israel de-legitimisation. Although these frameworks deserve further exploration, three examples will be provided here. The first example is the publication of a book called *Ongoing Ethnic Cleansing – Judaising the Naqab*, which derides Israeli activities as acts of ethnic cleansing.[105] The book is part of a series that was promoted by the BDS Movement. It aimed to convince international bodies in general and Jewry in particular to distance themselves from Israel and the Jewish National Fund.[106]

Another example is Ahmad Amara's call for boycott in an article he published in *Jadal*, titled 'Towards a Complete Boycott by the Negev Arabs on the Judicial System.' Amara, a member of a Bedouin advocacy team, claimed that 'the boycott is now the better move and that efforts towards international advocacy and public recruitment can bring with them achievements that Israel's courts cannot offer.'[107] The last example is a short film produced by Physicians for Human Rights titled 'Fiddler with no Roof.' In the film, Theodore Bikel compares the expulsion of Jews in 19th century-Russia to Israeli activities vis-à-vis the Bedouin against the backdrop of music from Fiddler on the Roof.[108]

Discussion

This article revealed an expanding international interest in Israeli Bedouin affairs and an increasing amount of material submitted to human rights committees. The activities at the UN committees were accompanied by an effort to engage foreign states. Since 1998, when the issue was first introduced to UN bodies, the discussion surrounding Bedouin issues has become a permanent feature, at times even a key subject in UN human rights committees. It developed a focal point for criticism regarding Israel's human rights violations. The international coverage was incorporated by NGOs with the Palestinian nationalist agenda and BDS anti-Israeli NGOs.

The Bedouin issues were advanced in the international arena by multiple NGOs, each with its own agenda, as depicted from the reviewed reports.

ACRI was the first to incorporate Bedouin issues in their international advocacy. Its reports presented the 'Bedouin' issue in the 'Negev' as one of the many other issues that Israel needs to address. A more critical perspective was raised by RUCV, a grassroots NGO organisation that submitted a report in 2003. RUCV used the terms 'Palestinian Bedouin' and 'Negev' within the text. As previously mentioned, initially, the Bedouin topic was marginal, and 'Negev' was the name of the geographic region. In the second period, two NGOs joined the discussions concerning Bedouin with two different agendas. Namely, NCF with its joint Jewish-Arab agenda of 'Negev Bedouin' unique indigeneity, and Adalah as an Israeli-Palestinian NGO with 'Palestinian Bedouin' and the 'Naqab' agenda. Later, NCF joined RUCV to publish a combined report adopting the 'Naqab-Negev' and Bedouin 'indigeneity'. Nevertheless, they did not embrace the 'Palestinian-Bedouin' narrative.

During the third period, the Bedouin topic gained momentum on the international level. Additional NGOs sent reports, most of them foreign organisations. During this period, NCF accepted Adalah's lead and together

SOFT THREATS TO NATIONAL SECURITY

promoted the nationalist narrative of 'Palestinian-Bedouin' of the 'Naqab'. The Bedouin unique 'indigeneity' became part of Palestinian indigeneity. Amnesty, an international NGO, with its UN prestige, provided global exposure to the Bedouin case. Bimkom, like Amnesty, became involved with a specific aim, to halt the promotion of the Begin-Prawer Bill. When their mission succeeded, both organisations avoided any further international involvement in the Bedouin affairs. Other foreign organisations, such as Habitat, COHRE and the prominent Palestinian Badil, put forward their Palestinian agenda. The latter was associated with the BDS movement.

In the last period since 2017, the role of the Palestinian nationalist agenda was carried out by additional anti-Israeli NGOs that joined Badil with their accusations of 'ethnic cleansing.' Palestinian unity was also presented in the joint report by Adalah. While Adalah did not incorporate the 'ethnic cleansing' terminology, it nevertheless took pride in its achievements in CERD, where Israel's actions were condemned as resembling apartheid on both sides of the 1967 border. Bedouin issues proved a useful tool in promoting the goal of Israel's condemnation.

The shift towards anti-Israeli discourse within the Bedouin international advocacy and additional direct publications cannot be explained solely by the concern for a new government policy. No Israeli plans to worsen the Bedouin situation were introduced in the last years. On the contrary, there has been development towards recognition of more illegal Bedouin settlements and large investments in improving their living conditions. As indicated, Amnesty and Bimkom, both recruited to advocate on the Bedouin's behalf in 2013, did not find it necessary to submit any further reports.

To recap, the change in the international HR committees' discourse on the Bedouin issue and the NGOs' involvement are directly correlated to the agendas of those NGOs and not directly to that of the Bedouin. The situation of Negev Bedouin human rights, being Israeli citizens, is different from that of West Bank Palestinians, who are not Israeli citizens and mostly live under the Palestinian Authority's rule. However, due to the international exposure of Bedouin issues, their problematic living conditions and the ongoing land dispute with the state, they became an asset for an Israeli de-legitimisation campaign, especially its misrepresentation as applying apartheid on both sides of the Green Line.

Disregarding Israel's detailed reports, human rights committees toed the Palestinian line and wrongly unified Negev Bedouin and Palestinian issues, while ignoring the Israeli government's spirited efforts to improve the Bedouin's situation and living conditions. It is highly likely therefore that the Negev Bedouin issue will continue to be exploited in the anti-Israel agenda for quite some time.

Notes

1. "For first time, UN body criticizes Israel's policies of racial segregation against Palestinians in Israel and OPT – as a single entity," *Adalah*, December 19, 2019. https://www.adalah.org/en/content/view/9873 (accessed July 17, 2020).
2. Adalah statement was not accurate. CERD did not use the terms "apartheid", CERD, CO, January 27, 2020. CERD/C/ISR/CO/17-19.
3. Ratcliffe, "The Battle for Recognition', and 'Bedouin Rights," 97-124; and Payes, *Palestinian NGO's.*
4. The topic was dealt in *NGO Monitor report*, "NGOs and the Negev Bedouin Issue in the Context of Political Warfare", November 6, 2013. https://www. ngo-monitor.org/reports/ngos_and_the_negev_bedouin_issue_in_the_con text_of_political_warfare/. (accessed July 17, 2020).
5. Dennis Ross, "Antisemitism and Delegitimization," http://jppi.org.il/en/arti cle/de-legitimisation/toc/overview/#.X7zDoGgzY2w (accessed July 17, 2020).
6. Ibid.
7. Steinberg, "The Politics of NGOs," 24-54.
8. Sharvit-Baruch and Aviram, "Delegitimization of Israel," 456-57.
9. Steinberg, "From Durban to the Goldstone," 372-88; Gerstenfeld, "Delegitimization currents in Europe"; Groiss, "De-legitimisation"; and Nisan, "In defence of the idea of a Jewish state," 259-72.
10. Giraut and Houssay-Holzschuch, "Place Naming," 1-21.
11. Azaryahu, "Hebrew, Arabic, English," 461-79; Bigon and Dahamshy, "An Anatomy of Symbolic Power," 606-21; Benvenisti, *Sacred Landscape*; Ben-Israel and Meir, "Renaming space and reshaping identities," 65-92; and Cohen and Kliot, 'Place-Names," 653-80.
12. See: Yahel, "The Conflict over Land Ownership and Unauthorized Construction in the Negev," 352-69 and "Beyond the Letter of the Law," 84-127.
13. Elmasi and Waisblay, *Bedouin Population in the Negev.*
14. Salzman, *Pastoralism;* Kark and Frantzman, "Empire, State and the Bedouin," 487-510; Khazanov, *Nomads and the Outside World*; Galilee and Kark, "Bedouin Cemeteries in the Negev," 113-32.
15. Khazanov, *Nomads and the Outside World.*
16. Yahel and Kark, "Land and Settlement of Israel's Negev Bedouin," 1-26.
17. Goldberg et al., *Din VeHeshbon.*
18. Prawer et al., *Hamlatzot.*
19. Government Resolution 3707, September 11, 2011.
20. Begin, "Regularization."
21. Several plans are dedicated to the economic and social development of the Negev Bedouin: Government Resolution 3708, September 11, 2011; Government Resolution 2397, February 12, 2017.
22. Sabel and Adler, *International Law*; and Ben-Naftali and Shani, *International Law.*
23. Lerner, *Group Rights*; Ben Naftali and Shani, *International Law*, 195, 205.
24. UN General Assembly, *Universal Declaration of Human Rights*, December 10, 1948, 217 A (III) https://www.ohchr.org/EN/UDHR/Documents/UDHR_ Translations/eng.pdf (accessed July 17, 2020).

25. "Human rights in international law," *Ministry of Justice website*. https://www.justice.gov.il/Units/YeutzVehakika/InternationalLaw/UnitWork/HumanRightsInternationalLaw/Pages/default.aspx (accessed July 17, 2020).
26. UN General Assembly, ICCPR, December 16, 1966, United Nations, Treaty Series, vol. 999, p. 171. https://www.ohchr.org/en/professionalinterest/pages/ccpr.aspx (accessed July 17, 2020). Ratified by Israel in October 1991, and entered into force in Israel on 3 January 1992; UN General Assembly, ICESCR, December 16, 1966, United Nations, Treaty Series, vol. 993, p. 3. https://www.ohchr.org/EN/professionalinterest/pages/cescr.aspx (accessed July 17, 2020). Ratified by Israel in October 1991, and entered into force in Israel on January 3, 1992; UN General Assembly, CERD, December 21, 1965, United Nations, Treaty Series, vol. 660, p. 195. https://www.refworld.org/docid/3ae6b3940.html (accessed July 17, 2020). Ratified by Israel in January 1979, and entered into force in Israel on February 2, 1979. Bedouin issues were also discussed within Universal Periodic Review and the Special Rapporteurs, but to less extent.
27. Medina, "Domestic Human Rights," 331.
28. See: Karsh, *Israel in the International Arena*.
29. ECOSOC, "List of non-governmental organisations in consultative status with the Economic and Social Council as of 1 September 2018," October 31, 2018. E/2018/INF/5.
30. UN General Assembly, *United Nations Declaration on the Rights of Indigenous Peoples*, October 2, 2007, A/RES/61/295. https://www.refworld.org/docid/471355a82.html (accessed July 17, 2020).
31. For further discussion, see: Frantzman et al., "Contested Indigeneity"; Yahel, Kark and Frantzman, "Negev Bedouin and Indigenous People," 121-44; Barzilai, *Communities and Law*. For different perspective see: Kedar, Amara and Yiftachel, *Emptied Lands*.
32. Israel Initial Report to CCPR, June 2, 1998. CCPR/C/81/Add.13 https://tbinternet.ohchr.org/_layouts/15/treatybodyexternal/Download.aspx?symbolno=CCPR%2fC%2f81%2fAdd.13&Lang=en (accessed July 17, 2020); Israel Initial Report to CESCR, January 20, 1998. E/1990/5/Add.39 https://tbinternet.ohchr.org/_layouts/15/treatybodyexternal/Download.aspx?symbolno=E%2f1990%2f5%2fAdd.39&Lang=en (accessed July 17, 2020).
33. Adalah's Statement to CESCR, November 1998. https://www.adalah.org/uploads/oldfiles/eng/intladvocacy/uncescr98.htm (accessed July 17, 2020).
34. Non-Profit Registration Certificate, Ministry of Interior, December 25, 1997; Payes, *Palestinian NGOs*, 111.
35. CESCR, "Summary Records of the 33rd Meeting," November 20, 1998. E/C.12/1998/SR.33.
36. CESCR, CO, December 4, 1998. E/C.12/1/Add.27.
37. Israel "Initial Report", April 9, 1998. CCPR/C/81/Add.13. https://undocs.org/CCPR/C/81/Add.13.
38. ACRI and B'Tselem, July 1998. https://law.acri.org.il/pdf/ICCPR1998.pdf (accessed July 17, 2020).
39. Non-Profit Registration Certificate, Ministry of Interior, January 26, 1983.
40. "About ACRI," *Palestinian NGO's*. https://www.english.acri.org.il/about-us (accessed July 17, 2020); Payes, *Palestinian NGO's*, 181.
41. CCPR-HRC, CO, August 18, 1998. CCPR/C/79/Add.93.
42. Adalah's Statement to CERD, March 1998. https://www.adalah.org/uploads/oldfiles/eng/intladvocacy/cerd-major-finding-march98.pdf (accessed July 17, 2020).

43. CERD, CO, March 30, 1998. CERD/C/304/Add.45.
44. AAHR & RCUV, "The unrecognised Villages in the Negev Update: 2003," Submissions to the CESCR; "Between Segregated inclusion, Transfer and Concentration," May 5, 2003.
45. CESCR, https://www.un.org/unispal/document/auto-insert-212995/ (accessed July 17, 2020).
46. Greenspan, *Mediating Bedouin Futures*, 62; and Payes, *Palestinian NGO's*, 177.
47. CESCR, CO, June 26, 2003. E/C.12/1/Add.90.
48. Adalah's reports, July 22, 2003: "State of Emergency," https://www.adalah.org/uploads/oldfiles/eng/intladvocacy/unhrc_03_emergency.pdf (accessed July 17, 2020); "The Use of Palestinian Civilians as Human Shields by the Israeli Army," https://www.adalah.org/uploads/oldfiles/eng/intladvocacy/unhrc_03_hum_shields.pdf (accessed July 17, 2020); "Family Unification and Citizenship," https://www.adalah.org/uploads/oldfiles/eng/intladvocacy/unhrc_03_fam_uni.pdf (accessed July 17, 2020); and "discrimination in representation in Governmental bodies," https://www.adalah.org/uploads/oldfiles/eng/intladvocacy/unhrc_03_fair_rep_gov.pdf (accessed July 17, 2020).
49. ICCPR-HRC, CO, August 21, 2003. CCPR/CO/78/ISR.
50. Frantzman et al., "Contested Indigeneity."
51. Boteach, "The indigenous Bedouin."
52. Avalon Project, "The Palestine Mandate."
53. Non-Profit Registration Certificate, Ministry of Interior, February 21, 1999.
54. NCF, "Written Reports to the years 2008-2017," Ministry of Justice, https://www.guidestar.org.il/VF_View_File?guid=b931c4b3790f983-975c92f830704158-41a393682520d73d9944a790a2a540b8b26286fc c51447ae97bba65326128bb9-d57b18a8679031f5-72ead815734edf84e (accessed July 17, 2020).
55. NCF website: https://www.dukium.org/education-advocacy/ (accessed July 17, 2020).
56. ECOSOC, List of non-governmental Organisations.
57. Adalah, "NGO Report to CERD – Israel," December 15, 2005. https://www.adalah.org/uploads/oldfiles/eng/intl06/CERD151205.pdf (accessed July 17, 2020).
58. Ibid.
59. Ibid.
60. Adalah, "Economic, Social and Cultural Rights" to the UN Economic and Social Council – Commission on Human Rights, March 1, 2006. E/CN.4/2006/NGO/124.
61. ACRI, January 2006, https://law.acri.org.il/pdf/CERD0106.pdf (accessed July 17, 2020).
62. NCF, RCUV, Recognition Forum, Physicians for Human Rights, "The Arab-Bedouins of the Naqab-Negev Desert in Israel" Submitted to CERD', May 2006.
63. CERD, CO, June 14, 2007. CERD/C/ISR/CO/13.
64. Israel Periodic Report, November 21, 2008. CCPR/C/ISR/3.
65. Badil website:http://www.badil.org/en/campaigning-networking/networking/coalitions-and-networks.html (accessed July 17, 2020).
66. Mac Allister, "Applicability of the crime."

SOFT THREATS TO NATIONAL SECURITY 139

67. Haia Noach et al., NCF, "The Bedouin-Arabs in the Negev-Naqab Desert in Israel," Shadow Report, August 2009. In collaboration with: Association for Support and Defence of Bedouin Rights in Israel, Recognition Forum and Physicians for Human Rights. Link:https://tbinternet.ohchr.org/Treaties/CCPR/Shared%20Documents/ISR/INT_CCPR_NGO_ISR_99_9205_E.pdf (accessed July 17, 2020).

68. NCF, "Supplementary Report," June 12, 2010. https://tbinternet.ohchr.org/Treaties/CCPR/Shared%20Documents/ISR/INT_CCPR_NGO_ISR_99_9201_E.pdf (accessed July 17, 2020).

69. Khalil Alamour, "Statement to the 99th session of the Human Rights Committee, 12-14 July 2010, Geneva," https://www.dukium.org/wp-content/uploads/2011/06/Khalil-statement-CPPR-review-of-Israel-July-2010-v3.pdf (accessed July 17, 2020).

70. Adalah, "The Rights of Palestinian Arab Citizens of Israel," August 10, 2009. https://tbinternet.ohchr.org/_layouts/15/treatybodyexternal/Download.aspx?symbolno=INT%2fCCPR%2fNGO%2fISR%2f99%2f9208&Lang=en (accessed July 17, 2020).

71. Adalah, "NGO Report to UN HRC: Palestinian citizens of Israel," June 24, 2010. https://tbinternet.ohchr.org/_layouts/15/treatybodyexternal/Download.aspx?symbolno=INT%2fCCPR%2fNGO%2fISR%2f99%2f9210&Lang=en (accessed July 17, 2020).

72. Badil, "Relevant Information for the compilation of the List of Issues," September 30, 2009. https://tbinternet.ohchr.org/Treaties/CCPR/Shared%20Documents/ISR/INT_CCPR_NGO_ISR_99_9203_E.pdf (accessed July 17, 2020); additional reports: Badil, "Updated Relevant Information," June 25, 2010. https://tbinternet.ohchr.org/_layouts/15/treatybodyexternal/Download.aspx?symbolno=INT%2fCCPR%2fNGO%2fISR%2f99%2f9211&Lang=en (Accessed July 17, 2020); Adalah, "Follow-Up," https://tbinternet.ohchr.org/_layouts/15/treatybodyexternal/Download.aspx?symbolno=INT%2fCCPR%2fNGO%2fISR%2f99%2f9211&Lang=en (accessed July 17, 2020).

73. CCPR, CO, September 3, 2010. CCPR/C/ISR/CO/3.

74. HIC website: https://www.hic-gs.org/mission.php.

75. LRC website: https://www.lrcj.org/about-16.html.

76. Michal Rotem et al., "Response to the Report of the State of Israel- CESCR," October, 2010 http://www2.ohchr.org/english/bodies/cescr/docs/ngos/NCFCE_Israel.doc (accessed July 17, 2020); Adalah, Response to the List of Issues, October 18, 2011. https://tbinternet.ohchr.org/_layouts/15/treatybodyexternal/Download.aspx?symbolno=INT%2fCESCR%2fNGO%2fISR%2f47%2f9143&Lang=en (accessed July 17, 2020).

77. NGO Information submitted by the Association for Civil Rights in Israel (ACRI) to CESCR, October 2010. http://www2.ohchr.org/english/bodies/cescr/docs/ngos/ACRI_Israel45.doc (accessed July 17, 2020).

78. Libby Lenkinski et al., "NGO Information submitted by the Association for Civil Rights in Israel (ACRI) to the Committee on Economic, Social and Cultural Rights: For Consideration when assessing the compliance of the State of Israel under the International Covenant on Economic, Social and Cultural Rights," October 2011. https://law.acri.org.il//he/wp-content/uploads/2011/10/ICESCR2011.pdf (accessed July 17, 2020).

79. CESCR concluding remarks December 16, 2011. E/C.12/ISR/CO/3.

80. Non-Profit Registration Certificate, Ministry of Justice, May 18, 2000. https://www.guidestar.org.il/VF_View_File?guid=66467b5d7fc6ad0-861ec26d0b860053-3f7f1fc66fba8d659c46e422042dcde6578e695f45a5f048bc76e3850825eb52-38b1d6f0a856268f-1eaba4aad0b14b033 (accessed July 17, 2020).
81. Mossawa et al., "Shadow Report: United Nations Committee Against All Forms of Racial Discrimination," January 2012. https://tbinternet.ohchr.org/_layouts/15/treatybodyexternal/Download.aspx?symbolno=INT%2fCERD%2fNGO%2fISR%2f80%2f9177&Lang=en (accessed July 17, 2020).
82. CERD, CO, 9 March 2012. CERD/C/ISR/CO/14-16.
83. Adalah, NCF, Bimkom, Amnesty International, Badil, NGO Monitor.
84. Amnesty, "Israel," September 2014.
85. It gained CS status in 1964. Amnesty website: https://www.amnesty.org/en/who-we-are/ (accessed July 17, 2020).
86. Sharon Karni-Kohn et al, "Violations of Civil and Political Rights in the Realm of Planning and Building in Israel and the Occupied Territories," September 2014. http://bimkom.org/eng/wp-content/uploads/shadow-report.pdf (accessed July 17, 2020).
87. Non-Profit Registration Certificate, Ministry of Interior, May 11, 1999.
88. CCPR, CO, November 21, 2014. CCPR/C/ISR/CO/4.
89. NFC and Adalah, 'Violations of the ICERD against the Arab Bedouin citizens of Israel living in the Naqab/Negev desert', September 12, 2019. https://tbinternet.ohchr.org/_layouts/15/treatybodyexternal/Download.aspx?symbolno=INT%2fCERD%2fNGO%2fISR%2f37260&Lang=en (accessed July 17, 2020).
90. Joint Parallel Report to CERD 100th Session, November 10, 2019. https://tbinternet.ohchr.org/Treaties/CERD/Shared%20Documents/ISR/INT_CERD_NGO_ISR_39700_E.pdf (accessed July 17, 2020).
91. "Concluding observations," January 27, 2020. CERD/C/ISR/CO/17-19.
92. Negev Coexistence Forum for Civil Equality Official Website: https://www.dukium.org/education-advocacy/.
93. "Join the Alternative Naqab Tours!," *Negev Coexistence Forum for Civil Equality Official Website*, https://www.dukium.org/tout-the-negev-with-ncf/ (accessed July 17, 2020).
94. Adalah, "Tours," https://www.adalah.org/en/content/view/7910 (accessed July 17, 2020).
95. "Adalah Leads Foreign Diplomat Tour of Arab Bedouin Unrecognized Villages in the Naqab, as part of "Stop Prawer" Campaign," *Adalah*, October 30, 2012, https://www.adalah.org/en/content/view/7859 (accessed July 17, 2020).
96. Ibid.
97. NCF, "U.S. Department of State 2017 Human Rights Report," https://www.dukium.org/wp-content/uploads/2019/03/NCF-Update-for-the-US-State-Department-2017.pdf (accessed July 17, 2020).
98. US Department of State, *2018 Country Reports on Human Rights Practices: Israel, Golan Heights, West Bank, and Gaza* https://www.state.gov/reports/2018-country-reports-on-human-rights-practices/israel-golan-heights-west-bank-and-gaza/ (accessed July 17, 2020).
99. "About us," *EuroMed Rights*, https://euromedrights.org/about-us/who-we-are/ (accessed July 17, 2020).
100. EuroMed Rights and OBS to Federica Mogherini, EU, June 7, 2016.http://euromedrights.org/wp-content/uploads/2016/06/EuroMed-Rights-OBS-letter

SOFT THREATS TO NATIONAL SECURITY 141

-on-the-continued-hostility-towards-human-rights-organisations-in-Israel-OPT.pdf (accessed July 17, 2020).

101. "About the HRA," *HRA*, https://arabhra.wordpress.com/arab-hra-updates/about-the-hra/ (accessed July 17, 2020).

102. Euro-Mediterranean Human Rights Network, Adalah and AHR, *The EU and the Palestinian Arab Minority in Israel*, Brussels, February 2011. https://www.adalah.org/uploads/oldfiles/eng/Arab_Minority_Rep.pdf (accessed July 17, 2020).

103. Ibid., 58.

104. "Achievements," *Adalah*, https://www.adalah.org/en/content/view/7716 (accessed July 17, 2020).

105. *JNF Colonising Palestine Since 1901: Ongoing Ethnic Cleansing – Judaising the Naqab* (Al-Beit: Association for the Defence of Human Rights in Israel) https://bdsmovement.net/files/2011/02/JNFeBookVol3.pdf (accessed July 17, 2020). Suliman Abu-Sitta, "Al-Araqib – All of Palestine," in JNF. Abu-Sita is the Founder and President of Palestine Land Society (PLS). http://www.plands.org/en/home (accessed July 17, 2020). His latest article titled "Massacres as a weapon of ethnic cleansing during the Nakba," June 12, 2020. http://www.plands.org/en/articles-speeches/articles/2019-(1)/when-the-denial-bubble-bursts-an-israeli-kibbutz-faces-the-nakba (accessed July 17, 2020).

106. Pappe et al., *Introducing the Jewish National Fund*. JNF eBook, Volume 1, January 2010. https://www.bdsmovement.net/files/2011/02/JNFeBookVol1ed2x.pdf (accessed July 17, 2020); See also Ghada Karmi, "Weapon of the Weak," *Haaretz*, July 16, 2007.

107. Amara, "Towards a Complete Boycott."

108. "Fiddler with no Roof," Production of Physician for Human Rights, 2103. Available at: https://www.youtube.com/watch?v=b8c57DEOji4 (accessed June 7, 2020); Ben-Dror Yemini, "The blood libel film," *The Times of Israel*, November 29, 2013.

Disclosure statement

The author was the Deputy District Attorney (Civil Matters), Southern District, in the Ministry of Justice, Israel until 2014.

Bibliography

Amara, A. "Likrat Herem Muhlat Shel Arviey HanNegev Al Ma'rechet HaMishpat [Towards a Complete Boycott by the Negev Arabs on the Judicial System]." *Jadal 13*, May 2012. [In Hebrew]. For Arabic version see: Accessed July 17, 2020. https://www.mada-research.org/wp-content/uploads/2012/Jadal13/Ara/ahmad-amara-f-a.pdf

Avalon Project. "The Palestine Mandate." Accessed July 24, 1922. https://avalon.law.yale.edu/20th_century/palmanda.asp

Azaryahu, M. "Hebrew, Arabic, English: The Politics of Multilingual Street Signs in Israeli Cities." *Social & Cultural Geography* 13, no. 5 (2012): 461-479.

Barzilai, G. *Communities and Law: Politics and Cultures of Legal Identities.* Ann Arbor: University of Michigan Press, 2003.

Begin, B. Z. *Regularization of Bedouin Communities in the Negev: Summary of the public hearing on the Draft Law and recommendations for policy and for amendments to the Draft.* Jerusalem: State of Israel, 2013.

Ben-Israel, A., and A. Meir. "Renaming Space and Reshaping Identities: The Case of the Bedouin Town of Hura in Israel." *Hagar* 8, no. 2 (2008): 65-92.

Ben-Naftali, O., and Y. Shani. *International Law between War and Peace.* Tel Aviv: Ramot, 2006. [In Hebrew].

Benvenisti, M. *Sacred Landscape: The Buried History of the Holy Land since 1948.* Berkeley: University of California Press, 2002.

Bigon, L., and A. Dahamshy. "An Anatomy of Symbolic Power: Israeli Road-Sign Policy and the Palestinian Minority." *Environment and Planning D: Society and Space* 32, no. 4 (2014): 606–621.

Boteach, E. *The Indigenous Bedouin of the Negev Desert in Israel.* Omer: NCF, 2005.

Cohen, S. B., and N. Kliot. "Place-Names in Israel's Ideological Struggle over the Administered Territories." *Annals of the Association of American Geographers* 82, no. 4 (1992): 653–680.

Elmasi, U., and E. Waisblay. *Bedouin Population in the Negev: Data Collection.* Jerusalem: Knesset, Center for Research and Information, November 16, 2020. [In Hebrew].

Galilee, E., and R. Kark. "Bedouin Cemeteries in the Negev: First Typology and Spatial Dispersion, 1990–1966." *The New East* 50 (2011): 113-132. [In Hebrew].

Gerstenfeld, M. "Delegitimization Currents in Europe." *Israel Affairs* 18, no. 3 (2012): 389–402. doi:10.1080/13537121.2012.689519.

Giraut, F., and M. Houssay-Holzschuch. "Place Naming as Dispositif: Toward a Theoretical Framework." *Geopolitics* 21, no. 1 (2016): 1–21. doi:10.1080/14650045.2015.1134493.

Goldberg, E., B. Givon, Y. Bar-Sela, F. Al-Haziyl, D. Al-Assad, Cohen, Y. Yishay, and S. Gambasho. *Din VeHeshbon HaVa'ada LeHatsa't Mediniut LeHasdarat Hityashvut HaBedu'im BaNegev [Commission's Report for Recommending Policy for the Regulation of Bedouin Settlement in the Negev] [In Hebrew].* Jerusalem: State of Israel, 2008.

Greenspan, I. "Mediating Bedouin Futures: The Roles of Advocacy NGOs in Land and Planning Conflicts between the State of Israel and the Negev Bedouins." MA thesis, York University, 2005.

Groiss, A. "De-legitimization of Israel in Palestinian Authority Schoolbooks." *Israel Affairs* 18, no. 3 (2012): 455–484. doi:10.1080/13537121.2012.689524.

Kark, R., and S. J. Frantzman. "Empire, State and the Bedouin of the Middle East, past and Present: A Comparative Study of Land and Settlement Policies." *Middle Eastern Studies* 48 (2012): 487–510.

Karsh, E., ed. *Israel in the International Arena.* London: Cass, 2004.

Kedar, A., A. Amara, and O. Yiftachel. *Emptied Lands: A Legal Geography of Bedouin Rights in the Negev.* Stanford: Stanford University Press, 2018.

Khazanov, A. M. *Nomads and the outside World.* 2nd ed. Madison, WI: University of Wisconsin Press, 1994.

Lerner, N. *Group Rights and Discrimination in International Law.* 2nd ed. The Hague: Martinus Nijhoff Publishers and Kluwer Law International, 2003.

Mac Allister, K. "Applicability of the Crime of Apartheid to Israel." *Badil website.* Accessed August 23, 2009. http://www.badil.org/en/publication/periodicals/al-majdal/item/72-applicability-of-the-crime-of-apartheid-to-israel.html

Medina, B. "Domestic Human Rights Adjudication in the Shadow of International Law: The Status of Human Rights Conventions in Israel." *Israel Law Review* 50, no. 3 (2017): 331–388. doi:10.1017/S0021223717000164.

Nisan, M. "In Defence of the Idea of a Jewish State." *Israel Affairs* 19, no. 2 (2013): 259–272. doi:10.1080/13537121.2013.778088.

Pappe, I., A. Hayeem, U. Davis, S. Tarbush, S. Karkar, B. White, R. Mizrahi, B. Williamson, and J. Goss. eds. *Introducing the Jewish National Fund.* JNF eBook no.1. Scotland, UK: Scottish Palestine Solidarity Campaign c/o Peace & Justice Centre, 2010. https://www.bdsmovement.net/files/2011/02/JNFeBookVol1ed2x.pdf

Payes, S. *Palestinian NGO's in Israel: The Politics of Civil Society.* London: IB Tauris, 2005.

Prawer, E., S. Asif, S. Gambasho, Y. Bibi, S. Dana, Y. Bachar, A. Heler, ans S. Ben-Salmon. *Hamlatzot Tzevet HaYisum LeDoh Goldberg LeHasdarat Hityashvut HaBedui'm BeNegev* [Recommendations of the implementation team for the Goldberg Report on formalizing Bedouin settlement in the Negev]. Jerusalem: State of Israel, 2011. [In Hebrew].

Ratcliffe, R. "The Battle for Recognition: Civil Society, Citizenship and the Political Rise of the Negev Bedouin." In *Civil Organizations and Protest Movements in Israel: Mobilization around the Israeli-Palestinian Conflict*, edited by M. Elisabeth, 209-231. London: Palgrave Macmillan, 2009.

Ratcliffe, R. "Bedouin Rights, Bedouin Representation: Dinamics of Representation in the Naqab Bedouin Advocacy Industry." *Journal of Holy Land and Palestine Studies* 15, no. 1 (2016): 97–124.

Sabel, R., and H. Adler. *International Law.* Jerusalem: Sacher Institute, 2010.

Salzman, P. C. *Pastoralism: Equality, Hierarchy, And The State.* Boulder, CO: Westview Press, 2004.

Sharvit-Baruch, P., and A. Keren. "Delegitimization of Israel: The Legal Framework." In *The Delegitimization Phenomenon: Challenges and Responses*, edited by E. Yogev and G. Lindenstrauss, 456–457. Petach-Tikva: INSS, 2017.

Steinberg, G. M. "The Politics of NGOs, Human Rights and the Arab-Israel Conflict." *Israel Studies* 16, no. 2 (2011): 24–54.

Steinberg, G. M. "'From Durban to the Goldstone Report: The Centrality of Human Rights NGOs in the Political Dimension of the Arab–Israeli Conflict." *Israel Affairs* 18, no. 3 (2012): 372–388. doi:10.1080/13537121.2012.689518.

Yahel, H. "Beyond the Letter of the Law: Process to Formulate a Compromise in the Negev Bedouin Ownership Claims in the 1970s." *Iyunim Bitkumat Israel* 38 (2017): 84-127. [in Hebrew].

Yahel, H. "The Conflict over Land Ownership and Unauthorized Construction in the Negev." *Contemporary Review of the Middle East* 6, no. 3–4 (2019): 352-369.

Yahel, H., and R. Kark. "Land and Settlement of Israel's Negev Bedouin: Official (Ad-hoc) Steering Committees 1948–1980." *British Journal of Middle Eastern Studies* 44, no. 3 (2017): 1-26.

Yahel, H., R. Kark, and S. J. Frantzman. "Negev Bedouin and Indigenous People: A Comparative Review." In *Societies, Globalization, and Marginalization: Marginal Regions in the 21st Century*, edited by R. Chand, E. Nel, and S. Pelc, 121-144. Cham: Springer, 2017.

The coalescence of anti-Zionist ideologies

Henri Stellman

ABSTRACT

This article examines the coalescence of the main anti-Zionist ideologies: Left, Jewish, Christian, Arab/Muslim and Conspiracy anti-Zionism. After a definition of anti-Zionism, its relationship to antisemitism and an overview of the historical origin of the coalescence drive, the article shows the extent of the synergy between representatives of the main anti-Zionist ideologies. It concludes that the accusation of a global conspiracy ascribed by antisemites to Zionism and Judaism can be turned on its head: it is in fact a feature of anti-Zionist ideologies that are otherwise in existential struggle with each other.

Ideologies that are trying to transform the world and replace it with a new order are in an existential struggle with other ideologies seeking to bring about their alternative new order. However, when it comes to Zionism and Israel, supporters of competing ideologies have colluded to advance an "anti-Zionist International."

There are five main anti-Zionist ideologies embedded in different cultures, communities and political movements around the world: Left, Jewish, Christian, Arab/Muslim and Conspiracy anti-Zionism.

Notwithstanding their differences, proponents of the five anti-Zionist ideologies have found common ground in their virulent opposition to Zionism and Israel. In what follows this article will define anti-Zionism and its relationship to antisemitism, review the historical origin of the anti-Zionist coalescence drive and examine the coalescence feature for each of the five anti-Zionist ideologies by focusing on a series of conferences that have taken place in Iran and attended by Holocaust deniers, conspiracy theorists, Anti-Zionists, BDS activists and others from around the word.

Defining anti-Zionism

Anti-Zionism is the opposition to Zionism and/or the state of Israel. When it aims at bringing an end to Israel's existence, it can be called Politicidal anti-Zionism.[1] When it aims at delegitimizing, dehumanising, and demonising the state of Israel it can be called anti-Israel anti-Zionism. De-legitimatisation is the attempt to take away the acceptance of Israel by the international community of nations. Dehumanisation is the attempt to deprive Israel and its inhabitants of positive human qualities. Demonisation is the attempt to portray Israel as wicked.[2] Each of the above two forms of anti-Zionism can stand alone or can appear in combination with the other.

Anti-Zionism should not be conflated with criticism of Israel's policies. One can legitimately disapprove of Israel's policies in the same way that one can legitimately disapprove of any other country's policies.

Anti-Zionism and antisemitism

The International Holocaust Remembrance Alliance's (IHRA) definition of antisemitism is rapidly becoming a benchmark definition, widely accepted by national and international institutions around the world. It gives the following contemporary examples of antisemitism whilst noting that those are not the only examples. Whilst the explanation and justification articulated by antisemites do not always contain an anti-Zionist element, often they do:

- Calling for, aiding, or justifying the killing or harming of Jews in the name of a radical ideology or an extremist view of religion.
- Making mendacious, dehumanising, demonising, or stereotypical allegations about Jews as such or the power of Jews as collective – such as, especially but not exclusively, the myth about a world Jewish conspiracy or of Jews controlling the media, economy, government or other societal institutions.
- Accusing Jews as a people of being responsible for real or imagined wrongdoing committed by a single Jewish person or group, or even for acts committed by non-Jews.
- Denying the fact, scope, mechanisms (e.g. gas chambers) or intentionality of the genocide of the Jewish people at the hands of National Socialist Germany and its supporters and accomplices during World War II (the Holocaust).
- Accusing the Jews as a people, or Israel as a state, of inventing or exaggerating the Holocaust.
- Accusing Jewish citizens of being more loyal to Israel, or to the alleged priorities of Jews worldwide, than to the interests of their own nations.

146   SOFT THREATS TO NATIONAL SECURITY

- Denying the Jewish people their right to self-determination, e.g., by claiming that the existence of a State of Israel is a racist endeavour.
- Applying double standards by requiring of it a behaviour not expected or demanded of any other democratic nation.
- Using the symbols and images associated with classic antisemitism (e.g., claims of Jews killing Jesus or blood libel) to characterise Israel or Israelis.
- Drawing comparisons of contemporary Israeli policy to that of the Nazis.
- Holding Jews collectively responsible for actions of the state of Israel.[3]

This article identifies five additional categories of antisemitic anti-Zionism: Zionism as Codeword, Consequential Antisemitism, Fellow anti-Zionist Travellers, Separate antisemitic and anti-Zionist views in same individuals and Unintentional Antisemitism in Anti-Zionism.

Zionism as a code word

Zionism is used as a code word for Judaism. Anti-Zionists often use the word "Zionists" or, alternatively "Zio," a term used by far-right antisemitic groups, when they refer to members of the diaspora Jewish community as a way to cover up an antisemitic statement. A few examples:

- In 1969, Hafez Ismael, former Egyptian ambassador to France said that as long as Israel would be a nation supported by "12 million Zionists" from all over the world, there would be something foreign in that part of the world. As there were approximately twelve million Jews outside Israel at the time, it is quite clear that Ismael's "12 million Zionists" meant the whole of world Jewry. Since he was afraid that the diatribe would create bad publicity, he substituted "Zionists" for "Jews."[4]
- In 1981, the-then president of the British National Union of Students David Aaronovitch, now a well-known journalist, was the victim of a campaign of forged letters alleging that he was in the pay of the Israeli embassy in London. The British anti-Zionist Organisation (BAZO) that published the letters claimed that Aaronovitch had a "Zionist" name. There is of course no such thing as a Zionist name, only a Jewish sounding name.[5]
- In 1972, the Soviet embassy in Paris was charged with circulating anti-semitic literature in one of its publications. The embassy used as its defence the argument that the article in question was directed at "Zionists," not Jews. Yet Grigory Svirsky, an expert in Russian antisemit-ism, produced for the Paris tribunal quotations from an antisemitic

SOFT THREATS TO NATIONAL SECURITY

publication of the infamous Cossack band, the Black Hundreds, which were identical to those of the Soviet embassy with one small but telling difference: in the embassy's publication each mention of the word 'Jew' had been replaced by the word 'Zionist.' The Paris tribunal found the embassy guilty and fined it heavily.[6]

- Khadim Hussain, a former Lord Mayor of Bradford, was suspended from Labour after he shared a Facebook post that referred to 'the six million Zionists that were killed by Hitler.'[7]
- Nazim Ali, director of the Islamic Human Rights Commission, organiser of the annual Al Quds anti-Zionist demonstration in London, said through a public-address system as he led the march on 18 June 2017:

We are fed up of the Zionists, we are fed up with all their rabbis; we are fed up with all their synagogues, we are fed up with their supporters. As we know in Grenfell [a high-rise tower in London where many of its tenants perished as the result of a fire] many innocents were murdered by Theresa May's cronies, many of which are supporters of Zionist ideology. Let us not forget that some of the biggest corporations who were supporting the Conservative Party are Zionists. They are responsible for the murder of the people of Grenfell, in those towers in Grenfell, the Zionist supporters of the Tory Party. It is the Zionists who give money to the Tory party, to kill people in high-rise blocks. Free Free Palestine.[8]

Consequential anti-Zionism

The substance of this theory is that since support for Zionism and the existence of the state of Israel is shared by an overwhelming majority of Jews around the world and since Israel is seen as an important, if not central dimension of Jewish identity, it follows that an attack on the state of Israel is an attack on Jews all over the world.

For Professor Shlomo Avineri of the Hebrew University of Jerusalem, it is a fact that most Jews today define themselves in some way or another, and in various degrees of intensity, in relation to Israel. Should Israel disappear, or a major catastrophe befalls it, practically all Jewish people would conceive it as a major tragedy for their own existence as Jews. Therefore, de-legitimisation of Israel is tantamount to the de-legitimisation of Jewish existence as understood today by most Jews.[9]

For Kenneth L. Marcus, Assistant Secretary for Civil Rights at the US Department of Education

certain forms of hostility towards Israel are anti-Semitic in the sense that they cause foreseeable harm to Jews based on a trait that is central to Jewish identity [...] Some abuse of Israel by the BDS campaign is profoundly offensive to Jews because of the intimate relationship between a person's Jewish identity and that person attachment to Israel. Indeed, for many Jews, a commitment to

Israel is so intrinsic to their religious belief as to be the paradigmatic case of a characteristic that a people should not be required to change. For those Jews who embrace Israel as part of their Jewish identity, the commitment may be of multi-generational duration, shared historically by many members of the group, inscribed centrally in the group's common literature and tradition, and pervasive of the culture.[10]

This is not an absurd claim by any means, writes Jonathan Freedland, from *The Guardian*:

> Jewish affinity with Israel is now so widespread and entrenched, across the political and religious spectrum, that it has indeed become a central part of Jewish identity ... This should give the anti-Zionist pause; much as they may insist that they condemn only Zionists, not Jews, this is not how Jews themselves experience it. The Jewish people has made up its mind since 1945 and it has embraced Zionism. To stand against that idea now is to stand against a core Jewish belief.[11]

If we look at the main themes of anti-Zionism over the past few decades, we note in particular the equating of Zionism with Nazism. Since most Jews identify closely with Israel, an anti-Jewish dimension can be seen in this charge. In other words, accusing Zionism and Israel of Nazism is tantamount to accusing the Jews of the world of being Nazis, a rather cynical inversion of yesterday's victims into today's perpetrators.

Fellow anti-Zionist travellers

The concept of anti-Zionists colluding with antisemites without being themselves antisemitic – originally developed in the context of the Bolshevik revolution – has been analysed by Anthony Julius:

> They are often found defending anti-Semites - not guilty of the offense themselves, but quick to champion others who are guilty of it ... They share space with anti-Semites, untroubled by the company they keep; they comprise a species of "fellow traveller" ... the kind of person ready to overlook or excuse everything that is vicious in the cause he supports, the protagonists he admires.[12]

In March 2009, the well- known British film director Ken Loach responded to a report on the growth of antisemitism since the Gaza War a couple of months earlier. Loach described the report as 'a red herring,' adding that '[i]f there has been a rise I am not surprised. In fact, it is perfectly understandable because Israel feeds feelings of anti-Semitism.'[13]

Jean Bauberot, a past leader of the French Christian Students Association wrote that to be against all forms of racism is as stupid as being against all forms of violence; that Palestinians have the right to appear antisemitic to 'us.' Bouberot then moves away from the position of an outside colluder when he writes that to demonstrate the intricacies of the Palestine problem

SOFT THREATS TO NATIONAL SECURITY

forces 'us' to treat the Jews as oppressors and that 'we' are allowed to use identical terms and parts of sentences used by Hitler even if we have nothing in common with that ideology.[14]

Separate antisemitic and anti-Zionist views

Researchers were interested to see how prevalent it is to simultaneously hold extreme anti-Israel and antisemitic views. Professors Edward Kaplan and Charles Small arrived at the conclusion that there was a correlation between the two:

> In the discourse surrounding the Israeli-Palestinian conflict, extreme criticisms of Israel (e.g., Israel is an apartheid state, the Israel Defence Forces deliberately target Palestinian civilians), coupled with extreme policy proposals (e.g., boycott of Israeli academics and institutions, divest from companies doing business with Israel), have sparked counterclaims that such criticisms are anti-Semitic (for only Israel is singled out) ... based on a survey of 500 citizens in each of 10 European countries, the authors ask whether those individuals with extreme anti-Israel views are more likely to be anti-Semitic. Even after controlling for numerous potentially confounding factors, they find that anti-Israel sentiment consistently predicts the probability that an individual is anti-Semitic, with the likelihood of measured anti-Semitism increasing with the extent of anti-Israel sentiment observed.[15]

Jackie Walker, a British leftwing Jewish anti-Zionist, has expressed antisemitic views distinct from her anti-Zionist views. She wrote on her Facebook that Jews were the 'chief financiers of the sugar and slave trade.'[16] British anti-Zionist politician and leader of his country's Labour Party until April 2020, Jeremy Corbyn, defended in 2012 a London mural that depicted Jewish bankers counting money around a board balanced on men with dark complexions.[17]

Unintentional antisemitism in anti-Zionism

According to British academic David Hirsh, it is now widely accepted among antiracist scholars and activists that 'acts, speeches, ideas, practices, or institutions may be racist or may lead to racist outcomes, independently of whether or not the people involved are judged to be self-consciously racist.'[18]

The report by Lord Scarman on the 1981 London Brixton riots, repeated and expanded by the British Judge Macpherson in 1999 in his enquiry on the Stephen Lawrence murder, accepted the existence of 'unwitting,' 'unconscious' and 'unintentional' racism.[19]

On 14 January 2002, the *New Statesman* weekly published on its front cover a star of David piercing a union jack flag with the headline 'A Kosher Conspiracy.' The issue featured two articles analysing the influence of the pro-

Israel lobby. The editor of the *New Statesman*, Peter Wilby, wrote subsequently that 'We (or more precisely, I) got it wrong' and that 'The cover was not intended to be anti-Semitic, the *New Statesman* is vigorously opposed to racism in all its forms. But it used images and words in such a way as to create unwittingly the impression that the *New Statesman* was following an anti-Semitic tradition that sees the Jews as a conspiracy piercing the heart of the nation.'[20]

In a message sent on Facebook, Rayhan Uddin who had been running for the post of general secretary of the London School of Economics Student Union, asserted that 'leading Zionists' had attempted to 'win back the LSE and make it right wing and Zio again.' In a subsequent message on Facebook, he apologised, writing 'it is utterly repugnant to me to think that I may have unwittingly appeared to endorse in any way the foul ideology of antisemitism.'[21]

Historical origin of the coalescence drive

The beginning of the anti-Zionist international coalescence movement can be traced to the much-hailed Bandung conference in Indonesia in April 1955, the first mass gathering of independent African and Asian states. Israel was not invited. Moreover, a critical communique issued at the end of the conference supported only 'the rights of the Arab people of Palestine.'[22]

From Bandung onwards, the joint animus gathered a momentum underwritten by such events as the 1967 Six-Day War, which provided ammunition to the charge that, unlike the Arab states and the Palestinians, Israel was treated as a 'Superdog' that was not subjected to opprobrium.

The next watershed was the resolution adopted by the 30th UN General Assembly in 1975 that equated Zionism with a 'form of racism and racial discrimination.'[23] Whilst the resolution was rescinded in 1991, the 1982 Lebanon War and subsequent events linked to the West Bank, the Gaza Strip and the Lebanon provided fodder for a further anti-Zionist push in other UN agencies, various international organisations and specialised conferences.

A further landmark was a forum of 775 Non-Governmental Organisations that met in parallel to the UN World Conference Against Racism, Racial Discrimination, Xenophobia and Related Intolerance that took place in Durban, South Africa in 2001. The forum published an NGO Declaration that referred to Israel's supposed brand of apartheid and ethnic cleansing methods, racist crimes against humanity, acts of genocide and announced a policy of complete isolation of the country and the imposition of sanctions and embargoes.[24]

The coalescence of anti-Zionist ideologies

There are three ways the collusion of competing anti-Zionist ideologies can be observed: through the use of the same means by different anti-Zionist ideologies to achieve their objective, through the borrowing of ideological elements from each other and through meetings where the representatives of the various anti-Zionist ideologies exchange views.

Means

Many anti-Zionists have used Boycott, Divestment and Sanction, or BDS, as a common denominator to achieve their goal.

The boycott of Israel can be defined as a refusal to buy from, do business or collaborate with companies or organisations associated with the State of Israel as an expression of protest to the existence of the state or to its policies, or as a means to coerce Israel to alter its policies. Divestment can be defined as the act of selling or disposing of an asset connected with Israel, with similar aims to those of the boycott. Sanctions are penalties or coercive measures against companies or organisations associated with Israel, also with aims similar to the boycott.[25]

Another mean is intersectionality

In the words of Ziva Dahl, '[p]roponents of intersectionality see a world of all-encompassing oppression, where racism, classism, sexism, homophobia and ableism constitute an intersecting system.' According to this view of the world,

> all injustices are interconnected, even if occurring in unconnected geographic, cultural and political environments ... This is the rationalization for building alliances among unrelated causes like LGBTQ rights, fossil fuel divestment, prison reform, racial discrimination and immigration. The anti-Israel BDS campaigns have successfully injected the Palestinians into this intersectional mix as victims of colonialist oppression by pro-Western Israel. The marriage of intersectionality with the Arab-Israeli conflict allows any victim group to make common cause with the Palestinians. [26]

A recent example of how Intersectionality operates within the framework of anti-Zionism is the injection of accusations against Israel by demonstrators identified with the movement Black Lives Matter in the wake of the murder by police officers of George Floyd in May 2020.[27]

Borrowing of ideological elements from each other

Many anti-Zionists have also frequently relied on ideological themes that are extrinsic and even antithetical to the particular ideology to which they subscribe. Right-wing conspiracy theories have found a fertile terrain amongst Muslim, Arab, Christian and Left-wing anti-Zionists. Muslim, Arab, Christian and right-wing anti-Zionists attack Israel/Zionism as being 'capitalist,' 'colonialist' and 'imperialist' which is clearly left-wing in origin.[28]

Antisemitic and anti-Zionist meetings: a case-study

In 2005, a series of conferences in Iran were inaugurated, attended by Holocaust deniers, conspiracy theorists, anti-Zionists, BDS activists and others from around the world. Echoing this 'bizarre collage,' one academic has wryly commented on these meetings:

> At how many conferences can you be guaranteed to meet Iranian Revolutionary Guards, Russian imperialists, anti-Ukrainian fascists, Chinese spies, Qaddafi devotees, Corbyn fans, Assad apologists, neo-Nazis, Trump devotees, French Holocaust deniers, Western anti-war feminists, African American separatists, Venezuelan socialists and anti-Semites of every conceivable form and type? There is really only one, and it's run by an organization that the U.S. Treasury designates as a front for the Iranian regime's most hardline power-brokers.[29]

In what follows, this article examines each of the five main anti-Zionist ideologies through quotes from one or more participants at three of the Iranian conferences that took place in 2006, 2012 and 2014.

Left anti-Zionism

What were the respective explanation and justification advanced by the various proponents of this ideology?

Karl Marx never took a position on Zionism but uttered insulting remarks of the worst kind towards the Jews.[30] Karl Kautsky thought that Jews could not be considered a nation and their fate was irreversible self-dissolution. He saw Zionism as a reaction to the inevitability of Jewish disappearance and therefore as reactionary.[31] The Bund, a Jewish Workers' Union set up in in Vilna in 1887, argued for the rights of Jews to control their language, custom, way of life and culture as they saw fit in the diaspora. They opposed the Zionist stand that viewed Jews as alien in the Diaspora.[32] Eduard Bernstein called at times for the assimilation of Jews in their environment and referred to Zionist intoxication whose fate would be similar to an epidemic: it would vanish.[33]

Lenin advocated the assimilation of Jews in their environment. He argued that anyone resisting this trend, like the Bundists or the Zionists 'contemplates the rear aspect of Jewry with reverential awe.' He is an enemy of the proletariat, a supporter of all that is outmoded and connected with caste among the Jewish people; he is an accomplice of the rabbis and the bourgeoisie, 'a Jewish reactionary philistine, who want to turn back the wheel of history'[34] and 'foster the spirit of the ghetto.'[35]

Trotsky believed that to make the Jews a special topic of discussion or to engage in a particularistic struggle against anti-Semitism was superfluous as the advent of the classless, socialist society would automatically 'solve' the problem.[36] The attempts to solve the Jewish question through the migration of Jews to Palestine was a 'tragic mockery of the Jewish people.'[37]

Subsequently, Russia, its satellites and Communist parties in non-Communist countries have expanded a policy of vilification of Zionism (even though the Soviet Union did call for the return to the 1947 partition's borders).[38] Ideological groups that go under the banner of the illustrious forefathers of the Left: Marxists, Leninists, Trotskyists, Stalinists, Maoists and others, have continued that unremitted drive.[39]

Medea Benjamin

Medea Benjamin is the cofounder in 2002 of Codepink: Women for Peace, a feminist anti-war organisation with dozens of branches in the US, Canada, Germany and Japan. Amongst their objectives are BDS and bringing down the support for Israel. Codepink's hostility to Israel takes the form of attention-grabbing disruptions of major pro-Israel events.[40] Benjamin uses conspiratorial rhetoric to denounce Israel's American supporters and accuses the American Israel Public Affairs Committee (AIPAC) of having 'undue influence' and being a 'de facto agent for a foreign government.'[41] A core aspect of Codepink is its connection to the broader left-wing and antiwar movement and its ability to introduce anti-Israel initiatives to these constituencies.[42]

Benjamin was an active participant at the Iranian conference that took place in 2014. She was a panellist to one of the sessions titled 'The Gaza War and BDS Movement Strategies against the Zionist Regime' with a discussion on its economic, political, cultural and academic aspects. In another session she participated in a discussion on 'Resistance,' as Palestinian terrorism is often euphemised.[43]

The mayor of the German city of Beyreuth rejected granting the city's tolerance prize to Codepink over allegations of the group's antisemitism. Following this rejection, Benjamin wrote him a letter in which she attempted to justify her participation in the conference, claiming that when she heard conference speakers voicing over-the-top conspiracy theories and anti-Jewish statements she brought her concerns to these speakers as well as the organisers. She also asserted that some of her issues were addressed by clarifications from the podium by the organisers that the conference was not anti-Jewish or antisemitic and that it was important to make a distinction between Judaism and Zionism.[44]

Jewish anti-Zionism

Jewish anti-Zionists are not a homogeneous group. There are three main different ideological attitudes: Emancipationists, Orthodox and Left anti-Zionism. The latter was discussed in the previous section.

Emancipationist anti-Zionism was advocated by Jews who sought to assimilate into Gentile society, a feature called 'self-hatred.' Those Jews put great hopes in the new world that was opening its gates to them thanks to the Enlightenment, and every impediment to the assimilation of Jews – including Zionism – was considered by them anathema.[45] A similar anti-Zionism was also advocated by those Jews who wanted to integrate in Gentile society while maintaining completely or with some modifications their Jewish identity.[46]

For Orthodox Jews, the Zionist idea was anathema as it was seen as oblivious to Judaism's religious precepts, laws and regulations. A number of anti-Zionist rabbis energetically engaged in a forceful campaign to prove their point. They were called the Protest Rabbis, a label coined by Theodor Herzl, founder of political Zionism.[47] When the first Zionist Congress was planned to be held in 1897, German rabbis, in the name of the Association of Rabbis in Germany, an anti-Zionist organisation including representatives of different wings of Judaism, published a fierce attack on Zionism from a religious point of view.[48]

The Protest Rabbis were followed by numerous other rabbis. Agudat Israel has been the leading organisation of Orthodox anti-Zionists, but over time it has come a long way closer to the Zionist camp with representatives elected to the Israeli Knesset and joining ruling government coalitions.[49]

Rabbi Aaron Cohen and Rabbi Yisroel Dovid Weiss

Neturei Karta is a small, ultra-orthodox sect living mainly in Jerusalem – the name of Neturei Karta is Aramaic for 'Guardians of the City' – who broke away from Agudat Israel in 1935. It has lived in separation from the rest of Israeli society but has been tolerated as such by the state.[50]

Its ideology, in addition to the classical religious anti-Zionist arguments, is most radical. It has asserted that it will never accept the State of Israel, even if Arabs do,[51] has expressed willingness to ally itself with the PLO,[52] and has even called, in its resistance to state tax collection, for the killing of the tax collectors as it has claimed that this is sanctioned by religious law.[53]

Its articulate American supporters, based in Brooklyn, have engaged in diverse activities. They have sent letters to the UN Secretary-General stressing Zionist 'fraud, deception and usurpation'[54] and published books such as *Min Hameitsar* by Rabbi Michael Dov Weissmandel[55] and *The Holocaust Victims Accuse* by Rabbi Moshe Shonfeld[56] purporting to show that the Zionists have much to be reproached with for the Holocaust.

Rabbi Aaron Cohen, an Orthodox Jew from Manchester, and a leading member of Neturei Karta who participated in the 2006 Tehran conference, argued in his speech that while the Jews were promised the Holy Land, the

SOFT THREATS TO NATIONAL SECURITY

bible subjected the promise to certain conditions that, if unfulfilled, would lead to the Jewish People being dispersed across the world.[57] He also claimed that Jews were required to be loyal citizens of the countries in which they lived and were prohibited 'against the wishes of the All Mighty' to try to force their way out of the exile by their own hands to establish a Jewish state in Palestine.[58] He accused the Zionists of having cooperated with the Nazis and even cast doubt about the figure of six million Jews murdered during the Holocaust.[59]

At the 2012 conference, Rabbi Cohen argued that Zionism means apartheid, nationalism and sectarianism. He wanted Zionism exterminated and called for restoration peace and tranquillity in the Middle East.[60]

Also present at the 2012 conference was Rabbi Yisroel Dovid Weiss, another leading Neturei Karta activist. In his speech at the gathering he depicted Zionism as an evil philosophy and ideology that rebelled against God and repressed the people.[61] He also attacked Holocaust denial but absolved the Iranian President Mahmoud Ahmadinejad, claiming that he was not an enemy of the Jews and that he 'does not deny the Jewish Holocaust,' ignoring altogether the Ahmadinejad's well-documented systematic Holocaust denial.[62]

Christian anti-Zionism

Above anything else, Jews are blamed by Christian anti-Zionism for the crime of deicide, considering the Jews culpable for the death of Jesus Christ. It is mainly on this basis that the Church has persecuted the Jews. This has been the most powerful and widespread agent in the history of antisemitism.[63] Zionism being the product of Jews, it is opposed by Christians, just like Judaism, also for deicidal reasons.

Zionism is also opposed on the basis of the non-belief of Jews in the Christian religion. A significant foundation of Christian theology is the idea of spreading itself as much as possible in the world by Christianising mankind. The liberation of man or woman is only considered possible in a world where all men and women have chosen to follow Christ. This belief has been used in the framework of anti-Zionism. The state of Israel, when established, would represent an achievement and symbol of the Jewish unbelievers, an antithesis, an obstacle to the universal mission of the Church and is therefore opposed.

In 1904, Theodor Herzl had an audience with Pope Pius X who told him: 'We cannot give approval to this movement. We cannot prevent the Jews from going to Jerusalem – but we could never sanction it. The soil of Jerusalem, if not always sacred, has been sanctified by the life of Jesus Christ. As the head of the Church I cannot tell anything different. The

Jews have not recognised our Lord, therefore we cannot recognise the Jewish people [and its aspiration to a national existence].'[64]

Anti-Zionist Christians have also accused the Zionists of crucifying the Palestinians. Here their opposition does not rise from the far distant past. It derives from the contemporary Arab-Israeli conflict.[65]

Reverend Stephen Sizer

Reverend Sizer, a Church of England vicar, is at the forefront of the Christian opposition to Zionism and the state of Israel. He is particularly up in arms against Christian Zionism, a world movement that supports the State of Israel on theological grounds. He has expanded on this theme in his PhD thesis, various publications and other activities on his website.[66] Reverend Sizer's views are evident from his choice of links on his website which include the purveyors of antisemitic material including a website claiming that Jews and Israel had a role in the 9/11 terrorist attack,[67] another espousing Holocaust denial[68] and a third featuring an image of a Nazi flag with a swastika superimposed on the Star of David.[69]

Reverend Sizer was an active participant at the Annual International Conference of Independent Thinkers and Filmmakers that took place in Tehran in 2014. The conference programme lists him as part of a panel discussion at the Iranian Foreign Office, as a speaker on 'Christian Jihad versus Christian Zionism' at the opening ceremony and as giving a talk on 'The Israel Lobby in England' at another session.[70] In a video of one of his conference speeches on Youtube, Sizer articulates the case against the Christian support for Zionism and Israel and asserts that Islam's interpretation of Jihad is misunderstood.[71]

Conspiracy anti-Zionism

One of the sources of right-wing attack of Israel and Zionism is the so-called antisemitic conspiracy theory, the origin of which lies in the *Protocols of the Elders of Zion* – an early 20th century antisemitic Russian document allegedly narrating the minutes of the supposed secret deliberations of the leaders of world Jewry plotting word domination. The first Zionist congress in Basle in 1897 was considered the framework for these demonic consultations.[72] There are four groups of Conspiracy anti-Zionists: Christians, Nazis, Neo-Nazis and Holocaust Deniers.

According to a Christian conspiracy theory propagator, 'Jew-Zionism is the spearhead of the anti-Christ on this earth, dedicated to the evaporation of the Christian religion, the Christian population and the governmental authority of nations that are predominantly Christian.'[73] 'The enemies of Christ are determined to capture through the United Nations, not through what people call a World Government, but through the manipulating political, financial and military power of World Zionism.'[74]

The idea of Jewish lust for power has been adopted by Nazi ideology and is intrinsic to its attack on Zionism, considered a product and a means of the conspiracy and thus wicked.[75] The exposure of the evil of Nazism has not prevented their ideas from being advocated after WWII until today. The British National Front, created in the late 1960s, offers a good example of neo-Nazism. It has gone so far – perhaps the ultimate in anti-Zionism – as to claim that by way of achieving their goals, Zionists have staged attacks on their fellow Jews.[76]

Completing this pantheon of visceral hate are Holocaust deniers who are unhappy about what they see as the immunity given to Zionism and/or Israel thanks to the Holocaust. To overcome this, they 'examine critically' the Holocaust with a view to proving that much of it has never happened but has rather been inflated by Zionism/Israel in order to get support and immunity for their illegitimate deeds.[77]

Robert Faurisson

The late Robert Faurisson is perhaps the most well-known Holocaust denier, frequently mocking it unapologetically. A professor of French literature and author, he travelled to various historical revisionist conferences around the world and even managed to get an article published in the prestigious *Le Monde*. Faurisson has had regular brushes with French justice. He was convicted of Holocaust denial, fined and lost his position at the University of Lyon, but the French legal system was unsuccessful in stymieing his abuses and activities.[78]

Faurisson has summarised his controversial views in a number of succinct points:

- Hitler's gas chambers never existed and the genocide of Jews never took place – both are lies.
- The narrative of the supposed extermination of European Jewry is a 'gigantic political-financial swindle' invented by the Zionists.
- Israel has been the chief beneficiary of this narrative while its main victims have been the German and the Palestinian peoples.
- The power of the Jew-controlled international media has ensured the success of this lie and censored the freedom of expression of those who expose the lie.
- Supporters of the Holocaust hoax distort the meaning and nature of revisionist research and search for historical truth.[79]

At the Tehran conference of 2012, Faurrison argued that 'Hollywood was the one that created the fake image of some myths – like holocaust, gas chambers and the massacre of six million Jews during WW2 by Nazi Germany – in people's minds.'[80] Praising 'Revisionism' as a method through which the truth will be uncovered, he argued that

> The general idea of the west towards [the] holocaust has been Zionism's sword and shield. But today revisionism has threatened this idea. I, as a revisionist, came through my researches to this idea that those Jews who are claimed to be massacred in fact have died of Typhus and Jewish holocaust is nothing except a big lie. The claim about killing 6 millions Jews in German furnace is not true ... The biggest achievement of Hollywood was invention of holocaust. Holocaust is a lie at American scale (sic).[81]

Arab and Muslim anti-Zionism

The main impetus of Arab and Muslim anti-Zionism is based in the Middle East but it is also widespread among Arabs and Muslims based in the West. Statements of politicidal anti-Zionism, which seeks to destroy the state of Israel, and of its anti-Israel anti-Zionism corollary, which seeks to delegitimize, dehumanise, and demonise the Jewish state, are a permanent and widespread feature of Palestinian and wider Arab and Muslim societies, as expressed through official spokesmen, the media, culture, the education curriculum and various civil organisations. At times the goal is expressed in explicit language but more often (especially when directed to Western audiences) it is presented in a more indirect and ambiguous fashion so to camouflage its murderous nature.[82]

There is a rich catalogue of scurrilous libels brought by Arabs/Muslims against Zionism and the state of Israel, from their depiction as a cancerous colonialist implant in the Middle east, to accusing them with horrendous crimes (e.g., deliberately spread Aids, murdering Palestinians to harvest their organs, etc.), to using medieval blood libels (e.g., Jews as well-poisoners, murdering non-Jews and using their blood for ritual purposes, etc.), to the most far-fetched conspiracy theories (e.g., seeking world domination a la *The Protocols of the Elders of Zion*, carrying the 9/11 attacks, etc.), to Holocaust denial and equating Zionism with Nazism, apartheid, and similar forms of fascist oppression. It was Arab/Muslim anti-Zionism that has given birth to the BDS movement and has spearheaded it in the West in general, and on Western campus in particular.[83]

Dieudonné M'Bala M'Bala, Sean Stone and Iranian President Mahmoud Ahmadinejad

Dieudonné M'Bala M'Bala is a French stand-up comedian and aspiring politician of mixed Cameroon and French parentage who espouses a leftist, pro-Palestinian position. He has come to prominence for his provocative stand-up routines, statements and articles that deliberately use antisemitic narratives, puns and gestures disguised as humour such as offensives jokes about Jews and the Holocaust. Amongst his infamous stunts are the 'quenelle' gesture, an inverted Nazis salute, as well as the reference to 'Shoananas' or Holocaust pineapples. This, perceived as a cock a snoot to the French establishment and the Jewish community, has garnered interest and support among young people, in particular those identifying themselves as disenfranchised.[84]

Dieudonné's's idiosyncrasies have in turn lead to considerable interest on the part of the French and international media. He has been the subject of many talk shows, televisions and radio programmes, articles and editorials. Claiming the right of freedom of speech, he has flouted laws in France that are meant to represent an effective judicial arsenal available to deal with Dieudonné's types of outré provocations. And yet, though he has been sued many times and banned in various countries, the French courts have dealt with him leniently, with the authorities seemingly unable to put a stop to his activities.[85]

At the 2012 conference in Tehran, Dieudonné's expressed his views in poorly spoken English, reproduced in the conference documents as follows:

> I do believe in freedom of speech. And I respect everybody who exercises this right. Under the Zionist lobby pressure they are taking away my right. In Hollywood backstage there are some negative Propaganda underway against other people who are against Israel. All this propaganda are (sic) in line with Israel's interest . . . . Hollywood doesn't like any movie to be produced against Zionism ... Discussions against Zionism should be taken serious (sic) ... Zionism should be regarded as an illness. That's why Jews carry most responsibilities to introduce Zionists to the world. Zionism has put man kinds in peril. This illness should be cured by Jews. World public opinion is Zionism. People around the world are determined to abolish Zionism. I as an African feel the need for many movies which intend to reveal different aspects of Zionism. That is what I have done personally to produce documentaries. I will try to focus an American Jews. You know that American Jews are at service of Israel and they are trying to force and encourage others to give service to Israel's interests ... I hope we would be able to meet out human originality and do our social tasks towards revealing Zionists. Real identity and myth of holocaust. Zionist lobby in France is stepping in line with Israel's interests.[86]

Also present at the conference was Sean Stone, son of the famous Hollywood director Oliver Stone, an actor, director, producer, cinematographer and screenwriter in his own right. He converted to Shiite Islam during his visit to Tehran and was quoted as saying that 'Israel and Zionism are not solely supported by Hollywood. Actually, they have bigger and more powerful allies. You see, there are many movies in Hollywood in which the bad guys are Muslims, Chinese or Russians. They are always shown to be threats or the enemies of the world. But I believe the enemies of the US are inside the US.'[87]

The closing session of the conference was addressed by Iranian President Ahmadinejad who reassured the participants that 'just as the Soviet Union was wiped out and today does not exist, so will the Zionist regime soon be wiped out.'[88]

Conclusion

This above analysis and evidence of coalescence is based on available sources appertaining to the programmes and the presentations at these conferences. However, it is fair to assume that aside from the official sessions at these conferences, delegates had the opportunity to mingle, compare notes, exchange tips, enhance their collaboration and learn from each other about successful tactics and strategies they can copy and incorporate in their own individual strategies.

What conclusion can be drawn from this bizarre convergence of ideologies that are otherwise in existential struggle with each other? Awareness of the synergy among representatives of the main anti-Zionist ideologies might help to focus, redefine and improve the fight against anti-Zionism. One may well turn the age-old accusation of a global conspiracy ascribed by antisemites to Jews and Zionists on its head by showing that such collaboration is in fact a significant feature of the anti-Zionist movement. Perhaps this could suggest a clue to a strategy of turning the tables on enemies of Israel, Zionism and Judaism.

Notes

1. Harkabi, *Arab Attitudes to Israel*, 37.
2. Sprinzak, "Anti-Zionism."
3. Resolution adopted by the *International Holocaust Remembrance Alliance*.
4. Press Conference on 12 August 1969.
5. *Jewish Observer*.
6. Ages, *Anti-Semitism versus Anti-Zionism*. See also Litvinoff, *Soviet Anti-Semitism*.
7. http://www.bbc.co.uk/news/magazine-36160928.
8. *The Jewish Chronicle*, 23 June 1917.
9. Avineri, "Anti-Semitism Today: A Symposium," 4, 5.
10. Marcus, "Is the Boycott, Divestment and Sanctions Movement Anti-Semitic?"
11. Freedland, "Is Antizionism Anti-Semitism?"
12. Julius, *Trials of the Diaspora*: 522.
13. "EU-wide rise in anti-Semitism described as 'understandable', *EU Politics News*, 4 March 2009.
14. Bauberot, "La Vie de l'Alliance."
15. Kaplan and Small, "Anti-Israel Sentiment Predicts Anti-Semitism in Europe"; and Staetsky, "Antisemitism in contemporary Great Britain."

16. *Jewish Chronicle*, 2 June & 7 October 2016; *The Times*, 5 October 2016; and Rich, *The Left's Jewish Problem*: 242–6.
17. *Haaretz*, 25 March 2018.
18. Hirsh, *Hostility to Israel and Antisemitism*, 1413.
19. Macpherson, "Report of the Stephen Lawrence Inquiry."
20. *New Statesman*, 11 February 2002.
21. http://www.thejc.com/node/154476.
22. Curtis and Gitelson, *Israel and the Third World*: 335.
23. Troen, "The Campaign to Boycott Israeli Universities," 314.
24. https://www.ngo-monitor.org/reports/ngo_forum_at_durban_conference_/
25. Stellman, *What is Antizionism?* 22.
26. Dahl, *The Observer*, 15 March 2016, http://observer.com/2016/03/intersection ality-and-the-bizarre-world-of-hating-israel/.
27. Freedland, "The Sacking of Long-Bailey shows that, at last, Labour is serious about antisemitism."
28. Stellman, "Christian Anti-Zionism."
29. Ross, "The anti-Semitism Fest."
30. Marx, *On the Jewish Question*, 1–40.
31. Stellman, *What is Antizionism?* 29–33.
32. Ibid, 34–7.
33. Ibid, 38.
34. Lenin, "Critical Remarks on the National Question," 20, 26–9.
35. Lenin, "The Position of the Bund in the Party," 101.
36. Wistrich, *The Jewish Chronicle*, 15 February 1980.
37. Nedava, *Trotsky and the Jews*:209.
38. Stellman, *What is Antizionism?* 43–8.
39. Ibid, 49,50.
40. https://www.adl.org/sites/default/files/documents/assets/pdf/israel-interna tional/israel–middle-east/Top-Ten-2013-Report.pdf#page6
41. Ibid.
42. Ibid.
43. https://archive.md/enCx0
44. https://www.ngo-monitor.org/ngos/codepink/; https://www.codepink.org/let ters_to_mayor_brigitte_merk_erbe
45. Laqueur, *A History of Zionism*, 385–407.
46. Ibid.
47. Zieve, "This Week in History: Herzl, Rabbis Clash on Zionism."
48. Press release by the "Protest Rabbis," in *Theodor Herzl, A Portrait for his Age*.
49. Stellman, *What is Antizionism?* 76–7.
50. *Encyclopaedia Judaica*, vol. 12, 1002,1003.
51. *Yediot Ahronot*, 21 February 1975.
52. Ibid.
53. *Jerusalem Post International Edition*, 2–8 November 1980.
54. *United Nations General Assembly*, 30th Session, 1975, Agenda item 68,A/10,341, Annexe.
55. Weissmandel, *Min Hameitsar*.
56. Shonfeld, *The Holocaust Victims Accuse*.
57. https://www.nkusa.org/activities/Speeches/2006Iran-ACohen.cfm
58. Ibid.
59. Ibid.

60. https://www.scribd.com/document/119868007/Hollywoodism-2nd-Conference
61. Ibid.
62. Ibid.
63. Poliakov, *Histoire de* l'antisemitisme, vol. 1955, 1961, 1977.
64. *The Complete Diaries of Theodor Herzl*, vol. 4: 1602–3.
65. *Message de Sa Beatitude Maximos V Hakim, Conference Mondiale des Chretienspour la Palestine, Cahier du Temoignage Chretien,22.*
66. Stephensizer.com.
67. https://www.independent.co.uk/news/uk/home-news/vicar-investigated-over-facebook-post-linking-to-anti-semitic-article-911-israel-did-it-10012794.html.
68. https://www.jpost.com/Jewish-World/Jewish-News/Group-says-Church-of-England-vicar-anti-Semitic
69. Ibid.
70. https://archive.md/enCx0
71. https://www.youtube.com/watch?v=kgQSPcLKS_c
72. Cohn, *Warrant for Genocide.*
73. Smith, *The Cross and the Flag*, 20 March 1973, in Forster and Epstein: 297.
74. Ibid., 19 April 1973.
75. Stellman, *What is Antizionism?* 54–5.
76. "Nazi Terror Scare a Zionist Hoax" *National Front News*, November-December 1980, 1.
77. Stellman, *What is Antizionism?* 58–9.
78. https://cst.org.uk/news/latest-news/2018/10/23/an-obituary-for-holocaust-denial.
79. Robert Faurisson, text sent to a number of personalities in Thion, 'Verite Historique ou Verite Politique', 93.
80. https://www.scribd.com/document/119868007/Hollywoodism-2nd-Conference
81. Ibid.
82. Stellman, *What is Antizionism?*81-2.
83. Ibid, 83–93.
84. https://jcpa.org/article/french-jewry-dieudonne-affair/
85. Ibid.
86. https://www.scribd.com/document/119868007/Hollywoodism-2nd-Conference
87. Ibid.
88. https://www.independent.co.uk/news/world/middle-east/defiant-ahmadinejad-revels-at-holocaust-event-428232.html

Disclosure statement

No potential conflict of interest was reported by the author.

Bibliography

Ages, A. "Anti-Semitism versus Anti-Zionism." *Conservative Judaism* 31, no. 4 (1972 Summer).

Avineri, S. "Anti-Semitism Today: A Symposium." *Patterns of Prejudice* 16, no. 4 (1984 October).

Bauberot, J. 1969. "La Vie De l'Alliance." *Herytem*, May-July

Cohn, N. *Warrant for Genocide, the Myth of the Jewish World Conspiracy and the Protocols of Zion.* Harper & Row, London, 1966.

Curtis, M., and S. A. Gitelson, ed.. *Israel in the Third World.* Transaction Books, New Brunswick, New Jersey, 1976.

Dahl, Z. 2016. *The Observer*, March 15. http://observer.com/2016/03/intersectional ity-and-the-bizarre-world-of-hating-israel/

"EU-wide Rise in anti-Semitism Described as "Understandable." 2009. *EU Politics News*, March 4.

Encyclopaedia Judaica. Vol. 12. The Macmillan Company,1971.

Faurisson, R. *Text Sent to a Number of Personalities in Thion, S. Verite Historique Ou Verite Politique.* La Vielle Taupe, Paris, 1980.

Freedland, J. "Is Antizionism Anti-Semitism?." In *A New Antisemitism? Debating Judeophobia in 21st-Century Britain*, edited by P. Iganski and B. Kosmin. Profile Books, 2003.

Freedland, J. 2020. "The Sacking of Long-Bailey Shows That, at Last, Labour Is Serious about Antisemitism." *The Guardian*, June 26.

Haaretz, 2018 March 25.

Harkabi, Y. *Arab Attitudes to Israel.* Transaction Books, 1974.

Hirsh, D. "Hostility to Israel and Antisemitism: Toward a Sociological Approach." *Journal for the Study of Antisemitism* 5, no. 1 (2013).

https://archive.md/enCx0

https://cst.org.uk/news/latest-news/2018/10/23/an-obituary-for-holocaust-denial

https://jcpa.org/article/french-jewry-dieudonne-affair/

https://www.adl.org/sites/default/files/documents/assets/pdf/israel-international/ israel–middle-east/Top-Ten-2013-Report.pdf#page6

https://www.codepink.org/letters_to_mayor_brigitte_merk_erbe

https://www.independent.co.uk/news/uk/home-news/vicar-investigated-over-facebook-post-linking-to-anti-semitic-article-911-israel-did-it-10012794.html

https://www.independent.co.uk/news/world/middle-east/defiant-ahmadinejad-revels-at-holocaust-event-428232.html

https://www.jpost.com/Jewish-World/Jewish-News/Group-says-Church-of-England -vicar-anti-Semitic

https://www.ngo-monitor.org/ngos/codepink/

https://www.ngo-monitor.org/reports/ngo_forum_at_durban_conference_/

https://www.nkusa.org/activities/Speeches/2006Iran-ACohen.cfm

https://www.scribd.com/document/119868007/Hollywoodism-2nd-Conference

https://www.youtube.com/watch?v=kgQSPcLKS_c

Jewish Chronicle, 2016. June 2 and October 7.

Jewish Observer.

Julius, A. *Trials of the Diaspora – A History of Anti-Semitism in England.* Oxford University Press, 2010.

Kaplan, E. H., and C. E. Small. "Anti-Israel Sentiment Predicts Anti-Semitism in Europe." *The Journal of Conflict Resolution* 50, no. 4, August.

Laqueur, W. *A History of Zionism*. Schocken, 2003.

Lenin, V. I. "Critical Remarks on the National Question." *Collected Works* 7 (1961).

Lenin, V. I. "The Position of the Bund in the Party." *Collected Works* 20 (1964).

Litvinoff, E. *Soviet Anti-Semitism: The Paris Trial*. Wildwood House, 1974.

Macpherson, W. 1999. "Report of the Stephen Lawrence Inquiry." February 24 . https://www.gov.uk/government/publications/the-stephen-lawrence-inquiry.

Marcus, K. L. "Is the Boycott, Divestment and Sanctions Movement Anti-Semitic?." In *The Case against Academic Boycotts of Israel*, edited by E. Nelson and G. N. Brahm. MLA Members for Scholar Rights, 2015.

Marx, K. *On the Jewish Question, Karl Marx Early Writings*, ed. T. B. Bottomore. McGraw-Hill, 1963.

Message de Sa Beatitude Maximos V Hakim. *Conference Mondiale des Chretiens pour la Palestine, Cahiers du Temoignage Chretien*. no. 52.

"'Nazi' Terror Scare A Zionist Hoax." *National Front News* no. 28 (1980 November-December).

Nedava, J. *Trotsky and the Jews*. Jewish Publication Society of America, 1972.

New Statesman, 2002 February 11.

November 1. http://www.bbc.co.uk/news/magazine-36160928

2016. November 1. http://www.thejc.com/node/154476

Patai, R., ed.. *The Complete Diaries of Theodor Herzl*, 1602,1603. Vol. 4. Herzl Press and Thomas Yoseloff, 1960.

Poliakov, L. "*Histoire de* l'antisemitisme." *Calmann-Levy* 1955, (1961). 1977.

Press release by the 'Protest Rabbis'. *Theodor Herzl, A Portrait for His Age*, edited by L. Lewisohn, 1955.

Reb Shonfeld, M. *The Holocaust Victims Accuse*. Neturei Karta of U.S.A., 1977.

Reid Ross, A. 2019. "The anti-Semitism Fest Where Russian Spies, Code Pink, David Duke and the Nation of Islam Make Friends and Influence People." *Haaretz*, March 14.

"Resolution Adopted by the International Holocaust Remembrance Alliance." https://www.holocaustremembrance.com/working-definition-antisemitism

Rich, D. *The Left's Jewish Problem: Jeremy Corbyn, Israel and Antisemitism*. Biteback Publishing, 2016.

Smith. 1973. *The Cross and the Flag*, March 20. Forster, A. and Epstein, B. R. *The New Anti-Semitism*, McGraw-Hill Company, 1974.

Sprinzak, E. "Anti-Zionism: From Delegitimization to Dehumanization." Fall *Forum* no. 53 (1984).

Staetsky, D. I. 2017. "Antisemitism in Contemporary Great Britain – A Study of Attitudes Towards Jews and Israel." *JPR Report*, September.

Stellman, H. "Christian Anti-Zionism." *The Wiener Library Bulletin* no. 34 (1981). new series nos. 53 54.

Stellman, H. *What Is Antizionism? (...and Is It Antisemitic?) A Short Handbook for Activists and Analysts*. Aspekt, 2019.

Stephensizer.com

"The Jewish Chronicle." 1917. June 23.

"The Jerusalem Post International Edition." 1980. November 2-8.

The Times. 2016 October 5.

Troen, I. "The Campaign to Boycott Israeli Universities: Historical and Ideological Sources." In *The Case against Academic Boycotts of Israel*, edited by E. Nelson and G. N. Brahm. MLA Members for Scholar Rights, 2015.

"United Nations General Assembly." 1975. 30th Session. Agenda item 68, A/10341, Annex.

Weissmandel, M. D. *Min Hameitsar*. Nitra Yeshiva, 1960.

Wistrich, R. S. 1980. "The Jewish Chronicle." February 15

Yediot Aharonot, 1975 February 21.

Zieve, T. 2012. "This Week in History: Herzl, Rabbis Clash on Zionism." *Jerusalem Post*, July 15.

The Covert War: From BDS to De-legitimization to Antisemitism

Lev Topor

ABSTRACT
The Boycott, Divestment and Sanctions (BDS) movement, a Palestinian-led anti-Israel international campaign, seems necessary to many 'progressive' activists, especially from the radical left. However, it promotes antisemitism through boycotting; legitimisation of terrorism through whitewashing; the destruction of Israel via support for the Palestinian 'right of return'; and acceptance of antisemitic anti-Zionism by associating Jews, all Jews, with Israel.

The Boycott, Divestment and Sanctions (BDS) movement, a Palestinian-led anti-Israel international campaign, has been enthusiastically embraced by many progressive activists, especially from the radical left. The BDS campaign de-legitimises the State of Israel and seeks its eventual destruction through its endorsement of the Palestinian 'right of return,' the standard Palestinian euphemism for Israel's destruction via demographic subversion.[1] This denial of the Jewish right to national self-determination is a hallmark of antisemitism, as defined by the widely accepted working definition antisemitism by the International Holocaust Remembrance Alliance (2016),[2] as is its collective association of all Jews, regardless of their worldviews and ideologies, with Israeli policies, thus holding them culpable for its supposed misdeeds. Hence the designation of the BDS movement as antisemitic by several states, notably by the German parliament.[3]

This article views the BDS as a form of soft power used to de-legitimise an opponent in the international arena. Palestinians adopted this non-violent strategy after the traditional hard measures of military attacks and terrorism failed to undermine the Jewish state. Equally important, 9/11 made Palestinian terrorism highly unpopular thus putting a premium on non-violent challenges to Israel.

The article has three parts. The first explains how the Palestinians and their supporters decided to embrace soft power, the second discusses the soft power tools deployed against Israel, such as BDS, which has led to de-legitimisation and antisemitism, while the third part looks at the activities of the BDS movement as a two-dimensional effort with a respectable and politically-correct façade and a darker covert sphere. The former serves as a platform for intersectionality, where human rights activists, civil society advocates, and minority groups sympathisers can unite in support of the Palestinian cause. The latter comprises the covert and less savoury activities of the BDS, including terror groups and their state patrons. Such a bifurcated structure helps to deceive the well-meaning 'virtuous' members of the pro-Palestinian coalition.

The BDS movement and the utilisation of soft power

In his seminal 1990 study, Joseph S. Nye, Jr. noted that after the end of the Cold War the definition of power had changed; instead of hard power and coercion, a softer and yet at times much more effective use of power came into vogue. As he put it, there was a shift in perception from the utility of guns and bombs towards economy, culture, political values, and global ethics. While used mostly in International Relations (IR) and International Security (IS), the concept of soft power is also valid in national movements and even terror organisations.[4]

The Palestinians were quick to make the transition from hard power terrorism to the soft power of global ethics and human rights issues, of which Boycott, Divestment, and Sanction (BDS) was their signature achievement. Leila Khaled, the terrorist who hijacked TWA Flight 840 in 1969 and attempted another hijacking the following year, is a good example in this context. Nowadays, Khaled, who has a road named after her in the south African town of Johannesburg, acts as a public speaker and fund raiser for the BDS and its affiliates.[5]

The ideational origins of the BDS movement can be found in the Arab-Israeli conflict and the subsequent direct engagement of the Palestinians with Israel. The defeat of the Arab states in the 1967 war strengthened the Palestinian belief that there would be no significant results without the intensification of the political and armed struggle. Yasser Arafat and Khalil Wazir, the two main founders of Fatah in the late 1950s, decided on an all-out terror campaign. Fatah pioneered terror attacks against Israel and later joined other terror groups into the PLO (created in 1964), seizing its leadership in February 1969, with Arafat becoming PLO Chairman, a post he held till his death in November 2004.

Never abandoning terrorism despite his ostensible commitment to peace through the Oslo process, in September 2000 Arafat launched an all-out war of terror (euphemised as the 'al-Aqsa Intifada'), which lasted for nearly five years.[6] However, several factors worked against the continuation of this form of hard power, not least Israel's gradual suppression of the Palestinian terror campaign and its unilateral disengagement from the Gaza Strip in the summer of 2005, which by and large terminated the Palestinian terror war.[7]

Though Hamas and the Palestinian Islamic Jihad chose to sustain their terror strategy from its enclave in the Gaza Strip, the PLO and the PLO-dominated Palestinian Authority (PA) came to appreciate soft power tactics. Taking a page from the black struggle in South Africa against apartheid, a number of activists such as Omar Barghouti, a graduate of Tel Aviv University in Israel, decided to launch in 2004 the Palestinian Campaign for the Academic and Cultural Boycott of Israel (PACBI). Israeli academics such as Adi Ophir and Rachel Giora who had toyed with the boycott idea for some time provided additional inspiration.[8]

Noting Israel's 'refusal to accept the inalienable rights of the refugees and displaced stipulated in and protected by international law' (i.e. the Palestinian 'right of return'), the PACBI manifesto vowed to 'contribute to the struggle for Palestinian freedom, justice and equality. It advocates for a boycott of Israeli academic and cultural institutions for their deep and persistent complicity in Israel's denial of Palestinian rights that are stipulated in international law.'[9] In the summer of 2005, the BDS was officially launched. As Barghouti recalled in his book: 'On 9 July 2005, Palestinian civil society launched what is now widely recognised as a qualitatively different phase in the global struggle for Palestinians freedom, justice, and self-determination against a ruthless, powerful system of oppression.'[10] In a nod to the civil nature of the struggle, more than 170 Palestinian civil society groups, political parties, refugee rights associations, trade union federations, woman's unions, NGO networks and other grassroots organisations signed up to support the BDS movement.

The BDS movement and its activists demand three, seemingly non-violent things from the state of Israel: to end 'the occupation and colonization of all Arab lands' and dismantle the security barrier; to recognise the rights of Israel's Arab-Palestinian citizens to full civil equality; to allow Palestinian refugees to return to their homes and properties as allegedly stipulated in UN Resolution 194 (i.e. leading to Israel's demographic subversion).[11]

The language of the demands indicated that movement had identified the Jewish state's weakest link – public support in the international community. The goal of the project was to use the South African model to de-legitimise and ostracise Israel from the international community under the broad umbrella of boycotts, sanctions and divestments. For instance, PACBI's guideline for the international cultural boycott of Israel states that even normalisation projects are 'boycottable.' In other words, unless Israel accedes to the maximalist demands of the Palestinians (i.e. its effective demise), it should be considered a pariah state.[12]

Ironically, as Robert Fine and Phillip Spencer argue, the anti-Israel project started by reviving the historical 'Jewish Question,' which, as is well known, had generated considerable sympathy for the homeless Jews. For thousands of years Jews were persecuted, discriminated against, blamed for each and every wrong or evil event. As the renowned antisemitism scholar, Robert Wistrich wrote, the road from deicide to genocide was not linear but was tenacious. To tackle the millenarian 'Jewish problem,' which culminated in the Holocaust, the international community acquiesced in the establishment of a Jewish state, as stipulated in the November 1947 UN General Assembly partition resolution.[13]

The hard-won legitimacy of the Jewish state did not last long. The radical left, especially post-colonialists, Marxists, and other leftist activists rushed to proclaim the new state a racist endeavour. They perceived Israel as a colonialist, imperialist, racist, and aggressive state. The 1975 UN General Assembly resolution 3379 equated Zionism with racism. And while the resolution triggered a large body of writings, its anti-Jewish implications were not sufficiently realised at the time. Since most Jews supported Israel, a 'racist state,' they should be considered racists, according to the radical leftist circles. As the BDS campaign evolved, its growing antisemitic character has emerged (beyond its openly pronounced antisemitic goals noted above, which are largely undecipherable to western audiences).[14]

For instance, local BDS initiatives have created the so-called 'Israeli Apartheid Free Zones' (IAFZ). The IAFZ is a contemporary initiative to isolate and boycott Israeli goods, as stated in the BDS website:

> Building on a rich history of Nuclear Free Cities and Apartheid Free areas during the campaign against South African Apartheid, Israeli Apartheid Free Zones is a new initiative that aims to build community support for the Palestinian struggle and for BDS. In Spain, community activists are inviting shops, restaurants, community centers, businesses, trade unions and other civil society organizations to declare themselves to be an Israeli Apartheid Free Zone.[15]

These BDS activities carry the uncomfortable echoes of the first stage of de-legitimisation of Jews in Nazi Germany. Businesses were marked with yellow Stars of David, and Jew-Free Zones (JFZ) were created. Filip Friedman, the renowned historian who testified in the Nuremberg trials wrote: '[T]he Nazi propaganda machine still needed time to present to the outside world its justification for the isolation of the Jews.'[16] The BDS movement also tries to justify Israeli and Jewish isolation, using the IAFZ-JFZ equivalent. Attuned to its Nazi past, in May 2019 the German Bundestag ruled that the BDS movement was antisemitic. The resolution explained that the 'Don't Buy' stickers were reminiscent of the Nazi-era boycott of Jewish businesses, 'Judenboykott.'[17]

From BDS to de-legitimisation to antisemitism

Scholarly literature on the soft-power-driven change in international perceptions indicates a complex and multilayered phenomenon. In the BDS case, three factors affected the transition from a boycott movement to de-legitimisation to antisemitism. The first is ideational, stemming from the critical philosophy best personified by Michel Foucault. The noted French philosopher was a strident critic of European hegemony, colonialism, and imperialism, and while he did not address the Jews or Israel, his legions of followers in the BDS circles were quick to argue that Israel is heir to the West's colonial-imperialist policy. In their tendentious rendition of history, Israel was an aggressive colonial state with no indigenous stakes in the region, which colonised the weak Palestinian populations, inflicting a lasting damage on their descendants.[18]

A number of scholars have amplified this approach. Brian Klug from Oxford University argues that Jews were actually the weak and oppressed ones but since the establishment of Israel they became the oppressors and the Palestinians were relegated to the role of the oppressed. While Jews established their own state and simultaneously climbed the social ladder in many Western countries, the Palestinians continued to suffer from various forms of Western colonisation. Thus, they could not progress and evolve. In the view of Klug (himself a Jew), the Jews managed to become the 'Privileged Whites' and the Arabs and Palestinians the 'Coloured Slaves.'[19]

Radical-leftists such as Professor Jacqueline Rose from the Birkbeck Institute for the Humanities argue that Jews and Israelis are obsessed with the Holocaust and use its memories to execute controversial policies. Congresswoman Rashida Tlaib, a freshman representative in the US Congress took this argument further by blaming the Holocaust for the misfortunes of the Palestinians: 'There's always kind of a calming feeling I tell folks when I think of the Holocaust ... and the fact that it was my ancestors – Palestinians – who lost their land and some lost their lives, their livelihood ... all of it was in the name of trying to create a safe haven for Jews, post-Holocaust ... and I love the fact that my ancestors provided that in many ways.'[20]

It is easy to see how Foucault's reasoning helped with the negative transition. Since his post-colonial thought sanctifies the weaker actors no matter their actions, while vilifying the stronger ones, it drives the BDS movement against the 'stronger Jews.' In turn, some BDS events openly promote antisemitism, including the July 2017 'Temple Mount' demonstration in London where Israeli flags were burnt, Hezbollah flags were waved, and antisemitic tropes were widely promoted. In recent years, radical-leftists and even violent Islamists have joined ranks to help with BDS under the banner of anti-globalisation, anti-capitalism, and anti-Zionism. Interestingly, the Islamists added an eschatological reason to the news coalition: they consider the Jewish state an alien implant on Islamic land and an obstacle to the restoration of the Islamic Caliphate.[21]

The second reason for the negative transition is circumstantial and emotional. De-legitimisation and antisemitism can be the outcome of a legitimate attempt to criticise Israeli policies. As the sociologist David Hirsh explains, a racist act is clear and it is perceived as such, but a racist effect is not perceived as a racist act. A racist effect can be perceived as harmless and legitimate at the beginning but exerting the wrong influence at the end. Thus, antisemitism can be the outcome of a non-racist, legitimate, criticism. In addition, some radical-leftists find an antisemitic 'alibi' by focusing on Israel instead of Jews as their main target, though still using common antisemitic stereotypes and tropes.[22]

Emotions and tempers come into play as well. Some radical-leftists, such as the famous British film director Ken Loach, argue that antisemitism can be 'understandable' or even 'justified' since there is a certain push-factor for 'progressive' critical radical-leftists and many others. Antisemitism by itself is not socially acceptable but if it comes as an act of anger at Israeli policies it is more understandable. They claim to simply lose their temper because of their emotional distress at Palestinian suffering. It is impossible of course to empirically assess this 'emotional outburst' argument, but, according to one observer, it makes the BDS-driven propaganda more palatable because antisemitism is perceived as a negative but anti-Zionism is considered a badge of honour in the radical left.[23]

The third reason for the negative transition is the indirect legitimisation of racism and the acceptance of it. Hirsh's sociological theory of act and effect postulates that non-racist acts can generate negative, racist, outcomes. Such an outcome is especially probable when leading public figures and politicians influence public discourse. Their non-racist, legitimate actions can cast a protective shadow over racist acts in cases where both the non-racist and racist acts share common themes. For instance, if the common motif is criticism of Israeli policies, then it can be made legitimately by politicians or it can be made in a racist manner by extremists. However, if the two public figures support each other, then legitimate politicians can cast a protective shadow over racist extremists. In other words, they can whitewash the racist arguments and make their purveyors socially acceptable. Even a simple action such as providing a platform, hosting a speech or being photographed with racists can increase the level of social tolerance for racist figures. The Venn diagram below (Figure 1) describes how antisemitism can become socially legitimate; the 'legitimate' circle is slightly larger than the 'non-legitimate' one.[24]

Jeremy Corbyn, the former leader of the British Labour Party who holds some radical leftist views, exemplifies this situation. Corbyn, a longtime critic

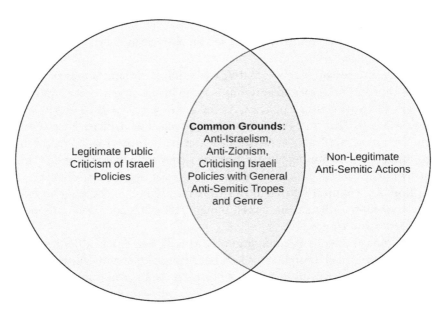

Figure 1. Common grounds between legitimate criticism and antisemitism. *Note that the 'legitimate' circle is slightly larger than the 'non-legitimate' one.

of Israel and supporter of the Palestinians, is not openly antisemitic though he made some antisemitic statements for which he was forced to apologise. Corbyn's statements were emotional and circumstantial at times. He even campaigned for the fight against antisemitism and racism. However, Corbyn is also known for his connections to terror organisations, such as Hamas, Hezbollah, the IRA and to extremists such as the openly antisemitic Raed Salah and Holocaust denier Paul Eisen. In October 2014, Corbyn was photographed posing with extremists, terrorists and antisemites, while laying a wreath in honour of the terrorists who carried out the 1972 Munich Olympic massacre. Following a report by the British Equality and Human Rights Commission (EHRC) in late 2020, which concluded that Labour party leadership did not sufficiently tackle antisemitism, acting party leader Sir Keir Starmer, Corbyn's successor, suspended his predecessor for downplaying antisemitism during his term.[25]

Bobby Gillespie from the alternative rock band Primal Scream is another example in this category. Before the 2019 Eurovision song contest in Tel Aviv, he commented that Israel should not exist. He also derided Madonna, the Queen of Pop, as a 'total prostitute' for preforming in Israel. At the same time, Gillespie expressed admiration for at least two famous Jews, Bob Dylan and Karl Marx, apparently to show that he was not antisemitic – only a harsh critic of Israel. In practice, Gillespie de-legitimised the right of Jews for their own state, associated Israel with negative tropes, and labelled Israel supporters as enemies of humanity. Since Gillespie has many admirers, they could be influenced by his antisemitism.[26]

From words to actions: covert events, masquerading activists, and deceived leftists

As noted above, antisemitism frequently masquerades itself as anti-Israelism, anti-Zionism, or some other inane 'anti' cause. Radical-leftists in particular are adamant that their BDS activity has nothing to do with antisemitism. For them, antisemitism is either religiously motived or follows Nazi ideology. Listening to the former London Mayor Ken Livingstone, former Labour leader Corbyn, or the former leader of the British Respect Party, George Galloway, one can be fooled into believing that antisemites still wear Nazi uniforms and salute with a *Seig Hail*.[27]

It is thus hardly surprising that supporters mask the antisemitic and anti-Zionist foundations of the BDS movement with slogans taken from the post-colonial, anti-globalisation, anti-capitalist, and anti-Western ideologies.[28]

This duality is best understood by looking at the BDS movement as a two-dimensional affair – a respectable façade that is politically-correct and see-mingly legitimate and a darker covert sphere. The public dimension of the BDS movement includes all of its public relations, events, press releases, calls for actions, and so on. In most cases, the radical-leftists preside over the public dimension, but the covert dimension is filled with a core network of foundations and organisations in the Middle East and Western Asia. Past and present convicted terrorists hold key positions in the BDS movement and while they try to avoid using explicit antisemitic actions in the front sphere, they certainly do so in the back sphere.[29]

One of the most significant examples of a covert event was the Durban (South Africa) World Conference Against Racism in September 2001. Following the December 1997 UN General Assembly resolution 52/111, which implemented the continuation of the programme of actions to combat racism and racial discrimination, the Iranian authorities organised a regional anti-racism conference in Iran that set the agenda for Durban. The Durban event, named 'World Conference against Racism, Racial Discrimination, Xenophobia and Related Intolerance' hosted thousands of representatives from over 1500 organisations. The public dimension of the conference was legitimate as few could disagree with its stated goal: 'We declare that for the purpose of the present Declaration, the victims of racism, racial discrimina-tion, xenophobia and related intolerance are individuals or groups of indi-viduals who are or have been negatively affected by, subjected to, or targets of these scourges.'[30]

The covert dimension included Durban's organisers and influencers from anti-Zionist countries like Iran, Syria, and other Middle Eastern states that deny Israel's right to exist. These backstage activists inundated the conference with allegations of human rights violations, war crimes and racism, allegedly made by Israel. The declaration of the Durban conference reflected these charges: Article 164 stated that Israel targeted mostly children, women, and refugees, article 425 called for a complete political embargo on Israel, article 426 condemned Israel's supporters. In protest, the American and Israeli delegation withdrew from the conference after a few days.[31]

The Iranian-backed annual Al-Quds Day rally that took place in London on 2 June 2019 is another example of a covert event. The Islamic Human Rights Commission (IHRC) stated that "'The Quds Day is a universal day. It is not an exclusive day for Quds itself. It is a day for the oppressed to rise and stand up against the arrogant" – Imam Khomeini.' The language of the website sounds reasonable enough for people, specifically from the left, in order to embrace the rally. They would never reject a rally made for the 'oppressed to rise and stand up against the arrogant.' The front sphere was fully legitimate, just as with the Durban example.[32]

However, the average participant was not aware that the rally was organised and funded by anti-Zionist Iran, and organisations such as the IHRC and the Palestine Solidarity Campaign (PSC). For instance, the IHRC named the French newspaper Charlie Hebdo 'Islamophobe of the Year' in 2015, just two months after Islamic terrorists massacred twelve of its staff in Paris. The PSC, which has Corbyn's support, constantly shared antisemitic cartoons and conspiracy theories against Jews and Israel.[33]

The annual Al-Quds Day rally itself is promoted to the European public as a legitimate rally. The 2019 rally itself, however, was filled with antisemitism and anti-Zionism. As in the past, participants burnt Israeli and American flags, chanted Hamas-like slogans such as 'From the river to the sea, Palestine will be free' (i.e. a Palestinian state established on Israel's ruins), 'Death to Israel', 'Death to America', and waved Hamas and Hezbollah flags. Foreign agents, terrorists and radical-leftists marched together against Israel and the Jews. The rally was secured and guarded by the British Metropolitan police. The rally bore a similarity to the Battle of Cable Street in East London (October 1936), when the Metropolitan police protected the antisemitic, fascist march of Oswald Mosley's British Union of Fascists. Both rallies were led by seemingly legitimate organisations, both were protected in the name of free speech, both were viciously antisemitic.[34]

There are numerous examples of activists posing as legitimate human rights activists and attracting the support of radical-leftists in their front sphere while acting in a non-legitimate manner in the covert space. The above-noted Leila Khaled is one of them. Ismail Patel, founder of the Friends of Al-Aqsa organisation is another significant example. Patel is strongly associated with Hamas, he was on board the violent Mavi Marmara flotilla in May 2010, and met and endorsed Hamas leader Ismail Haniyeh in 2011. Yet Patel operates in Britain, raising funds, and mobilising supporters.[35]

The radical left and even parts of the European and American mainstream left have been deceived by the covert war of the extremists. Because they value anti-racism, anti-capitalism, and promote human rights, notably Palestinian human rights, they are easy targets. They either ignore or are unaware of the fact that the foundations that promote these events are infected with antisemitism, anti-Zionism, and still harbour dreams of violent elimination of Israel. In this sense, the shift from hard power to Nye's soft power is apparently only tactical since the goal of 'disappearing' Israel is still on the agenda. As the former terrorist Khaled stated in a public speech in Germany in 2016: 'Nevertheless, our people has proven, day in and day out, that it is much greater than those (leaders), and that negotiations will be held only with knives and weapons.'[36]

This deception is even deeper than expected because the BDS movement has close relations with hard-power groups such as Hezbollah, Hamas, and the Popular Front for the Liberation of Palestine (PFLP). For instance, in June 2019 the German Bank for Social Economy closed the account of a pro-BDS group after the *Shurat HaDin* Law Centre revealed that the group helped finance the PFLP, which the United States and European countries define as a terrorist entity. Iran, Syria and Turkey, known human right violators, have been also known to support BDS through covert means that preserves the façade of the human rights movement.[37]

Conclusion

This article sought to explain how the BDS movement covertly promotes de-legitimisation and antisemitism against the State of Israel and Jews. Having failed to achieve their goals through terrorism, the Palestinians turned to soft power in the form of the BDS movement to promote their original goal. As PACBI co-founder Omar Barghouti stated, the movement signalled a new phase in the Palestinian struggle against Israel. It is not clear whether Barghouti and his cohorts understood the negative transformative dynamics of their movement, but, as the article demonstrates, the BDS campaign generated Israel de-legitimisation and antisemitism. This negative transition occurred because of a number of factors that worked in favour of the Palestinians, notably the widely popular Foucauldian philosophy and the related post-colonial theory. The latter presented the Palestinians as the poster children of oppressed indigenous people and Israel as their oppressive hegemon. With such a starring role, the Palestinians achieved the permanent status of victimhood and garnered the sympathy of the 'progressive' community worldwide. By the same token, Israel and by extension, the Jews, were cast as the eternal villains in the post-colonial drama.

Having seized upon the human rights and post-colonial narrative, the BDS movement and its supporters enacted it in countless activities ranging from simple rallies to elaborate performances such as the Apartheid Week staged on university campuses. While the public space of BDS activity is designed to project a benign and humane façade, the covert part harbours the antisemitic and violent supporters of the movement. It is more than a passing irony that many of the covert actors, including terror groups and Iran that sponsors the al Quds Day rallies, are violent entities and serial human rights violators.

Exposing these build-in contradictions is the first step to unravel the elaborate deception architecture that the BDS movement has erected. Furthering research into the negative transitions that turned legitimate criticism of Israel into a modern form of antisemitism is also essential in order to combat the BDS phenomenon.

Notes

1. This was already expressed in the BDS's launching announcement that called inter alia for "Respecting, protecting and promoting the rights of Palestinian refugees to return to their homes and properties as stipulated in UN resolution 194." See: "Palestinian Civil Society Call for BDS."
2. IHRA, "Working Definition of Antisemitism."
3. Reuters, "Germany designates BDS Israel boycott movement as anti-Semitic," May 17, 2019.
4. Nye, "Soft Power."
5. Jerusalem Post Staff, "Johannesburg Names Road After Palestinian Terrorist Leila Khaled."
6. Karsh, *Arafat's War*.
7. Kabha, *The Palestinian People* 255-331.
8. Barnett, "Neo-Marxist Israeli academics."
9. PACBI Statement.
10. Barghouti, *BDS* 4-5.
11. Ibid., 6.
12. Sharansky, "3D Test for Antisemitism"; and Radoshitzky, "Containing the Link Between BDS and Antisemitism."
13. Fine and Spencer, *Antisemitism and the Left*; Wistrich, *A Lethal Obsession* 104-5.
14. Topor, "Explanations of Antisemitism."
15. Apartheid Free Zones, BDS Movement, https://bdsmovement.net/apartheid-free-zones.
16. Friedman, "The Jewish ghettos of the Nazi era," 73.
17. Bennhold, "German Parliament Deems BDS MovementAnti-Semitic"; and Michman, *The Emergence of Jewish Ghettos* 1-14.
18. See note 14 above.
19. Klug, "Interrogating 'New Antisemitism'."
20. Liebovitz, "Rashida Tlaib's Unbelievable Lies"; and Heni, "Antisemitism in UK Academia."
21. Karagiannis and McCauley, "The emerging red-green alliance"; Zieve, "Protesters burn Israeli flag in London Temple Mount demonstration"; and Topor, "Explanations of Antisemitism."

22. Geras, "Alibi Antisemitism"; and Hirsh, "Hostility to Israel and Antisemitism."
23. MacShane, *Globalising Hatred* 1-18; and Paul, "British Film Director."
24. Kantor Centre, "Antisemitism Worldwide 2018"; and Hirsh, "Hostility to Israel."
25. Simcox, "Jeremy Corbyn Has a Soft Spot for Extremists"; Sabbagh, "Jeremy Corbyn: I was present at wreath-laying but don't think I was involved"; and Stewart, Elgot and Parveen, "Keir Starmer denies Jeremy Corbyn Labour whip despite end of suspension."
26. Moore, "The Venn diagram of misogyny."
27. See note 14 above.
28. Karagiannis and McCauley, "The emerging red-green alliance."
29. Ministry of Strategic Affairs, "Terrorists in Suites."
30. Report of the World Conference against Racism, Racial Discrimination, Xenophobia and Related Intolerance.
31. Steinberg, "From Durban to the Goldstone Report."
32. Islamic Human Rights Commission, "Al Quds Day 2019."
33. Richards, "Charlie Hebdo given 'Islamophobe of the Year' award"; and Sleigh, "Swathe of anti-Semitic abuse is uncovered at pro-Palestinian group backed by Jeremy Corbyn."
34. Tazpit News Agency, "Anti-Israel Marchers in the Center of London Espouse Antisemitism"; and Thurlow, "The Straw that broke the Camel's back: Public order, civil liberties and the battle of Cable street."
35. See note 29 above.
36. Visser, Lubbers and Kraaykamp, Jaspers, "Support for radical left ideologies in Europe."
37. Weinthal, "German Bank and BDS Group"; *Times of Israel*, "UN condemns 'severe' human rights violations in Iran."

Acknowledgments

The author wishes to thank Prof. Jonathan Rynhold and Prof. Jonathan Fox for their guidance and support during his research. He would also like to thank Dr. Dana Barnett for her helpful and pleasant editorial work for this issue.

Disclosure statement

No potential conflict of interest was reported by the author.

ORCID

Lev Topor ⓘ http://orcid.org/0000-0002-1836-5150

Bibliography

Al-Krenawi, A. *Building Peace Through Knowledge*. Cham: Springer, 2017.

Barghouti, O. *BDS: Boycott, Divestment, Sanctions: The Global Struggle for Palestinian Rights*. Chicago: Haymarket Books, 2011.

Barnett, D. "Neo-Marxist Israeli Academics: From post-Zionism to Antisemitism." *Israel Affairs* 25, no. 1 (2019): 102–117. doi:10.1080/13537121.2018.1554867.

Bennhold, K. "German Parliament Deems B.D.S. Movement Antisemitic." *The New York Times*. Accessed May 17, 2019. https://www.nytimes.com/2019/05/17/world/europe/germany-bds-antisemitic.html

Fine, R., and P. Spencer. *Antisemitism and the Left- on the Return of the Jewish Question*. Manchester: Manchester University Press, 2018.

Foucault, M., and F. Ewald. *"Society Must Be Defended": Lectures at the Collège De France, 1975-1976*. New York: Picador, 2003.

Friedman, P. "The Jewish Ghettos of the Nazi Era." *Jewish Social Studies* 16, no. 1 (1954): 61–88.

Geras, N. 2013. "Alibi Antisemitism." *Fathom*. http://fathomjournal.org/alibi-antisemitism/

Heni, C. "Antisemitism in UK Academia." *Journal for the Study of Antisemitism* 5, no. 1 (2013): 112–127.

Hirsh, D. "Hostility to Israel and Antisemitism: Towards a Sociological Approach." *Journal for the Study of Antisemitism* 5 (2013): 1401–1422.

International Holocaust Remembrance Alliance (IHRA). *Working Definition of Antisemitism*. 2016. https://www.holocaustremembrance.com/resources/working-definitions-charters/working-definition-antisemitism

Islamic Human Rights Commission. "Al Quds Day 2019." https://www.ihrc.org.uk/activities/events/21700-al-quds-day-2019/

Jerusalem Post Staff. "Johannesburg Names Road After Palestinian Terrorist Leila Khaled." *The Jerusalem Post*. Accessed December 3, 2018. https://www.jpost.com/Arab-Israeli-Conflict/Johannesburg-names-road-after-Palestinian-terrorist-Leila-Khaled-573416

Kabha, M. *The Palestinian People: Seeking Sovereignty and State*. Boulder, Colorado: Lynne Rienner Publishers, 2013.

Kantor Center. "Antisemitism Worldwide 2018- General Analysis." http://www.kantorcenter.tau.ac.il/sites/default/files/Antisemitism%20Worldwide%202018.pdf

Karagiannis, E., and C. McCauley. "The Emerging Red-green Alliance: Where Political Islam Meets the Radical Left." *Terrorism and Political Violence* 25, no. 2 (2013): 167–182.

Karsh, E. *Arafat's War*. New York: Grove Atlantic, 2003.

Klug, B. "Interrogating 'New Antisemitism'." *Ethnic and Racial Studies* 36, no. 3 (2013): 479–480.

Lappin, S. "The Re-Emergence of the Jewish Question." *Journal of Contemporary Antisemitism* 2, no. 1 (2019): 29–46.

Liebovitz, L. "Rashida Tlaib's Unbelievable Lies." *Tablet Magazine*. Accessed May 13, 2019. https://www.tabletmag.com/scroll/284748/rashida-tlaibs-unbelievable-lies

MacShane, D. *Globalising Hatred: The New Antisemitism*. London: Hachette UK, 2008.

Michman, D. *The Emergence of Jewish Ghettos during the Holocaust*. New York: Cambridge University Press, 2011.

Ministry of Strategic Affairs. "Terrorists in Suites. The Ties between NGOs Promoting BDS and Terrorist Organizations." https://4il.org.il/wp-content/uploads/2019/02/MSA-Terrorists-In-Suits-English-1.pdf

Moore, S. "The Venn Diagram of Misogyny, Antisemitism and Support for Julian Assange Is a Very Strange Thing." *New Statesman*. Accessed May 21, 2019. https://www.newstatesman.com/world/2019/05/venn-diagram-misogyny-antisemitism-and-support-julian-assange-very-strange-thing

Nye, J. S. "Soft Power." *Foreign Policy* 80 (1990): 153–171.

"PACBI Statement: Call for an Academic and Cultural Boycott of Israel." Accessed July 6, 2004. https://bdsmovement.net/pacbi/pacbi-call

"Palestinian Civil Society Call for BDS." BDS Website. https://bdsmovement.net/call

Paul, J. "British Film Director: Rise in Antisemitism Understandable." *The Jerusalem Post*. Accessed March 17, 2009. https://www.jpost.com/International/British-film-director-Rise-in-antisemitism-understandable

Radoshitzky, M. H. "Containing the Link between BDS and Antisemitism." *The Jerusalem Post*. Accessed June 3, 2015. https://www.jpost.com/Opinion/Containing-the-link-between-BDS-and-antisemitism-404964

Report of the World Conference against Racism, Racial Discrimination, Xenophobia and Related Intolerance. 2001. https://www.oas.org/dil/afrodescendants_Durban_Declaration.pdf

Richards, V. "Charlie Hebdo Given 'Islamophobe of the Year' Award." *Independent*. Accessed March 11, 2015. https://www.independent.co.uk/news/world/europe/charlie-hebdo-murdered-staff-given-islamophobe-of-the-year-award-10100317.html

Sabbagh, D. "Jeremy Corbyn: I Was Present at Wreath-laying but Don't Think I Was Involved." *The Guardian*. Accessed August 14, 2018. https://www.theguardian.com/politics/2018/aug/13/jeremy-corbyn-not-involved-munich-olympics-massacre-wreath-laying

Sharansky, N. "3D Test for Antisemitism: Demonization, Double Standards, Delegitimization." *Jewish Political Studies Review* 16 (2004): 3–4.

Simcox, R. "Jeremy Corbyn Has a Soft Spot for Extremists." *Foreign Policy*. Accessed October 3, 2018. https://foreignpolicy.com/2018/10/03/jeremy-corbyn-has-a-soft-spot-for-extremists-ira-hamas-hezbollah-britain-labour/

Sleigh, S. "Swathe of Antisemitic Abuse Is Uncovered at pro-Palestinian Group Backed by Jeremy Corbyn." *Evening Standard*. Accessed May 8, 2019. https://www.standard.co.uk/news/politics/swathe-of-antisemitic-abuse-is-uncovered-at-group-backed-by-jeremy-corbyn-a4136681.html

Steinberg, M. G. "From Durban to the Goldstone Report: The Centrality of Human Rights NGOs in the Political Dimension of the Arab–Israeli Conflict." *Israel Affairs* 18, no. 3 (2012): 372–388. doi:10.1080/13537121.2012.689518.

Stewart, H., J. Elgot, and N. Parveen "Keir Starmer Denies Jeremy Corbyn Labour Whip despite End of Suspension." *Guardian*. Accessed November 18, 2020. https://www.theguardian.com/politics/2020/nov/18/jeremy-corbyn-refused-labour-whip-despite-having-suspension-lifted

Tazpit News Agency. "Anti-Israel Marchers in the Center of London Espouse Antisemitism." *Jewish Press*. Accessed June 3, 2019. https://www.jewishpress.com/news/global/uk/anti-israel-marchers-in-the-center-of-london-espouse-antisemitism/2019/06/03/

Thurlow, R. C. "The Straw that Broke the Camel's Back: Public Order, Civil Liberties and the Battle of Cable Street." *Jewish Culture and History* 1, no. 2 (1998): 74–94.

Times of Israel. "UN Condemns 'Severe' Human Rights Violations in Iran." Accessed December 18, 2018. https://www.timesofisrael.com/un-condemns-severe-human-rights-violations-in-iran/

Topor, L. "Explanations of Antisemitism in the British Post-Colonial Left." *Journal of Contemporary Antisemitism* 1, no. 2 (2018): 1–14.

Visser, M., M. Lubbers, G. Kraaykamp, and E. Jaspers. "Support for Radical Left Ideologies in Europe." *European Journal of Political Research* 53, no. 3 (2014): 541–558.

Weinthal, B. "German Bank and BDS Group Accused of Aiding Palestinian Terrorists." *The Jerusalem Post*. Accessed June 27, 2019. https://www.jpost.com/International/Israel-Law-Center-accuses-German-bank-and-BDS-group-of-aiding-PFLP-terror-593650

Wistrich, R. S. *A Lethal Obsession: Antisemitism from Antiquity to the Global Jihad.* New York: Random House, 2010.

Zieve, T. "Protesters Burn Israeli Flag in London Temple Mount Demonstration." *The Jerusalem Post*. Accessed July 23, 2017. https://www.jpost.com/Arab-Israeli-Conflict/Protesters-burn-Israeli-flag-in-London-Temple-Mount-demonstration-500535

The BDS as an example of Soviet political warfare

Nelly Atlan

ABSTRACT

This article seeks to underline the ideological filiation between the principles of Russian political warfare (disinformation, aggressive propaganda, manipulation, distortion, political isolation of the target (politicide), the anti-Zionist propaganda formulated by the Soviet Union and the BDS argument, conceived as a node around which anti-Israeli organisations and structure gravitate. To determine this filiation this article examines step by step; the principles of Russian political warfare; the development of that doctrine as expressed in the anti-Zionist propaganda formulated by the Soviet Union between 1897 and 1991 and finally the modalities of the application of the Russian political warfare in the BDS argument. The findings reveal a twin phenomenon of appropriation; first an appropriation of Russian political warfare as a strategy to delegitimise Israel and second, an appropriation of the arguments produced by the anti-Zionist propaganda formulated by the Soviet Union.

Since the beginning of the 2000s, Israel and Jewish communities worldwide have been confronted with anti-Israeli information warfare, the BDS (Boycott, Divestment Sanctions Movement) personifies this activity by applying the rules of Russian political warfare known as the Gerasimov doctrine defined as a form of war by non-military means.

[1] According to Stephen Blank and Yolanta Darczewska, Russian information warfare may encompass 'broad sociopsychological manipulations'[2] [benefitting] Russian interests and taking nourishment from the Russian traditional military doctrine comprising of 'disinformation, aggressive propaganda.'[3] Investigating the concept of Russian political warfare, Adamsky suggests the validity of the concept of 'cross-domain coercion' based on the power generated by the exploitation of a plurality of non-military domains of influence.[4] The integration of the principles of Russian political warfare into Palestinian strategy was born from a military and ideological cooperation between the former Soviet Union and the Arab League, which has been in place since the creation of the State of Israel.

The second enabling factor is the research by the Palestinian side to overcome the reality of the asymmetry of forces by creating power by non-military means (Gerasimov doctrine). By attacking Israel and the Jewish people on the question of the Holocaust, religion, ethnicity, indigeneity, the BDS illustrates the Russian Information warfare. In order to demonstrate the effective appropriation of the Russian doctrine, this article examines the principles of Russian information warfare, in terms of terminology and significance in the first part of the article. The second part of the article examines the developments of the doctrine as expressed in the anti-Zionist propaganda formulated by the Soviet Union between 1897[5] and 1991.[6] The last part of the article identifies the modalities of the application of the Russian political warfare in the BDS argument, by deconstructing its competitive narrative[7] based on the cognitive subversion of Jewish and Israeli significant events and doctrine (Zionism) and their replacement by alternative spatio temporal markers: e.g. Nakba (1948), Occupation (1967).[8]

Russian political warfare: a theoretical clarification

At the theoretical level it is important to clarify the definition of Russian political warfare and its specific use in the present article. In its broadest definition, political warfare is the employment of all the means at a nation's disposal, short of war, to achieve its national objectives. That said, this broad definition of 'Political Warfare' has been renamed by Frank Hoffman as 'hybrid warfare'.[9] Hybrid warfare connotes a combination of non-kinetic or irregular military tactics with conventional military means, rather than a combination of military and civilian tools to achieve effects. The preponderance of tools in political warfare are non-kinetic in nature, and their combination with conventional military means constitutes the 'hybrid' aspect. In addition to this, as explained by Dima Adamsky, the concept of hybrid warfare as mainly based on the Israeli and Western combat experiences has not really penetrated the Russian military thought, which prefers the concept of New Generation warfare (voini novogo pokoleniia), and the theory of victory. In contrast, this Russian acceptance of the concept minimises kinetic fighting but seeks to defeat the adversary, emphasising non-military forms of influence, and maximising cross-domain coercion.[10]

This study is focused on the political warfare aspect rather than on the admixture of the overall concept of NGW or of the Doctrine Gerasimov. As explained by Adamsky, the 'informational psychological struggle' first takes a leading role while the moral-psychological-cognitive-informational suppression of the adversary's decision-makers and operators assures conditions for achieving victory. Adamsky explains that in this perspective there is a will to activate world public opinion that eventually dissuades the adversary from initiating aggression. In his understanding of the Russian political warfare, General Yevgenniy Korotchenko refers to the concept of 'information

SOFT THREATS TO NATIONAL SECURITY

psychological confrontation' (IPC) stressing that 'if left unopposed, [IPC] may allow forces to achieve objectives without unleashing military operations.'[11]

For Adamsky,[12] Kuzio[13] Giles,[14] Franke,[15] Darczewska[16] Russia's adoption of information warfare concepts represents an attachment 'to old methods (sabotage, diversionary tactics, disinformation, state terror, manipulation, aggressive propaganda, exploiting the potential for protest among the local population).'[17] In addition,

> cunning indirectness, operational ingenuity, and addressing weaknesses and avoiding strengths are expressed in Russian professional terminology as military stratagem (voennaia khitrost) and have been, in the Tsarist, Soviet, and Russian Federation traditions, one of the central components of military art that complement, multiply or substitute the use of force to achieve strategic results in military operations.[18]

To transpose the concept to our present time, it might be highly relevant to stress Korotchenko's remark that the human psyche can be exploited more easily in the information age than previously because of the availability of cellular phones, TV, or the Internet, all of which can reach or integrate individuals into powerful groups.[19]

In this enterprise of disinformation, aggressive propaganda, manipulation, distortion, and political isolation of the target (politicide) Russia uses formal (diplomatic) and informal (proxy) ties with a wide range of foreign organisations as its key means of influence in foreign countries.[20] This part of the concept explained by the researchers of RAND, introduces the role of the BDS movement and also its operational structure as a movement that operates as common denominator between different entities linked by religious, political or cultural reasons. At the international level it has been shown that NGOs, like the BDS movement, are a source of soft power due to their transnational nature and activity.[21] In this article, I consider the BDS movement not as the movement born officially between 2001, at the Durban UN Conference against racism, and 2008[22] with the establishment of the BDS National Committee in Ramallah, but rather as a node around which different anti-Israeli organisations and structures gravitate. This dynamic relation obeys the very strategic competitive concepts of 'intersectionality'[23] or, in a more aggressive manner, the concept of 'cross-domain coercion.'[24] All are driven by the goal of coercing Israel legally, economically, academically, and culturally, and the BDS movement is only the node of this ideological conglomerate.

Moreover, their activity is not subjected to the rhythm of war punctuated by periods of fighting and lull, but is waged during peacetime and wartime simultaneously in the domestic, the adversary's and international media domains and in all spheres of new media.[25] Being deprived of the kinetic power of Russian new generation warfare (NGW), Russian political warfare emerges as a perfect

Russian political warfare: an ideological basis for the detestation of Israel between 1897 and 1991

As recalled by Simoni in an article published in the Israel Hayom in 1952, 'the fact that anti-Semitism has been officially prohibited in the USSR, [does not mean] that anti-Semitism disappeared there.'[26] This state of affairs forced the USSR to find ideologically acceptable concepts to express its anti-Semitism freely, which was then related to the challenge that was posed by a specific ethnic religious group called 'the Jews'; a group with a thousand years' history linked by religion and ethnicity; a fact in perfect contradiction to the goal of the socialist/communist theory, that sought to present humanity as a sole part only differentiated by its social posture in society. As always in strategy 'the nature of the threat shapes the nature of the response'.[27]

Therefore if the threat was identified as an incompatibility between the characteristics of the Jewish people – religion, a long history punctuated by discriminations and massacres, a never-ending link with a land in the Middle East from which it draws its language and sometimes its physical appearance – 'the Jews' seen as a specific group would consequently be attacked on these specific grounds, with the help of replacement concepts and theories, acceptable 'salonfahig',[28] according to the social norms of the society under study. If these norms look salonfahig and politically correct at first glance, they are fundamentally anti-Semitic because they attack the identity elements (ethnicity, faith, language, history and related political claims) of the Jewish people. These attacks do not exclude the most grotesque distortions of reality and the most hateful fantasy.

In a historical perspective, we should consider the Russian anti-Semitic paradigm of 'the cosmopolitan Jew' which plays a pivotal role in the construction of anti-Semitism and anti-Zionism in Russia, according to which the Jew is forever a foreigner with a specific agenda – sometimes 'tsarist', sometimes 'bourgeois', 'capitalist' or 'Zionist' and his agenda is immutably in contradiction with the will of the 'honest', 'loyal', 'pure' Russian.[29]

Grüner explains in an evolving perspective of antisemitism that:

> If the Jews as "cosmopolitans" were already seen in the thought processes of the Russian Right before 1917 as "unreliable, unpatriotic companions", who were infected with non-Russian, Western rationalist thinking and who placed themselves outside of Russian nationalism, under Stalin they were as "cosmopolitans" or Zionists part of a concrete international conspiracy against the Soviet Union. Viewed in this light, the anti-cosmopolitanism paradigm completely merged into the anti-Zionism concept, but in addition a further aspect developed that politically cemented it and, from a Soviet perspective, to

a certain extent, radicalised it. The 'cosmopolitan' did not completely disappear in the post-Stalinist rhetoric, but the anti-Zionism concept essentially took on its function.[30]

Considering the development, acknowledged by Robert Wistrich,[31] and Ben Cohen,[32] of anti-Zionism *per se*, a study written in 1977 by an American soldier, M. Daniel Goldberg, from the US Army entitled '**Anti-Zionism as a theme in Soviet Propaganda 1967–1977**' might be particularly informative on the subject. A very exhaustive literature was published after the second world war within the Russian state administration designed to demonise Zionism; Goldberg focused on, among others, 'classics' of the genre such as '**Caution: Zionism**' by Yurij Ivanov and '**Zionism: Theory and Practice**' edited by I. I. Mints; '**Zionism in the service of Anti-communism**' by V, Bolshakov; '**the Secret Weaponry of Zionism**', by S. Krylov; '**In the Name of the Father and the Son**' by I. Shevtsov; '**The Promised Land**' by Yu, Kolesnikov and '**the Prince of this World**' by G. Klimov. To this list should be added, for the sake of historical consistency, the infamous '**Protocols of the Learned Elders of Zion**' fabricated by Russia around the First Zionist Congress in 1897. In these protocols, the authors misrepresented the spirit of the Zionist Congress as a Jewish Plot to rule the World. These protocols, which have been long regarded as a fraud by the world, have been used by various anti-Semites everywhere as anti-Semitic propaganda. An important fact to mention is that during the Hitler regime Julius Streicher (in charge of Nazi Propaganda) exploited them heavily. Simoni even reports that, by order of Hitler, these protocols were translated into Arabic.[33] This information is important for the process of fabrication of the anti-Israeli propaganda by the BDS movement.

For Goldberg, the Anti-Zionist campaign in its most institutionalised form, started after the Six Day War, when the Soviet Union was challenged by the desire of Russian and Soviet Jews to reach Israel and by the defeat suffered by its Arab clients in the 1967 Arab-Israeli War.[34] As it was embarrassing for the Former Soviet Union to blame this defeat on the efforts of Israel alone, it decided to portray Israel as a party of a much larger force menacing world peace and progress. Israel then was portrayed by the Former Soviet Union, and by the European left-wing embarrassed by the ideological traumatism of decolonisation and the influence of Edward Said's Orientalism in 1978, as 'aggressive, expansionist, imperialist'.

In a more general analysis, Goldberg notices that in the overall Soviet anti-Jewish literature Zionism was depicted as follows: (1) Zionism has always been an implacable ideological foe of socialism, (2) Zionism is at base a racial supremacy theory, (3) Zionism will go to any lengths to achieve its goals, (4) Zionism is imperialistic by nature; and (5) Zionism has actively sought (...) to undermine the Soviet Union and other Socialist states.[35]

In order to discourage the Zionist feeling among Russian Jews already bled dry by the Stalinist purges in 1953[36] – a Russian political episode in need of a 'traumatism of replacement'[37] to clean its international image – anti-Zionist articles appeared in history, popular sciences, ideological, literary and cultural and military Journals.[38]

In the works '*Caution: Zionism*' and '*Zionism: Theory and Practice*', the authors present Lenin as opposing the Jewish Zionist organisation 'The Bund[39]', supposedly linked with the Nazi/fascist parties to boost the immigration to Israel.[40] In a general way Goldberg explains that:

> The essence of the Soviet charge against Zionism in this regard is that Zionism willingly, even gladly, used the Nazi racial policy to further immigration into Palestine, that Zionist leaders did not care about the fate of individual Jews and in fact collaborated with the Nazis in selecting which Jews would be sent to Palestine, and, consequently, which Jews would be left to die in Germany (.).[41]

The Soviet Propaganda went even further by stating that:

> (.) the Jewish Agency maintained an office in Nazi Berlin for the coordination of the selection process for prospective settlers, and that that office, under the directorship of Levi Eshkol, operated a series of "re-education camps" in Germany in which young Jews were trained for later work on agricultural kibbutzim.[42]

In the same vein, the idea of a distinct group related to the idea of choosiness or 'election' is in contradiction with the values of the socialist ideal, which is why the Soviet propaganda labelled it as 'racist':

> The current position is that there are more differences (language, culture, physical features) than similarities among the world's Jews, and that Zionist claims that there is some overriding, unifying relationship are groundless and founded upon a racist mystique.[43]

The idea of choosiness serves equally the biased link between Zionism and Nazism; indeed, the propagandist book '*In the Name of the Father and the Son*' is a good example of this as illustrated by the following quotation:

> Don't allow a New Hitler. He may exchange the Swastika for some other emblem and he will say that his nation is chosen by God to rule over the world, that his people is the most talented and worthy.[44]

The Soviet anti-Zionist propaganda already included a lawfare dimension, lawfare defined as 'the strategy of using or misusing law as a substitute for traditional military means to achieve a warfighting objective.'[45] This argument was taken as a substantiation of the Soviet charge for the 1975 United Nations Resolution 3379 equating Zionism with racism. Gerald Steinberg and Anne Herzberg explain that:

The UNGA also approved the creation of a special mechanism – the Committee on the Exercise of the Inalienable Rights of the Palestinian people – which among other activities expanded the legal attacks on the legitimacy of Israel.[46]

At that time it was already clear for Andrei Sakharov,[47] that 'If this resolution is adopted, it can only contribute to anti-Semitic tendencies in many countries by giving them the appearance of international legality.'[48]

Indeed, with the support of the NAM (Non Aligned Movement), which at the time was the largest political bloc in the UN, the Soviet Union and the Arab League were able to pass virtually any resolutions attacking Zionism and the Jewish people. In October 1964, Egyptian president Nasser with the help of the NAM wanted to secure a declaration branding Jewish self-determination as a form of racism. By 1973, the NAM conference went so far as to call for the eradication of Zionism itself and a full boycott of Israel and demanded the blocking of Jewish immigration to anywhere in the territory of Mandated Palestine west of the Jordan River.

A 1973 proposed International Convention of the Suppression and Punishment of Apartheid included a definition of apartheid that would encompass Zionism. In November 1974, UNESCO adopted a resolution condemning Israel for altering the historical features of Jerusalem and rejected a motion to include Israel in the Europe regional group. To go even further in their anti-Semitic attempt, the UN's 1975 World Conference on Women held in Mexico City again called for the elimination of Zionism and, 'equated Judaism with the nastiest forms of racial and group oppression.'[49]

A logical pendant of the idea of Zionism equating racism is the rich and baseless paradigm of Zionism equating Imperialism. This accusation against Zionism is not only ideologically oriented but also metaphorically oriented. In other terms, the Soviet Union is a 'Goliath' that wanted to demonise 'David'. In this conflict, to reverse the asymmetry of forces the Soviet Union 'is forced' to mentally increase the threat represented by a small group bled dry by the Stalinian purges of 1953 and the process of dejudaization and Russification.[50]

Regarding the imperialistic accusation, historically speaking, during the nineteenth and early twentieth centuries, Zionist leaders such as Herzl and Weizman actively sought the support of various European Powers in their effort to establish a Jewish national homeland. In fact, all the areas in which such a homeland might be established were under the direct control of one or other of the great colonial powers. Logically, the Zionist leaders tried to contact such leaders in order to expose them to the Zionist project of the creation of a Jewish state. As explained by Goldberg this was certainly not the interpretation of the Soviet propagandists who presented these contacts as the clear will to establish a 'British Jewish loyal-European outpost' standing in front of the 'volatile Arab population.'[51] In this context as Goldberg reports – on the basis of Soviet propaganda – the Zionists were involved in: 'sabotaging the economic development of Egypt, a developing nation, [by] bombings, kidnappings, and murder[ing] German scientists in Egypt during the early sixties.' In reality, the scientists were former Nazi rocket designers in charge of the development of explosive surface-to-surface rockets for Egypt, and among these scientists stood Hans Eisele who had conducted human guinea pig experiments at Buchenwald.[52]

From a more anthropological perspective, the Soviet propaganda supported this belligerent representation of the Zionists by explaining that it draws from the Ancient Israelites depicted as 'a rapacious horde, unlike the Mongols, who poured out of Arabia to destroy the existing cities and culture of Palestine and then imposed a Jewish Yoke on the region.'[53]

If sometimes the Soviet propaganda attacks the 'Ancient Israelites', it might also in other works, such as in '*The Prince of this World*' by Klimov, postulate that the Zionists are in fact 'Fake Jews' an example of the most hateful fantasy. In this book it is written that:

> All criminals, free-thinkers, intellectual avant-gardists, decadent philosophers (...) are said to be Jews or part Jews. In cases in which no Jewish ancestors can be found for these people, Klimov said that they are the result of artificial insemination. Thus even Soren Kierkegaard is classified as a Jew. The thrust of the story is that Stalin, even though he himself may have been the product of such artificial insemination, sought to wipe out all these agents of the Devil with the aid of the Novel's main character. The only lesson which the reader can draw from this work is that all of these evil Jews, Freemasons, Intellectuals, et al must be exterminated in order to save [the] humanity. As proof of the fact that Klimov is not alone in this lunacy, the book contains a foreword and an afterward by two Russian professors, one of [the] contemporary Soviet Literature, the other of social psychology, at two universities presumably in Britain. Both professors praise the book and engage in the same vein [of] mad ravings and specious arguments as used by Klimov.[54]

This example shows the perfect line between traditional antisemitism, tainted with grotesque science-fiction, and anti-Zionism, as a more politically correct construction.

Illustrating the pattern of disinformation,[55] the paradigm of usurpation as the basis of the imperialist accusation is particularly pregnant in both the Soviet Propaganda and the BDS propaganda, as we will see later in this article. Soviet propagandists explained that the Zionist settlers purchased lands from absentee landowners, and, consequently, the *Fellahin* found themselves deprived of their goods and homes. Of course, the Soviets omitted to mention the fact that the settlers were actually buying the lands by cash as the result of negotiations with the same *Fellahin*.[56]

Later, the Israeli-Arab conflict in its military aspects provided additional examples to demonise the Israelis and to make the Palestinians 'the victims of the victims, the refugees of the refugees[57]' to quote Edward Said. Goldberg reports that:

SOFT THREATS TO NATIONAL SECURITY 189

Menachem Begin [was] frequently identified in Soviet sources as a racist murderer who organized the notorious raid and subsequent massacre in the Arab village of Deir Yassin in April 1948 (...).[58]

These infamously imaginative arguments developed by the Soviet anti-Zionist propagandists testify in their form, content and structure to the direct link between traditional antisemitism symbolised by the attack on 'Ancient Israelites', 'Cosmopolitan Jew' becoming the 'Capitalist/Bourgeois Jew' and evolving into the 'Imperialist Jew' according to a process of adaptation to the norms of society and the need of the attackers, embarrassed by a conflict of the David and Goliath type. This need – although related to an irrational threat – enables the mental cultural, political and economic construction of '*salonfahig*' anti-Zionism based on disinformation, and on the 'moral desacralization' of the Holocaust making the Zionists, collaborators of Nazi and fascist ideologies becoming themselves the monsters of the new victims: the Arab world or the Palestinians. This process is exactly a process of replacement based on the observation that the characteristics of the enemy, 'the Jews', are extremely difficult to compete with in a spiritual, sociological, historical, even linguistic and, above all, emotional level of conflict.

In a chronological perspective, the BDS movement, as will be demonstrated in the last part of this article, only continued the historical timeline of anti-Semitic attacks from the depreciation of 'Ancient Jews' to the culminating idea of 'Zionist murderers of Palestinians,' for the simple reason that the BDS movement and its sympathisers is, as demonstrated by the historian Alex Joffe,[59] a result of pan-Arabism and communism.

Political exploitation of the methods and arguments of Russian political warfare by the BDS movement (Boycott Divestment Sanctions).

Paradoxically, it is interesting to observe the fact that if the Soviet Union had to fight a David (Russian Jews/Israel) and Goliath (the Soviet Union/Arab States) confrontation that forced them to increase mentally the power of a small group in order to demonise them, many of their arguments have been integrated into the ideological arsenal of the BDS movement. That said, in both cases the Soviet camp as well as the Palestinian camp – although ideologically and military linked in their geopolitical ensembles – had to compete with the Jewish people, the people that gave the Bible and the first moral and spiritual laws to this world and that on the emotional level endured the worst persecutions from ancient times up until the Holocaust. In one of his seminal works Robert Wistrich reports what Fidel Castro said in jest while arguing with his Iranian counterparts:

I don't think anyone has been slandered more than the Jews. I would say they have been slandered much more than the Muslims because they are blamed and slandered for everything. No one blames the Muslims for anything.[60]

The transmission of the arguments and even of the literature produced by Soviet propaganda was explained by the fact that these parameters of the conflict had not changed.

The accurate circumstances of the birth of the Boycott Divestment Sanction movement are actually unknown. For Joel Fishman, the movement would be born on 9 July 2005, after a group of Palestinian activists, joined by 170 signatories, met in Ramallah and launched the BDS movement.[61] Actually the BDS movement as explained earlier in this article should be seen as a node around which different anti-Israeli organisations and structures gravitate.

Omar Barghouti one of the thinkers of the BDS[62] summarises the BDS programme as follows:

> In parallel, the entire Palestinian conceptual framework and strategy of resistance [Muqawama] must be thoroughly and critically reassessed and transformed into a progressive action program capable of connecting the Palestinian struggle for self-determination and justice with the international social movement. The most effective and morally sound strategy for achieving these objectives is one based on gradual, diverse, context-sensitive, and sustainable campaigns of [the] BDS – political economic, professional, academic, cultural, athletic and so on and other forms of popular resistance, all aimed at bringing about Israel's comprehensive and unequivocal compliance with international law and universal human rights.[63]

A lexical analysis enables the ideological structure of the resistance [Muqawama] to be understood. Indeed, in Arabic it is a component of the name of the Palestinian terrorist organisation Hamas 'harakat al-muqâwama al-'islâmiya' related to Barghouti's expression 'and other forms of resistance' and supports the fact that the armed struggle is part of the global strategy of resistance (Muqawama). To that dimension you have to add, as explained by Barghouti, the 'political economic, professional, academic, cultural, athletic' dimensions considered as theatres of operations for the BDS movement. This multidimensional vision presented by Barghouti is a perfect illustration of Adamsky's conceptualisation of the 'cross-domain coercion.'[64] This implies that in these different scenes, the BDS sought to coerce Israel in order to achieve political means.

In Barghouti's lexicon there is also a reference to the sociological parameters of the formulation of the propaganda: 'The most effective and morally sound strategy for these objectives is one based on gradual, diverse, context-sensitive, and sustainable campaigns of the BDS'. In fact, if propaganda is to be convincing, it has to be self-explanatory by the fact that it interacts mentally or emotionally with a specific context or series of significant events. Taking this point into consideration, it is just one step away from understanding the chronological attraction supplied by the Apartheid context in South Africa for the BDS movement. To seize this opportunity, Barghouti on the first page of the third chapter of his book, '***BDS Boycott, Divestment, Sanctions, the global struggle for Palestinian rights***', entitled '***The South Africa Strategy For Palestine***' quoted the Guardian's award-winning Middle East correspondent, Chris McGreal stating that:

> Many Israelis recoil at the suggestion of a parallel because it stabs at the heart of how they see themselves and their country … Some staunch defenders of Israel's policies past and present say that even to discuss Israel in the context of Apartheid is one step short of comparing the Jewish state to Nazi Germany, not least because of the Afrikaner leadership's fascist sympathies in the 1940s and the disturbing echoes of Hitler's Nuremberg laws in South Africa's racist legislation. Yet the taboo is increasingly challenged.[65]

In this extract presented by Barghouti, it is possible to identify the tactics that became the pillars of the argument developed by the BDS movement and its sympathisers. First Barghouti used a third person speaker presented as 'the Guardian's award winning' in order to give more credence to his argument. Second at the beginning of the quote, 'Many Israelis recoil at the suggestion' the argument as low as it is would not come from the Palestinian/Arab/Muslim side but from the opponent's side 'the Israelis'. This tactic is, in fact, a well-known BDS tactic. Interestingly, the protagonists cited in the works produced by the Soviet propaganda are intentionally Jewish as in the infamous '***Protocols of the Learned Elders of Zion***', or in the book '***In the Name of the Father and the Son***' by Shevtsov, which reports the discussion between an 'enlightened Jewish father and his son'. This old method to convey critics of the Jews as being Jews themselves, is actually a 'big leaf or an alibi for latter-day anti-Semites who seek to come across exculpated from one of the most ancient hatreds in the world.'[66]

The question of Apartheid is particularly prolific in the propaganda created by the BDS movement, Omar Barghouti, Abigail Barkan and Yasmeen Abu Laban in their article '***Palestinian resistance and international solidarity: the BDS campaign***' present the argument:

> We argue that the effectiveness of such a civil society initiative, as a strategy of resistance and cross-border solidarity, can be usefully framed as an anti-racist movement that contests a post-second world war hegemonic construction of state ideology, in which Zionism plays a central role and serves to enforce a racial contract that hides the apartheid-like character of the state of Israel.[67]

In this specific formulation it is very easy to recognise both the 'strategic usefulness' clearly intended by the BDS movement and its sympathisers as well as the reminiscence of the 'communist discourse' in the reference to 'post-second world war hegemonic construction of state ideology' that would place Israel in a reprehensible and regressive hegemonic posture as described by the Soviet Union.

In the same vein, Claudia Baumgarte-Ochse reports the following appeal made by a consortium of 170 Palestinian organisations to:

> [...] international civil society organizations and people of conscience all over the world to impose broad boycotts and implement divestment initiatives against Israel similar to those applied to South Africa in the apartheid era. We appeal to you to pressure your respective states to impose embargoes and sanctions against Israel.[68]

Here again the language tends to imply a logical connection between the South African case and Israel. This accusation was already promoted in 1973 by the Soviet Union and its Arab clients. At the analytical level, the political connection with apartheid is particularly productive; it helps to confront the emotionality of the persecution and the discrimination endured by the Jewish people by inducing a reversal. In addition to that it enables a context-reaction, necessary for an efficient propaganda. In fact, this accusation resurfaced after the Soviet Union 'political prime', with the erection of a security fence between Israel and the Palestinian territories, designed to prevent incursions into Israeli territory by Palestinian terrorists.[69] Alas, rationale has no place in a propagandist intention.

The following element that appears in Barghouti's speeches is the ultimate connection with the Shoah; this element was already part of the Soviet Union anti-Zionist propaganda. As explained earlier in this article the works '*Caution: Zionism*' and '*Zionism: Theory and Practice*', present Lenin as opposing the Jewish Zionist organisation, 'The Bund', supposedly linked to the Nazi/fascist parties to boost the immigration to Israel.[70]

The BDS movement attacked the Shoah, of course, to compete with one of the most recent industrial and inhuman persecutions of the Jewish people in order to imply a strategy of reversal, making the Palestinians the victims of the 'Nazi Jews'. Again, rationally there is no supportive argument that can accredit this historical parallel; the Palestinians were never subjected to the annihilation of their culture or religion by the burning of their books or any other spiritual or intellectual production, in the way the Jews were up until the burning of their own bodies. The use of the Holocaust has another goal in the BDS discourse as shown by James Wald:

> A new discourse of remorse holds that the creation of Israel was a mistake founded on an injustice, with further proof retroactively adduced through denunciations of current Israeli policy that often assumes an anti-Semitic character. The argument may be summarized as follows: (1) Israel's purported right to exist derives from the Holocaust; (2) Europe created Israel based on emotions of guilt rather than reasons and fairness; (3) Palestinians thus paid the price for the crimes of Europeans; (4) Israel has failed to learn the lessons of the Holocaust and has itself become an oppressor; and (5) in the most extreme instances of Israel acting oppressor, Israelis become latter-day Nazis.[71]

Subsequent to this distortion of history, the method used by the Russian political warfare, the BDS movement and its sympathisers are trying to make the Palestinians 'the new Auschwitz' prisoners', to cancel politically the moral debts purportedly contracted by Europe and the West towards Jews in general in the hope of creating a new ideological debt, but not towards the real prisoners of Auschwitz but towards the intended new ones.

Another dimension which is central in the concept of 'cross-domain coercion' is the logical integration of the different dimensions around a very consistent narrative. For Adamsky: 'Its role of systemic integrator is expressed both verbally and graphically in Gerasimov's programmatic speech.'[72] This creation of a specific language supportive of a specific narrative is another dimension of propaganda set up by the BDS movement.[73] Julie Peteet, Professor of Anthropology and Director of Middle East & Islamic studies at the University of Louisville, in the United States published an interesting article in the Journal of Palestine Studies, an incubator of anti-Israeli ideas, entitled '**Language Matters in Palestine**' in order to suggest a

[shift] to academic discourse particularly [in] anthropology (...) to confront media's discursive strategies handmaiden of violence enabling and legitimizing colonial relations of displacement.[74]

For Peteet, 'the bundled linguistic repertoires and categories are deeply entangled with power and until recently unquestionably accompanied the colonial endeavour in Palestine.'[75] In this relation of power, a highly strategic thought, Peteet suggests a new discourse creating well intended confusion:

While there is no singular model of settler colonialism, Israel-Palestine has enough in common with settler colonialism in the Americas, Australia, and South Africa to constitute a branch on the family tree. Each is unique, but there are sufficient resemblances to allow us to speak of them as a type of social formation. In general, the parameters of settler colonialism involve a more technologically and militarily powerful entity imposing itself on less powerful and less technologically sophisticated communities and appending their economy to that of the settlers and their metropole.[76]

In this quotation – unfortunately originating from an 'anthropologist', but after all the Soviet Union as explained earlier used 'professors in Britain' to advance their thesis of 'artificial insemination to create Jews',[77] – the author explains that there is enough resemblance to 'speak' of Israel as a form of 'settler colonialism'. When such aberrant theses are advanced, it is important to recall the basic parameters of colonialism and why these ideational and linguistic inferences are baseless: (1) the Jewish people for their two most preponderant and well-known recognised groups (Sephardi and Ashkenazi branches) are a Semite people, and for that reason, as recalled by the historian Avi Bareli, the Jews were rejected in Europe since the Jews' foreignness in Europe involved an Oriental and Semitic element, [it] was one of the causes for the emergence of anti-Semitism,[78] (2) the Jewish settlement in Palestine transferred capital in an opposite direction to that of colonization projects; it invested Jewish capital in Palestine and did not withdraw natural resources and capital from it to benefit an empire or enrich investors,[79] (3) the Zionist socialists, the main Zionist group in the country, were determined to prevent their society from developing along the lines of colonial exploitation, and to this end they used the development of Jewish autonomy under British patronage, the gradual separation of the economies of the two national groups, and the circumstances of the national conflict from the 1920s onwards (.) all these factors fostered separation and the creation of a sustainable Jewish working class and prevented the development of a society based on exploitation of the Palestinian Arabs.[80]

Besides this allegation, there is also the attempt to impose specific language 'apartheid'[81]; 'settler colonialism,'[82] 'ethnic cleansing'[83] and its use as a specific narrative, as well as the recreation of a different History. In a pedagogic way, the BDS movement and its sympathisers used the episodes of the '*Nakba*' (the Catastrophe) 1948[84] and the episode of the Occupation (1967)[85] repeatedly. To those episodes we could add the 1st *Intifada* (1987–1993), the 2nd *Intifada* (2000–2006)[86] and the very visual events of the killing of Mohammed Al Dura (2000).[87]

This orchestrated repetition of concepts and dates, which aims to create an alternative coherent narrative by imposing through 'indoctrination' the use of temporal markers and inferential ideas reactivated in specific sociological, historical and political contexts supported by powerful images, acquires significance in people's minds. This idea lies at the core of the Russian political warfare or cross-domain coercion.[88]

Another legacy of the Anti-Zionist Soviet Propaganda is the continuation of lawfare commencing with the UN and UNGA (United Nations General Assembly) and UNESCO, as the NAM and the Soviet Union did to continue with the UNHRC (United Nations Human Rights Council) and the establishment of the UNRWA (The United Nation Relief and Works Agency for Palestinian Refugees). For Cohen and Freilich, this trend is more than clear:

> The UN has been a central venue for the delegitimization campaign, including the General Assembly (UNGA), Security Council (UNSC), various councils and commissions, and specialized agencies - indeed, virtually every UN forum. Facing an automatic Arab, Muslim, and third-world majority, Israel has been mostly unable to prevent this onslaught, including an unprecedented three UNGA emergency sessions regarding Israel in 2003. Most years, four or five nations are the target of one UNGA resolution condemning alleged breaches of human rights; in both 2004 and 2005 there were eighteen resolutions related to Israel, and there were nineteen in 2007. In 2012, of the twenty-six resolutions criticizing states passed by the UNGA, twenty-two focused on Israel. In 2013, the UNGA passed twenty-five resolutions, twenty-one of which were against Israel, and declared 2014 to be the "Year of Palestine." The UNGA has also criticized the

US for maintaining relations with Israel. In contrast, terrorism against Israel has been condemned in just one resolution. [89]

At the economic level, the BDS movement and its sympathisers, attacked different companies under contract with Israel and succeeded in 2015 in imposing a policy in the EU requiring that goods imported to Europe from the West Bank, East Jerusalem, Gaza, and the Golan Heights would no longer be labelled 'Made in Israel'. In addition to that:

> A number of European supermarkets and companies have stopped selling Israeli goods from the West Bank, a number of banks have begun to boycott Israeli counterparts or question their involvement in the settlements, and pension funds have begun to halt investment in Israeli banks and companies over their funding of construction in the West Bank. This measure had, as an impact, the loss of 8.88 USD billion annually until 2024, which was in addition to nearly 6 USD billion lost due to instability and decreased tourism. [90]

> At the academic and cultural level, an important tactic has been to convince academic associations to boycott contact with Israeli institutions and scholars and to pass resolutions critical of Israel. In Britain, several schools and academic associations have voted to boycott Israeli universities. In October 2015, 343 academics from 72 institutions from across Britain called for a boycott of all Israeli institutions, though not individual Israeli academics. In 2016, 168 Italian academics and researchers from seven institutions called for a boycott of the Israeli university Technion, though not for a broader boycott. The American Studies Association passed a resolution endorsing an academic boycott in 2013. They were followed shortly after by the Association for Asian American Studies, the Association for Humanist Sociology, and the Native American and Indigenous Studies Association, and in 2014 by the Modern Language Association, the Peace and Justice Studies Association, and the Critical Ethnic Studies Association.[91]

The other overall dimensions mentioned by Barghouti 'sustainable campaigns of BDS – political, economic, professional, academic, cultural, athletic and so on and other forms of popular resistance' show the BDS movement and its sympathisers' will to silence Israel and the Jews; this is not only a question of coercion but the ultimate goal is '**politicide**'. Fishman advanced this term rightly, explaining that:

> The BDS movement has its own distinctive message and political programme. Its adherents make no pretence of supporting Palestinian reconciliation with the Jewish state but openly call for the politicide of Israel, which they seek to destroy and replace with a single Palestinian state ruled by a Muslim majority. The advocates of BDS accuse Israel of being a racist and apartheid state, hence a criminal entity that has neither a legitimate place in the community of nations nor a raison d'être. If justice must be done, Israel should be destroyed and replaced. This constitutes BDS's basic, literal message and provides the unifying and guiding principle of the movement.[92]

Conclusion

The imposition of a specific language, based on distorted ideas, such as 'Zionist as colonialism', 'Jews as Nazis', 'Jews as promoters of a new form of apartheid' echoed the Soviet Union imaginative *leitmotiv* 'Cosmopolitan Jew', 'Tsarist Jew', 'Capitalist Jew', 'Bourgeois Jew', 'Imperialist Jew' in number and also in significance. The aim to reverse the emotional charge related to the persecution of the Jews by making the Palestinians 'the victims of the victims, the refugees of the refugees'[93] illustrates the transmission of an infamous legacy from Soviet Union propaganda and confirms an antisemitism badly disguised by the awkward and hypocritical formulation of '*salonfahig*' ideas. The reliance on Lawfare also shows a continuation in the instrumentalization of legal international bodies seen by the Soviet Union and the Non-Aligned (NAM) as a stage of choice for nothing other than the death sentence of Western values. Instrumentalization of Western values and institutions, normalisation of an anti-Semitic vocabulary and ideas designed to deny Israel the right to exist and, logically, the liberalisation of anti-Semitic violence in Israel and elsewhere, are solid enough reasons to stop blinding ourselves by granting a political tribune to the BDS and its sympathisers by pretending 'to preserve freedom of expression' in our 'Western democratic societies.' To persist on this path is nothing but a fool's bargain that endangers Israel, the Middle East and the entire Western world.

Notes

1. Giles, "The next phase of Russian," 4.
2. Blank, "Signs of New Russian Thinking," para.4.
3. Darczewska, "The Devil is in the Details," 7.
4. Adamsky, "Cross Domain coercion," 1–43.
5. Date of publication of the infamous *Protocols of the Learned Elders of Zion* fabricated around the First Zionist Congress in 1897.
6. Date of the collapse of the Soviet Union and the start of massive immigration of Russian Jews to Israel.
7. Peteet, "Language Matters," 24–40.
8. Barghouti, *Boycott Divestment Sanctions*, 56, 62, 67, 112, 129, 137, 141, 147, 187, 198, 239; MAKDISI, "Intellectual Warfare and the Question," 40, 43, 46 –57, 74 and ABU-LABAN, "Palestinian Resistance and International solidarity," 34, 39, 45, 51.
9. Hoffman, "Conflict in the 21st Century," 14.
10. Adamsky, "Cross Domain coercion," 22.
11. Thomas, "Russia's information warfare structure," 167.
12. See note 4 above.
13. Kuzio, "Old Wine in a New Bottle," 485–506.
14. See note 1 above.
15. Franke, "War by non-military means, Understanding Russian," 1–60.
16. See note 3 above.
17. Ibid.

18. Adamsky, "Cross Domain coercion," 25.
19. See note 11 above, 167.
20. Robinson et al., *Modern Political Warfare, Current Practices*, 56–57.
21. Demars, and Dijkeul, *The NGO Challenge*, 1–358.
22. Barghouti, *Boycott Divestment Sanctions*, 5.
23. Forward.com, "To Combat BDS, You Need to Understand," para. 2.; Prager, "Achievements According to the BDS Movement," 41.
24. See note 4 above.
25. Adamsky, "Cross Domain coercion," 29.
26. Wilhelm Marr, the German journalist who popularised the term antisemitism in the late nineteenth Century, did so because he wanted to move away from Christian anti-Judaism and transform Judaeophobia into a kind of modern political concept. Fuchshuber, "From Wilhelm Marr to Mavi Marmara, Antisemitism and Anti-Zionism," 29; See also Yedioth Hayom, "Soviet Antisemitism and the Prague Trial," 19, December 1952.
27. Adamsky, "Cross Domain coercion," 26.
28. The German term "salonfahig" means socially acceptable. It comes from the 17th and 18th centuries in France when the Enlightenment started to gather in specific parlours "salons" in French.
29. Gruner, "Russia's battle against the foreign," 445–472.
30. Ibid., 461.
31. Wistrich, *Le socialisme et les Juifs*, 189–199.
32. Cohen, "The ideological Foundations," 1–14.
33. Yedioth Hayom, "Soviet Antisemitism and the Prague Trial," 19 December 1952.
34. Goldberg, *Anti-Zionism as a theme in Soviet*, 4.
35. Ibid., 11.
36. By dint of a total numerus nullus, Jews were barred from the Soviet civil service in all fields of foreign relations and trade, being expelled not only from the ministries and legations, but even from all related institutions of higher learning (both as teachers and students). The number of Jews in the leadership of the many internal ministries and governing agencies (both all-Union and RSFSR) declined from 516 in January 1946 to 190 in 1952 (from 12.9% to 3.9% of the total). Similarly, of the 98 directors of ministerial departments functioning in 1946, only 25 were identified as Jews six years later by the Central Committee tasked to monitor the ethnic composition of personnel in the government and Party (…).WINSTON, "Reflections on the Anticipated Mass," 476.
37. Giles, "The next phase of Russian," 7. (*Giles reports that to dissimulate the Massacre of Katyn in 1940, a massacre perpetrated by the Russian troops on Polish individuals purportedly hostile to the regime, the Soviet propaganda emphasised the confusion in the media and written sources with the Khatyn massacre in Belorussia perpetrated by the Nazi troops.*)
38. Goldberg, *Anti-Zionism as a theme in Soviet*, 6.
39. Jewish socialist party founded in Russia in 1897; after a certain ideological development it came to be associated with devotion to Yiddish, autonomism, and secular Jewish nationalism, envisaging Jewish life as lived out in Eastern Europe, sharply opposed to Zionism and other conceptions of a world-embracing Jewish national identity. Jewish Library, "The Bund".
40. Goldberg, *Anti-Zionism as a theme in Soviet*, 9.
41. Ibid., 16.
42. Ibid., 17–18.

43. Ibid., 13.
44. Ibid., 14.
45. Kittrie, *Lawfare, Law as a weapon*, 4.
46. Steinberg, and Herzberg, "The Role of International Legal and Justice Discourse," 124.
47. www.nobelprize.org, "Sakharov Andrei Dimitrievitch," para. 1–2. (*Andrei Dimitrievich Sakharov (21 May 1921–14 December 1989) was a Russian nuclear physicist, dissident, Nobel laureate, and activist for disarmament, peace and human rights.*)
48. Moynihan, *A Dangerous Place*, 213.
49. Ibid., 172.
50. Starting earlier than purges in other sectors, Jews were systematically repressed and discriminated against in all creative fields under the banner of Russification and "purification" of the literature, music, theatre, and the variety of all other entertainment and art forms. In literature, discussed exhaustively in Boris Frezinskiy's Pisateli i sovetskiye vozhdi (Writers and Soviet Leaders; Frezinskiy 2008), and Maxim Shrayer's (2007) two-volume Anthology of Jewish-Russian Literature, the nearly complete suppression of Yiddish poets and writers. Winston, "Reflections on the Anticipated Mass," 476.
51. Goldberg, *Anti-Zionism as a theme in Soviet*, 26.
52. Ibid., 26–27.
53. Ibid., 27.
54. Ibid., 52.
55. Darzcewska, "The Devil is in the Details," 7.
56. Goldberg, *Anti-Zionism as a theme in Soviet*, 29.
57. New York Times, *The One-state Solution*, January 1999.
58. Goldberg, *Anti-Zionism as a theme in Soviet*, 46.
59. Times of Israel, *Why the origins of the BDS*, 31 August 2016.
60. Wistrich, "The Anti-Zionist mythology of the Left," 194.
61. Fishman, "The BDS Message of anti-Zionism, anti-Semitism," 416.
62. Ibid., 416.
63. Barghouti, *Boycott Divestment Sanctions*, 58.
64. See note 12 above.
65. Barghouti, *Boycott Divestment Sanctions*, 63.
66. Ribak, "There was no uncorrupt Israel," 257.
67. Abu-Laban, and Bakan, "Palestinian Resistance and International solidarity," 32.
68. Baumgarte-Ochse, "Claiming Justice for Israel/Palestine," 1175.
69. General Security Service, "Features of Terrorist Attacks."
70. Goldberg, *Anti-Zionism as a theme in Soviet*, 9.
71. Wald, "The New Replacement Theory, Anti Zionism, Antisemitism," 6.
72. Adamsky, "Cross Domain coercion," 30.
73. Hitchcock, Jennifer, "Social Media Rhetoric of the Transnational Palestinian-led Boycott," 1–12.
74. See note 7 above.
75. Peteet, "Language Matters," 25.
76. Ibid., 32.
77. Goldberg, *Anti-Zionism as a theme in Soviet*, 52; YEMINI, *Industry of Lies*, 1–354.
78. Bareli, "Forgetting Europe," 106.

SOFT THREATS TO NATIONAL SECURITY

79. Ibid., 107.
80. Ibid., 108.
81. Barghouti, *Boycott Divestment Sanctions*, 3, 5, 11, 12, 14, 15, 16, 17, 18, 20, 21, 24, 25, 26, 28.
82. Peteet, "Language Matters," 31–37; BAUMGARTE-OCHSE, "Claiming Justice for Israel/Palestine: The Boycott, Divestment, Sanctions (BDS) Campaign and Christian Organizations," 1175, 1177, 1183.
83. Barghouti, *Boycott Divestment Sanctions*, 2, 11, 12, 14, 16, 44, 64, 67, 72, 95, 107, 108, 110.
84. Ibid., 44, 47, 62, 67, 95, 108, 112, 137, 152, 194, 198.
85. Ibid., 6,7,8,9,11,12,14,20,22,23,25.
86. Ibid., 52,63,64,72,162,270,271,273,282.
87. The role played by the media in the mechanism of Israelophobia and Palestinophilia as direct reactions to the media representation of Tsahal as a "ruthless army" that is historically referring to the image of the "Cruel Jew" in the traditional anti-Semitic European Christian literature opposed to the image of the young Al Durah child who symbolised innocence and victimhood. Taguieff, *The New Judaeophobia,[French]*, 82.
88. See note 12 above.
89. Cohen, and Freilich, "The Delegitimization of Israel," 32.
90. Cohen, and Freilich, "War by other means," 48.
91. Ibid., 7.
92. See note 61 above, 412.
93. See note 57 above.

Disclosure statement

No potential conflict of interest was reported by the author(s).

Bibliography

Abu-Laban, Y., and A. B. Bakan. "Palestinian Resistance and International Solidarity: The BDS Campaign." *Institute of Race Relations* 51, no. 1 (2009): 29–54. doi:10.1177/0306396809106162.

Adamsky, D. "Cross-domain coercion: The current Russian Art of Strategy." *IFRI Security Studies Centers*, Proliferation paper no 54 (2015): 1–44. https://www.ifri.org/sites/default/files/atoms/files/pp54admasky.pdf

Bareli, A. "Forgetting Europe: Perspectives on the Debate about Zionism and Colonialism." *The Journal of Israeli History* 20, no. 2–3 (2001): 99–120. doi:10.1080/13531040108576162.

Barghouti, O. *Boycott Divestment Sanctions, the Global Struggle for Palestinian Rights.* Chicago: Haymarket Books, 2011.

Barghouti, O. "Opting for Justice: The Critical Role of Anti-colonial Israelis in the Boycott, Divestment, and Sanctions Movement." *Settler Colonial Studies* 4, no. 4 (2014): 407–412. doi:10.1080/2201473X.2014.911656.

Baumgarte-Ochse, C. "Claiming Justice for Israel/Palestine: The Boycott, Divestment, Sanctions (BDS) Campaign and Christian Organizations." *Globalizations* 14, no. 7 (2017): 1172–1187. doi:10.1080/14747731.2017.1310463.

Bolshakov, V. V. *Sionizm Na Sluzhbe Antikommunisma, (Zionism in the Service of Anti-communism)*. Moskva: Politizdat, 1972.

Clausewitz, V. C. *On War*. Trans. Howard, Michael, PARET, Peter. Princeton, New Jersey: Princeton University Press, 1989.

Cohen, B. "The Ideological Foundations of the Boycott Campaign against Israel." *American Jewish Committee* (2007): 1–14. https://www.bjpa.org/search-results/publication-261/

Cohen, B., and C. D. Freilich. "The Delegitimization of Israel: Diplomatic Warfare, Sanctions, and Lawfare." *Israel Journal of Foreign Affairs* 9, no. 1 (2015): 29–48. doi:10.1080/23739770.2015.1015095.

Cohen, B., and C. D. Freilich. "War by Other Means: The Delegitimization Campaign against Israel." *Israel Affairs* 24, no. 1 (2018): 1–25. doi:10.1080/13537121.2017.1398458.

Darzcewska, Y. "The Devil Is in the Details: Information Warfare in the Light of Russia's Military Doctrine." *OSW Point of View*, no. 50 (2015): 1–39. https://www.files.ethz.ch/isn/191967/pw_50_ang_the-devil-in_net.pdf

Demars, W., and D. Dijkeul. *The NGO Challenge for International Relations Theory*. London: Routledge, 2015.

Fishman, J. S. "The BDS Message of anti-Zionism, anti-Semitism and Incitement to Discrimination." *Israel Affairs* 18, no. 3 (2012): 412–425. doi:10.1080/13537121.2012.689521.

Franke, U. "War by Non-military Means, Understanding Russian Information Warfare." *FOI* (2015): 1–63. https://www.foi.se./rest-api/report/FOI-R–4065–SE

Frezinskiy, B. *Pisateli I Sovetskiye Vozhdi. Izbrannyye Syuzhety 1919-1960 Godov [Writers and Soviet Leaders], Selected Topics, 1919-1960*. Moscow: Ellis-Lak, 2008.

Fuchshuber, T. "From Wilhelm Marr to Mavi Marmara, Antisemitism and Anti-Zionism as Forms of Anti-Jewish Action." In *Anti-Zionism and Antisemitism, the Dynamics of Delegitimization*, edited by A. H. Rosenfeld, 30–52. Bloomington, Indiana: Indiana University Press,2019.

Giles, K. "The Next Phase of Russian Information Warfare." *NATO Strategic Communication Center of Excellence* (2016): 1–16. https://www.stracomcoe.org/download/file/fid/5134

Goldberg, D., *Anti-Zionism as a Theme in Soviet Propaganda 1967-1977*, Student Research Report, Army Institute for Advanced Russian and East European Studies, 1977.

Gruner, F. "Russia's Battle against the Foreign: The Anti-cosmopolitanism Paradigm in Russian and Soviet Ideology." *European Review of History—Revue européenne d'histoire* 17, no. 3 (2010): 445–472. doi:10.1080/13507486.2010.481943.

Hitchcock, J. "Social Media Rhetoric of the Transnational Palestinian-led Boycott, Divestment, and Sanctions Movement." *Social Media + Society* (January-March, 2016): 1–12. doi:10.1177/2056305116634367.

Hoffman, F. G. "Conflict in the 21st Century: The Rise of Hybrid Wars." *Potomac Institute for Policy Studies* (December, 2007): 1–65. https://www.potomacinstitute.org/images/stories/publications/potomac_hybridwar_0101.pdf

Ivanov, Y. S. *Ostorozhno: Sionizm! (Caution: Zionism!)*. Moskva: Politizdat, 1969.

Kittrie, O. *Lawfare, Law as a Weapon of War*. New York: Oxford University Press, 2016.

Klimov, G. *Knyaz Mira Sego, (The Prince of This World)*. New York: Newspaper, Rosiya Company, 1970.

Krylov, S. A. *Tajnoe Oruzhie Sionizma, (The Secret Weaponry of Zionism)*. Moskva: Voenizdat, 1972.

Kuzio, T. "Old Wine in a New Bottle: Russia's Modernization of Traditional Soviet Information Warfare and Active Policies against Ukraine and Ukrainians." *The Journal of Slavic Military Studies* 32, no. 4 (2019): 485–506. doi:10.1080/13518046.2019.1684002.

Makdisi, S. "Intellectual Warfare and the Question of Palestine." *Journal of PalestineStudies* 35, no. 3 (Spring, 2006): 78–82. https://www.jstor.org/stable/10.1525/jps.2006.35.3.78.

Mints, I. I., ed. *Sionizm: Teoriya I Praktika, (Zionism: Theory and Practice)*. Moskva: Politizdat, 1973.

Moynihan, D. P. *A Dangerous Place*. New York: Little Brown, 1978.

Pappe, I. *The Ethnic Cleansing of Palestine*. Oxford: Oneworld Publications, 2006.

Peteet, J. "Language Matters: Talking about Palestine." *Journal of Palestine Studies* 45, no. 2 (178) (Winter, 2016): 24–40. doi:10.1525/jps.2016.45.2.24.

Prager, A. "Achievements according to the BDS Movement: Trends and Implications." *INSS, Strategic Assessment* 22, no. 1 (April, 2019): 39–49.

Ribak, G. "There Was No Uncorrupt Israel, the Role of Israelis in Delegitimizing Jewish Collective Existence." In *Anti-Zionism and Antisemitism, the Dynamics of Delegitimization*, edited by A. H. Rosenfeld, 255–280. Bloomington, Indiana: Indiana University Press, 2019.

Robinson, L., T. Helmus, C. Cohen, S. Raphael, A. Nader, A. Radin, M. Magnuson, and K. Migacheva. *Modern Political Warfare, Current Practices and Possible Responses*. Santa Monica, California: RAND Corporation, Aroyo Center, 2018.

Schanzer, J. *Hamas Vs. Fatah, the Struggle for Palestine*. New York: Palgrave Macmillan, 2008.

Shevtsov, I. M. *Vo Imya Ottsa I Syna, [In the Name of the Father and the Son]*. Moskva, Moskovskij: Rabochiz, 1970.

Shrayer, M. D. *An Anthology of Jewish-Russian Literature*. Vol. 1. Armonk, NY: M.E. Sharpe, 2007.

Simoni, S. "Soviet Antisemitism and the Prague Trial." *Yedioth Hayom*, December 19 (1952). https://www.cia.gov/library/readingroom/docs/CIA-RDP65-006756R000500130006-7.pdf

Steinberg, G. M., and A. Herzberg. "The Role of International Legal and Justice Discourse in Promoting the New Antisemitism." In *Anti-Zionism and Antisemitism, the Dynamics of Delegitimization*, edited by A. H. Rosenfeld, 115–157. Bloomington, Indiana: Indiana University Press, 2019.

Taguieff, P.-A. *La nouvelle Judéophobie [The new Judeophobia]*. éditions Mille et une nuits-Arthème Fayard, Paris, 2002.

Taguieff, P.-A. *La Nouvelle Propaganda Anti-juive [The New anti-Jewish Propaganda]*. éditions PUF, Intervention Philosophique. Paris: Presse Universitaire de Frances, 2010.

Thomas, T. L. "Russia's Information Warfare Structure: Understanding the Roles of the Security Council, F.A.P.S.I, The State Technical Commission and the

Military." *European Security* 7, no. 1 (1998): 156–172. doi:10.1080/09662839 808407354.

Trinquier, R. (col), *La Guerre Moderne [The Modern War]*, Editions de La Table ronde, Paris, 1961 (rééd. Economica, 2008).. :, .

Wald, J. "The New Replacement Theory, Anti Zionism, Antisemitism, and the Denial of History." In *Anti-Zionism and Antisemitism, the Dynamics of Delegitimization*, edited by A. H. Rosenfeld, 3–29. Bloomington, Indiana: Indiana University Press, 2019.

Winston, H., . V. "Reflections on the Anticipated Mass Deportation of Soviet Jews." *Post-Soviet Affairs* 31, no. 6 (2015): 471–490. doi:10.1080/1060586X. 2015.1079961.

Wistrich, R. "The Anti-Zionist Mythology of the Left." *Israel Journal of Foreign Affairs* 9, no. 2 (2015): 189–199. doi:10.1080/23739770.2015.1037579.

Wistrich, R., ed. *Anti-Judaism, Antisemitism, and Delegitimizing Israel*. Vidal Sassoon International Center for the Study of Antisemitism (SICSA), University of Nebraska Press, Lincoln, USA, 2016.

Yemini, B.-D. *Industry of Lies; Media, Academia and the Israeli Arab Conflict*. New York, NY: ISGAP, 2017.

Yeor, B. "Antisemitism/Anti-Zionism: Primal Pillars in Europe's Decay." In *Anti-Judaism, Antisemitism, and Delegitimizing Israel*, edited by R. WISTRICH, 25–38, the Vidal Sassoon International Center for the Study of Antisemitism (SICSA), University of Nebraska Press, Lincoln, USA, 2016.

Index

Note: Page numbers followed by "n" denote endnotes.

Adamsky, D. 181–183, 193
Al Dura, Mohammed 194
Ali, Nazim 147
alleged Israeli war crimes 68–69, 77, 82
Al-Quds Day rally 174
Amara, Ahmad 134
American Jews 12–13, 32, 159
American public opinion 11, 13, 21
anti-Israel agenda 34, 43, 122, 135
anti-Israeli discourse 135
anti-Israeli platform 63
anti-Israeli resolutions 91, 94, 97, 101
anti-Israel sentiments 149
antisemitic meetings 152
antisemitism 1, 3–5, 30, 32, 34–35, 39–41,
    57–64, 144–146, 148–150, 152–153, 155,
    166–167, 169–176, 184, 188–189, 194
anti-Zionism 34, 144–149, 151–158, 160,
    170–171, 173–175, 184–185, 188–189;
    conspiracy 144, 156
anti-Zionists 5, 144, 146, 149–152;
    ideologies 144, 150; travellers 148
Arab anti-Zionism 158
Arab Association for Human Rights (AHR)
    126–127, 133
Arab-Israeli Conflict 8, 151, 167
Arab League 93, 97–101, 181, 187
Arabs 8–9, 11–21, 23, 60, 62, 109, 114–115,
    123, 127–128, 151, 154, 158
Arafat, Yasser 167
artificial insemination 188, 193
Association for Civil Rights in Israel
    (ACRI) 126, 128, 130, 134
authoritarian regimes 2, 81
Avineri, Shlomo 147

Balfour Declaration 15, 114–115
bargaining model 90

Bauberot, Jean 148
Bedouin: activities in UN human rights
    forums 124; issues 125–135
Begin-Prawer Bill 124, 131–132, 135
Benjamin, Medea 153
Ben-Natan, Asher 17
Bensouda, F. 43, 79–82, 106–108, 110,
    112–115
Berkowitz, P. 74
Bernstein, Robert 34
bias 35–38, 40, 44, 46, 70, 73, 75–76,
    81–82
Blitt, Robert Charles 35
Boycott, Divestment, and Sanctions (BDS)
    movement 2–5, 42, 45, 63, 133, 135, 151,
    153, 166–170, 173, 175–176, 181–185,
    189–196
Brumlik, M. 59
Bundy, McGeorge 11

Christian Anti-Zionism 155
Christian Zionism 156
coalescence 5, 144, 150, 160
Cohen, M. S. 194
Cohen, Rabbi Aaron 154
Committee of Economic, Social and
    Cultural Rights (CESCR) 125–128, 130
Committee on the Elimination of Racial
    Discrimination (CERD) 121, 124–126,
    128, 130–132, 135
Committees of Inquiry (COI) 68–69,
    72–79, 82
Corbyn, Jeremy 171
Covert War 166, 175

Dahl, Ziva 151
Davis, Mary McGowan 74
decolonisation 110–111, 185

204INDEX

de-legitimisation 2, 5, 122, 133, 147, 166–167, 170–171
Diène, Doudou 74
Dieudonné M'Bala 158–159
discrimination 35, 58, 70, 126, 184, 192

Eban, Abba 18–19
Economist Intelligence Unit (EIU) 5n3
Emancipationist anti-Zionism 154

Faurisson, R. 157
Fifth International 16–17
Foreman, Jonathan 37
Foucault, Michel 170
Foxman, Abraham 37
Frankfurt School of Marxism 13
Freedland, Jonathan 148
Freilich, C. D. 194
French Christian Students Association 148

gaza 27, 32, 37, 41–42, 44–45, 69, 71–78, 81–82, 108, 113, 116
General Assembly Voting 90
Gerasimov doctrine 181–182
Gillespie, Bobby 172
Goldberg, D. 185
Goldberg reports 129, 187–188
Goldman Affair 17
Goldstone commission 72
Goldstone Report 73–74, 76
Gramsci, Antonio 13

Hamas 37, 40, 42, 44, 69, 71–74, 76–79, 81, 168, 172, 174–175
hard power 69, 167, 175
Hasbara 19, 22; problem 18
Herzl, Theodor 154–155
Hirsh, David 149
holocaust 30, 35, 40–41, 44, 46, 60, 63, 145, 154–155, 157–159, 169–170, 189, 192
Hossein, Sara 77
Human Rights Watch (HRW) 34–37, 39–47, 72
Hussain, Khadim 147

international advocacy 134–135
international coalescence movement 150
international community 2, 9, 71, 75, 99, 108, 112, 115, 145, 168–169
international crimes 43, 75

International Criminal Court (ICC) 34, 41–43, 69, 72, 75, 77, 79–82, 100, 105–108, 111, 116
International Holocaust Remembrance Alliance (IHRA) 5n1, 145, 166
international humanitarian law 36, 38, 68, 72, 74, 76
international law scholarship 109
international organisations 68–69, 89, 100, 117, 150
international recognition 14–15, 109–110
international tribunal 77, 106, 111, 118
intersectionality 3, 151, 167, 183
Intifada 194
Islamic Human Rights Commission (IHRC) 174
Ismael, Hafez 146
Israel 2–5, 7–22, 27–32, 34–46, 57–64, 68–82, 90–100, 105–109, 114–116, 121–127, 129–135, 144–151, 153–160, 166–168, 170–172, 174–176, 181, 184–187, 190–196
Israel Defence Forces (IDF) 18, 36, 38, 73, 76–78, 149
Israeli Apartheid Free Zones (IAFZ) 169
Israeli atrocities 10
Israeli-Palestinian conflict 31, 61, 64, 90, 106, 110–111, 133, 149
Israelis 7–8, 11–12, 14, 20–21, 23, 28, 36–37, 42–44, 58–59, 61–64, 78–82, 107, 109, 128, 182
Israel-related resolutions 93

Jewish anti-Israelism 57
Jewish anti-Zionism 153
Jew-hatred 64n2
Jew-Zionism 156
Johnson, Lyndon 11
Judaeophobia 60–61

Kaplan, Edward 149
Klug, Brian 170

Lebanon War 37–38, 42, 150
legitimacy 2–3, 5, 8, 10, 16, 18, 20, 122, 187
Levi, Edward 30
Loach, Ken 148, 171
logical fallacies 111

Marx, Karl 152
Marxist hostility 16

modern Jewish identity 57
Munich Olympic massacre 172
Murungi, Kaari Betty 77
Muslim anti-Zionism 158

Nakba 194
Naqab 121, 123, 128–131, 133, 135
nationality 13
national liberation movement 14, 16
national security 2–5, 8–23, 28–31, 35–47,
    58–63, 69–83, 90–93, 100–101,
    106–117, 122–135, 145–159,
    167–175, 182–195
national self-determination 107,
    113, 166
negative transition 170–171, 175–176
Negev Bedouin 121–123, 127, 130,
    134–135
Negev Coexistence Forum (NCF) 121,
    127–134
Netanyahu, Benjamin 75
non-aligned movement (NAM) 69–70, 187,
    194, 196
Nye, Joseph S. Jr. 167

Occupied Palestinian Territories (OPT)
    74–75, 97, 107–108, 113–114

Palestine 27–28, 42–43, 59–61, 79–81,
    108–112, 114–116, 150, 153, 155,
    174–175, 186, 188, 191, 193–194
Palestine Liberation Organisation (PLO)
    15, 37, 74, 76, 82, 115, 154, 167–168
Palestine Solidarity Campaign (PSC) 174
Palestinian Campaign 68, 168
Palestinian-Israeli conflict 68–69, 82,
    113, 115
Palestinian Lawfare 105
Palestinian propaganda 13–16, 45
Palestinians 4, 14–15, 19, 21, 36–38, 61–62,
    69–71, 74–75, 77–79, 81–82, 106–108,
    111–116, 128–132, 150–151, 156–158,
    166–168, 170–172, 175, 188–190,
    192–193
Peteet, J. 193
Pius, Pope X 155
political contexts 69, 194
political warfare 181–184, 189, 193–194
Popular Front for the Liberation of
    Palestine (PFLP) 175
pro-Palestinian propaganda 16

Rabin, Yitzhak 13, 15
racial discrimination 121, 124, 128,
    150, 173
racism 36, 41, 44, 60, 74, 148, 150–151,
    169, 171–174, 183, 186–187
radical Left 13, 16–17, 166, 169, 171, 175
Rajkovic, N. M. 35
regional organisations (ROs) 89, 92–94, 97,
    100–101
Rose, Jacqueline 59, 170
Roth, K. 36, 38–46; biases 38
Russian Information Warfare 181–182
Russian political warfare 181–184, 189,
    193–194

Sand, S. 4, 59, 61
Schabas, William 74–75
Schabas-Davis investigation 74, 76
self-determination 4, 108, 113–117, 146,
    168, 190
settler-colonial state stigma 2
Shahada, Muhammad 78
Sharon, Ariel 42
Six Day War 21, 23
Sizer, Reverend Stephen 156
Skorzeny, Otto 17
Small, Charles 149
soft power 3, 35, 69, 166–167, 175, 183
Soviet political warfare 181
statehood law 109, 117
state ideology 191

tautologies 111

Uddin, Rayhan 150
unauthoritative authorities 112
UN General Assembly (UNGA) 70, 79–81,
    90–93, 95, 97, 112–113, 115, 187, 194;
    voting 70, 90–91
unintentional antisemitism 146, 149
United Nations Human Rights Council
    (UNHRC) 42, 68–70, 72, 74, 76–77, 79,
    81–82, 194
United States 2, 44, 81, 91, 106, 175, 193
universality 35–36, 43, 46–47
UN voting 90–92
UN Working Group on Indigenous
    Populations (UNWGIP) 127

variance 94–95, 97
Vennesson, P. 35

votes 9, 23, 89, 91–94, 96–98, 100
voting patterns 89, 91, 93–94, 98–99, 101

Walker, Jackie 149
war crimes trial 42
Washington Post 15
Wazir, Khalil 167
Weiss, Rabbi Yisroel Dovid 154–155
Whitson, S. L. 36, 44–46
Wilby, Peter 150

xenophobia 58, 60, 150, 173

Yariv, Aharon 15
Yovel, Yirmiahu 21

Zionism 10, 13, 15–16, 34, 36, 38–39, 41,
    57–62, 144–160, 169–171, 173–175, 182,
    184–189, 191–192
Zuckermann, Moshe 62
Zur, Yaakov 16

Lightning Source UK Ltd.
Milton Keynes UK
UKHW050811250722
406270UK00004BA/89